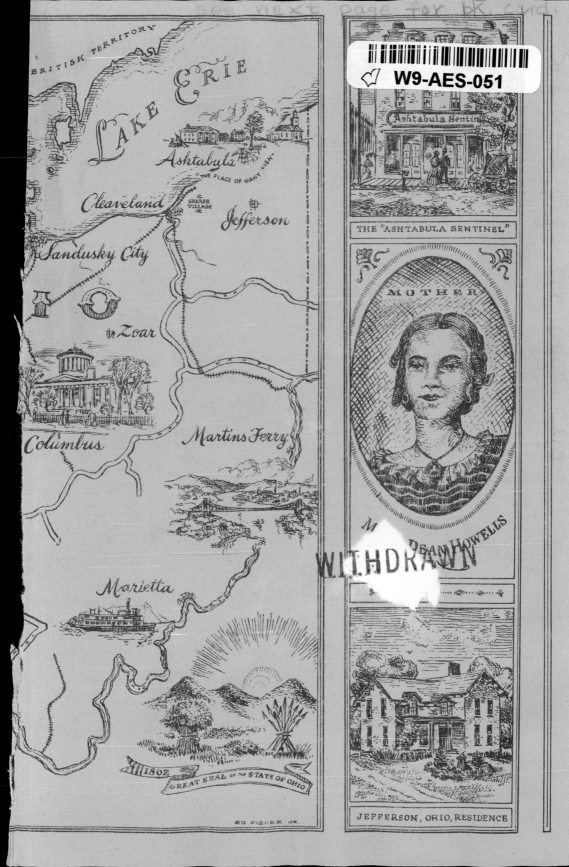

BRITISH TERRITORY

LAKE ERIE

Ashtabula
"THE PLACE OF MANY FISH"

Cleaveland

SHAKER VILLAGE

Jefferson

Sandusky City

Zoar

Columbus

Martins Ferry

Marietta

1802
GREAT SEAL OF THE STATE OF OHIO

ED FISHER JR.

Ashtabula Sentinel

THE "ASHTABULA SENTINEL"

MOTHER

M DEAN HOWELLS

JEFFERSON, OHIO, RESIDENCE

The Road to Realism

Edwin H. Cady

THE
ROAD TO REALISM

THE EARLY YEARS 1 8 3 7 - 1 8 8 5

OF

William Dean Howells

SYRACUSE UNIVERSITY PRESS

LIBRARY OF CONGRESS CATALOG CARD NO.: 56-11892

PS
2033
C25

© 1956 SYRACUSE UNIVERSITY PRESS

*Manufactured in the United States of America
by The Colonial Press Inc.*

To Norma

Preface

FOR WHATEVER REASONS, THERE HAS PREVIOUSLY BEEN NO BIOG-
raphy of William Dean Howells. Miss Mildred Howells' very
nearly unique achievement in bookmaking, *The Life in Letters
of William Dean Howells,* has been far more accurate, balanced, rich
and well-rounded in suggestion than the inexpert reader could know.
But it was never intended to serve the interpretive purposes of full-
scale biography, and no one has hitherto offered to present such
a work. Consequently the non-specialized understanding of Howells'
work, career, and significance has suffered from ancient errors of
distortion and misemphasis and from astonishing gaps of ignorance.
Our comprehension of American literary and cultural history has
suffered in turn.

Some readers will not need to be convinced of the importance
of Howells, whose place in the sun has grown larger year by year
in the past two decades. Others can only be referred to the story
which follows, since the man's life and achievement must demon-
strate their own importance or not be worth arguing. Basically,
this first part of Howells' biography is the story of a series of
intermingling lines of growth: the growth of an admirable personality, the growth of a great career in letters, the growth of a
penetrating mind, of a major command of literary art, of an influence of predominant importance to an age and to its legacy to
the present. Because its importance resides primarily in the novels
which the public is gradually rescuing from neglect, it has seemed
necessary to pay close attention to Howells' principal writings as the
true basis of his right to fame.

Over a period of years many individuals—in many ways—have
given me assistance with this book which it is a pleasure to record.
I am particularly grateful to Benjamin T. Spencer and Harry
Hayden Clark for early suggestions; and to George Arms, William
M. Gibson, Clara and Rudolph Kirk, and Louis Budd, among many
Howellsians. Thanks also to Albert J. George and Jack Lunn
Mowers, Ernest Gruenberg, Antonio Pace, Roy Harvey Pearce,
Clarence Clausen, Lars and Erna Ahnebrink, Walter Meserve, Sig-
mund Skard, and Chet Lampson. Miss Mildred Howells, William

viii *Preface*

White Howells, the late William Dean Howells, II, and his daughter Mrs. Wick have all been helpful.

This work would probably not have been finished without the aid of institutions, and I wish to thank the trustees and administrative officers, particularly William Pearson Tolley, Finla G. Crawford, Eric Faigle, and Sanford B. Meech, of Syracuse University for two subsidized research leaves and generous personal consideration. The John Simon Guggenheim Memorial Foundation also supported me with a Fellowship in 1953–54, administered with that tact and generosity for which the Foundation is famous.

And, of course, work like this could never have been done at all without the great libraries and their staffs. My thanks especially to the Houghton Library of Harvard University, Mr. William Jackson its director, and his staff; to the Syracuse University Library and its personnel, particularly Lester Wells; to the many Ohio libraries for their help—the Ashtabula Public; Cincinnati Historical and Public, and the University of Cincinnati Libraries; to the Dayton Public, the Rutherford B. Hayes in Fremont, the Ohio State Historical in Columbus, and in Cleveland the Public, Western Reserve Historical, and Western Reserve University Libraries.

The Newberry Library in Chicago, through Stanley Pargellis its director, staff, and the delightful policy of the Newberry Library Fellowships, was of extraordinary helpfulness. And then, nationally as well as internationally, great libraries have rendered me help which calls for further expressions of gratitude to the controllers and staffs of: the British Museum; Carolina Rediviva, Uppsala, Sweden; the Library of Congress, Columbia and Cornell Universities, the Huntington Library, the University of Leeds, the New York Public Library, Oslo University, the Pennsylvania Historical, University of Pennsylvania, the University of Wisconsin, and the Yale University Library.

I can thank Norma Woodard Cady for the long hours she has spent over typewriter and desk in the preparation of this and other manuscripts but not rightly for the far more important intangibles she has invested in the enterprise of which our books are a part.

For whatever of good may be found in this work all these persons and institutions may freely take their shares of credit—with my gratitude.

June, 1956

Acknowledgements

THE THANKS OF AUTHOR AND PUBLISHER ARE OFFERED FOR THE following permissions to quote privileged or copyrighted materials:

To Professor William White Howells, literary executor of the estate of William Dean Howells, and to the Committee of the Houghton Library on the Howells Papers, chaired by Mr. William Jackson, for permissions to quote from unpublished materials among the Howells Papers and from *In After Days, My Mark Twain,* and *Years of My Youth.*

To Miss Mildred Howells for permission to quote from *Life in Letters of William Dean Howells.*

To Appleton-Century-Crofts for quotations from "A Group of Aldrich Letters," *Century,* August, 1908.

To *The Atlantic Monthly* for quotations from Henry James, "Mr. and Mrs. James T. Fields," July, 1915.

To Harper and Bros. for A. B. Paine, editor, *Mark Twain's Letters;* and *The Portable Mark Twain* and *Mark Twain in Eruption,* both edited by Bernard DeVoto.

To The Rutherford B. Hayes Library, Fremont, Ohio, for C. R. Williams, editor, *The Diary and Letters of Rutherford B. Hayes.*

To Henry Holt and Co. for lines from *Complete Poems of Robert Frost.* Copyright 1930, 1949, by Henry Holt and Company. Copyright 1936, 1948 by Robert Frost.

To the Houghton Mifflin Co. for quotations from: Ferris Greenslet, *The Life of Thomas Bailey Aldrich;* Richards and Elliott, *Julia Ward Howe;* Rosamund Gilder, editor, *Letters of Richard Watson Gilder;* W. R. Thayer, editor, *Letters of John Holmes to James Russell Lowell and Others;* Bliss Perry, *And Gladly Teach;* M. A. D. Howe, *John Jay Chapman and His Letters.*

To Longmans, Green and Co. for William James, *The Varieties of Religious Experience.*

To The Macmillan Co. for Ethel F. Fisk, editor, *The Letters of John Fiske,* 1940; Rollo Ogden, editor, *Life and Letters of Edwin Laurence Godkin,* 1907.

The New Yorker magazine for Lionel Trilling, "The Moral Tradition," September 24, 1949.

To Ralph Barton Perry for *The Thought and Character of William James,* 1936.

Contents

Chapter One

THE HOWELLSES IN OHIO

WILLIAM DEAN HOWELLS WAS BORN IN WHAT WAS THEN THE raw boom town of Martins Ferry, Ohio, on March 1, 1837, the second child of a warm-hearted, Irish-German frontier girl and a most unusual Welsh printer. To understand the long and fascinating life then begun, it is best to start with a perspective look at its origins. But it is not easy to know at just what point to begin.

It might be with the time in 1808 when Joseph Howells, an eccentric Quaker convert, sold his little textile mill in Hay, Wales, and emigrated to America. Or it might be with the picture of William Cooper Howells, Joseph's son and William Dean's father, born in Wales in 1807, aged six and trudging beside the Conestoga wagon which carried the family's goods across the famous Wilderness Road to the Ohio Valley frontier. Or with the boyhood of William Cooper Howells and his growing to manhood on that rich and often lovely frontier landscape of which John James Audubon wrote so glowingly in his account of "The Ohio":

'When I think of these times, and call back to my mind the grandeur and beauty of those almost uninhabited shores; when I picture to myself the dense and lofty summits of the forest, that everywhere spread along the hills, and overhung the margins of the stream, unmolested by the axe of the settler; when I know how dearly purchased the safe navigation of that river has been by the blood of many worthy Virginians; when I see that no longer any Aborigines are to be found there, and that the vast herds of elks, deer and buffaloes which once pastured on these hills and in these valleys, making for themselves great roads to the several salt-springs, have ceased to exist; when I reflect that all this grand portion of our Union, instead of being in a state of nature, is now more or less covered with

1

villages, farms, and towns, where the din of hammers and machinery is constantly heard: that the woods are fast disappearing under the axe by day, and the fire by night; that hundreds of steamboats are gliding to and fro, over the whole length of the majestic river, forcing commerce to take root and prosper at every spot; when I see the surplus population of Europe coming to assist in the destruction of the forest, and transplanting civilization into its darkest recesses;—when I remember that these extraordinary changes have all taken place in the short period of twenty years, I pause, wonder, and, although I know all to be fact, can scarcely believe its reality.'

Thus, the frontier the Howellses knew was not that of Daniel Boone and Simon Kenton. The right culture-hero for their West was not Cooper's Leatherstocking but the half-legendary Swedenborgian saint and civilizer, Johnny Appleseed. In this guise Ohio and the West were of deep importance to the formation of Howells' character and qualities of imagination. Yet they came to him most through the men and women of his family and boyhood surroundings. And so perhaps the best way to set his life in its true perspective is to sketch in behind it the lives of those who did most to make him what he became.

I

In Howells' maturity he collaborated zestfully with Mark Twain in an effort to put the famous ne'er-do-well Colonel Beriah Sellers, of *The Gilded Age,* into a play. It was no accident that Howells could enter knowingly into the study of a hapless dreamer obsessed with the romance of boundless opportunities. For Joseph Howells had unmistakable Sellers traits which in turn he communicated to his sons. Like a character from Hawthorne, he was possessed by a romantic illusion of being different from other men, which estranged him from the everyday world. This led to oddities of behavior and belief and so to various degrees of isolation, sometimes even alienation, from the world. No single set of facts about Howells' background is more important than the family idiosyncrasies.

That Joseph Howells left his prosperous textile trade in the snug town of Hay, Wales, to come to America at all suggests Colonel Sellers. He seems to have had no trouble of poverty to bring him, only the beckoning of far horizons and the legend of a land green with opportunity. His own father had made a profitable voyage to sell Welsh flannels in America. The story was told that he trundled the proceeds, a cask of silver coin, back to the wharf in a wheelbarrow. He had talked with George Washington. And there was an intimate touch of Sellers in the family tradition that he had bought the deed of most of what later became the District of Columbia—if only the descendants could find a way to prove their right!

The Welshness of the family they retained with ardor. In childhood, William Cooper, moved also by the unpopular family Quaker pacifism and Federalism in the War of 1812, defied his patriotic Ohio playmates by proclaiming himself British. He reared his children to value their "Cymric" origins, and dream of possible descent from Welsh kings. His pride of Wales was allowed to leak out of the neighbors in Hamilton, Ohio, in the 1840's. And during the bitter newspaper fight he waged against the Mexican War in 1848 he found himself pilloried by his Democratic opponent as a subversive enemy alien. In boyhood William Dean Howells loved to dream of this romantic distinction, even though the family had completely lost Welsh as a language. He later thought seriously of finding a distinctive Welsh name for his first-born child. And when the frankness of old age came on him, his letters and even his writings responded often to the old pride and fascination in ancestral difference.

But the strain of Sellers in Joseph Howells went deeper than accidents of birth and geography. Economically, he drifted down, level by level. He left England a small entrepreneur, with his rating as "gentleman" officially established to permit him to evade the law against the emigration of weavers. In America he wandered from Boston to New York, then to Virginia, and at last in 1813 to the Ohio frontier. Moving mainly in Quaker circles, assisting other men to set up woolen mills, he was respected and favored but never found any opportunity quite golden enough. Eventually, his small capital spent, he became a factory hand, then a thoroughly unsuccessful frontier farmer, and finally reached equilibrium as a small-town drug, book, and "necessaries" storekeeper. The long strain of failure, descent, makeshift, and poverty left permanent marks on William Cooper, his eldest son.

Impecuniousness was made even harder for Joseph Howells and his family by their dreams of social superiority to the circumstances into which they fell. The father and mother could not abandon their sense of caste, of gentility. Joseph put his family onto a frontier farm originally to protect them against the vulgarity of Steubenville, Ohio, where he had become a mill hand. Then he and his wife were offended by the customs of their frontier neighbors. They could not forget their standards or depress their tastes. The effort to perpetuate them gave the children, said William Cooper, "a haughty notion of superiority"—and a sense of not belonging socially anywhere.

William Cooper's uncompleted memoirs, *Recollections of Life in Ohio, 1813–1840,* tell how he resented the burdens of responsibility and hard work shifted to him and his mother by the father's unworldliness in business and farming and by his otherworldliness in religion. In Wales Joseph Howells had become a Friend by Convincement. But this was really only a technicality, since he had been reared a Quaker by a father who had married a Methodist English girl and so been "read out of meeting" but not out of his faith or practice. Until his decline in Ohio, Joseph Howells remained a good Quaker, with all the social peculiarity that implied. As William Cooper remembered, "Till I was ten years old, I was taught to regard Quakerism as the true faith, and I very well remember wearing a new shad-bellied coat in the streets of Steubenville, and accepting the appellation Quaker with a feeling of cheap martyrdom." But by then they had left the Quaker communities for a settlement where there was no Meeting.

There, catastrophically, Joseph Howells recurred to his mother's faith. He forgot his economic dreams, cut down his work, moved his family out of town to a farm he visited only on alternate weekends, and became a passionate, shouting, soul-hunting Methodist class leader. It is not surprising that his efforts in taking William Cooper to camp meetings failed to win his son to conversion, or that, briefly before becoming Swedenborgian, William Cooper thought himself an infidel. After leaving Steubenville, Joseph Howells seems to have settled down to a compromise position of retaining Quaker garb and speech along with a theology and a tone which struck William Cooper and his family as "gloomy." The last record of his enthusiasm says that in Hamilton, Ohio, in the 1840's, he became a Millerite and, "Whenever he saw an especially black cloud in the sky he hastened home and donned his ascension-robes. . . ."

It was a part of Joseph Howells' Quakerism that he was in a way a radical, given to pacifism and abolitionism. He belonged to an abolition society as early as 1815 and brought his whole family, even eventually his daughter-in-law's Dean relatives, into the fold. The heritage of his radicalisms flowered in William Cooper. But it also affected the other sons, three of whom were later willing to plan a family Utopia with William Cooper at Eureka Mills. The family liberality resulted eventually in Howells' acquiring three distinguished Mohawk Indian cousins, among them the Canadian poetess, Pauline Johnson.

II

However alien he felt among its people, William Cooper became a child of the frontier. Nothing of all the family strangeness kept him from becoming altogether American, and he learned how to reap the benefit of his differentness by seeing more deeply into the life of the frontier around him than its better adjusted and less sensitive members could. He had been brought a rugged, crowded trip across the Wilderness Road, walking much of the way at the age of six and stopping for a bout of measles on the trail. Then by flatboat down the Monongahela to Pittsburgh and by keelboat down the Ohio. As a child in Steubenville he had rioted in the old wilderness plenty of wild grapes and nuts. But when as an adolescent he was moved out into the "new land" of Harrison County, just ten years settled, he came to the real thing.

Concerning the frontier and its people, William Cooper's memoir is an unusually human and penetrating record. He saw the overwork, privation, brutality, and cultural erosion from which the people suffered. They consumed incredible amounts of "white mule," raw corn-whiskey—women preferring the original "Old-Fashioned," made by dumping a spoonful of maple sugar into the bottom of a tin cup before filling it up with liquor and downing it. He felt the awful dullness of frontier farm-life and recorded how the people turned with a vim to politics, the church, and lawsuits for relief.

Nevertheless, his remembrance of the period is warm and mellow. Nature on the frontier he experienced as a glory. And the best in frontier life provided him with a permanent ideal of freedom and democracy. "Particularly remarkable," William Cooper said in old age, "was the general equality and the general dependence of all upon the neighborly kindness and good offices of others": the raisings, clearings, flaxings, and huskings which marked both the great social occasions and the cooperation for survival of frontiersmen.

Out on the early Ohio farms William Cooper got all too little formal education. His scattered months in country schools added up to only a year in all. His mother helped; there were sixteen nights in a grammar course, and the boy early learned Benjamin Franklin's trick of picking other men's brains. The family had a few books—best of all for him were the volumes of the English poets. Though he made no real record of his reading, his newspapers and Howells' testimony show that William Cooper managed somehow to make good use of an impressive list of books and to drink in many of the yeasty new ideas of the day. So that when Joseph Howells sometime about the turn of the year 1827–28 at length recognized his failure as a farmer and moved to Wheeling, Virginia, as a wool-grader, William Cooper was ready to begin his own career.

In town and with the possibilities of life all before him, he turned at once, with all Joseph Howells' gift for singularity, to one of the most romantic, certainly the most intellectually appealing, but the most estranging and insecure of the crafts open to a poor boy in that town-and-country civilization. William Dean Howells put it in 1893:

'The craft had a repute for insolvency which it merited, and it was at odds with the community at large by reason of something not immediately intelligible in it or at least not classifiable. I remember that when I began to write a certain story of mine, I told Mark Twain, who was once a printer, that I was going to make the hero a printer, and he said, "Better not. People will not understand him. Printing is something every village has in it, but it is always a sort of mystery, and the reader does not like to be perplexed by something that he thinks he knows about." This seemed very acute and just, though I made my hero a printer all the same, and I offer it to the public as a light on the anomalous relation the country printer bears to his fellow citizens. They see him following his strange calling among them, but to neither wealth nor worship, and they cannot understand why he does not take up something else, something respectable and remunerative; they feel that there must be something weak, something wrong in a man who is willing to wear his life out in a vocation which keeps him poor and dependent on the favor they grudge him.'

Though William Cooper was barred from an apprenticeship because at almost twenty-one he was too old, he elbowed his way into the shop of the *Virginia Statesman* with the proviso that he would be fired as soon as a new apprentice appeared. In the three months they gave him he learned a good deal about the tools and something about typesetting. Discharged, he went out into the country looking for a little shop that would give him more experience. For most of the next four or five years he was to be a wandering journeyman in an area rich in character and ferment. And he picked up his share of experiences. At the Quaker settlement of Mount Pleasant, Ohio, he saw the almost unique spectacle of a Quaker riot, when Orthodox and Hicksite groups split the Society of Friends into an unfriendly schism. He worked for the famous Alexander Campbell and later for Elisha Bates, a prime mover in the Orthodox Quaker wing and a pioneer in antislavery journalism.

In the autumn of 1828 he was back in Wheeling, founding, publishing, editing and printing a ladies' monthly literary miscellany called *The Gleaner.* With a hundred pounds of type and home-made equipment he slaved along with it for almost a year. Then he decided that the real reason for its unsuccess was that it did not appear often enough. What was needed was a weekly, a combination miscellany and newspaper. And so in December, 1829, he began to publish *The Eclectic Observer and Workingman's Advocate.*

The first part of that unusual title indicates the determination, which ruled all William Cooper's newspapers, to keep up the literary ideals of *The Gleaner.* But the new note of *Workingman's Advocate* was a deliberate sign of revolt. In the young editor-printer who had lost his religion and had been drinking in the heady New Thought, Joseph Howells' quixotism and radicalism had taken forms which must have been shocking to Joseph. Free thought, materialism, and anticlericalism in religion, total democracy, workers' rights, and a multitude of socio-economic reforms climaxing in what Arthur Bestor has called "Communitarian" socialism were all focused together for Westerners in Robert Owen and the New Harmony experiment. William Cooper's paper was primarily addressed to the "number of admirers" of Owen then in Wheeling. Its tone is suggested by the young publisher's observation that "I committed the grave mistake of addressing my efforts to the promotion of negative interests."

By this time there was plenty of romantic-reformer idealism eddying about in frontier Ohio. There were Shaker communities at Lebanon, Watervliet, Union Village, and Whitewater as well as at Shaker Heights; there were the Rational Brethren of Oxford, and the Cose Creek Community at Lebanon. Zoar, in Tuscarawus

County, was close to the area in which William Cooper grew up. When Owenism came after 1825, its main Western centers were Pittsburgh and Cincinnati: and Wheeling lay directly between them on the river by which they communicated.

Estranged from ordinary patterns as he was to begin with, it is not surprising that William Cooper, as he says, "was beset with the idea that the world was on the eve of some great social, political and civil revolution, at which the 'ills that flesh is heir to' were all to be cured." In addition to this Utopianism, he of course espoused Quaker abolitionism—most dangerous of all in what was then the western tip of Virginia. Altogether, he must have had a fine fling as a young frontier literary radical. But as is usual with such enterprises, he got "fair words, but very few dollars" from the other radicals. He worked hard, lived hard, and wore out his clothes—and the paper was "temporarily" suspended. Then appeared an "angel" with the manuscript of a visionary book, *The Rise, Progress, and Downfall of Aristocracy.* He promised to subsidize his book, to produce a volume the sales of which would rival those of *The Rights of Man,* and to hasten on Utopia as well as the prosperity of the printer. William Cooper put his stock and his back into the volume, saw the book fall dead from the press and the author slump after it into bankruptcy, and went out of publishing in Wheeling. On the strength of the book's promise, however, he had fortunately concluded his youth by marrying a Wheeling girl named Mary Dean.

III

Mary Dean, whom William Cooper met in January and married on July 10, 1831, was an attractive, passional girl with high cheekbones, thick brown hair, and blue eyes. Born in Lisbon, Ohio, on September 15, 1812, she was the child of a magnetic Irishman and a Pennsylvania Dutch mother. Of Dean himself there is scanty record. His inherited Catholicism was not transmitted to his children, but he must have had personality. To persuade Elizabeth Dock to go out for the cows one evening and elope away to the frontier with him, breaking away from the farmer's wealth and the tight-knit affections of her family, required enterprise, to say nothing of charm. And his sons, the steamboat captain "Dean uncles" so beloved by Howells, who was named for one of them, had an adventurous, robust masculinity which speaks well for John Dean.

The adventurousness which falling in love with the young Wheeling radical demanded of Mary Dean she was to need through all the thirty-seven years of her married life. Either through nature or nurture, courage and enterprise could have come to her by way of the Docks, too. Among her mother's ancestors was Conrad Weiser, the great frontier scout and captain. The Docks clearly provided the emotional richness she was able to pour out for her husband and children as well as her own parents. Mary Dean was given to paroxysms of homesickness, especially for her dialect-speaking, Luther Bible-reading mother. With a pioneer "female seminary" education, she could share her husband's love for poetry. Most of their common intellectual life was pooled in his readings and her songs. Their marriage appears to have been decidedly better than average. In joining the heritages of Welsh, Irish, and Pennsylvania Dutch; of Quaker, Methodist, Lutheran, and whatever John Dean was; of Old Country and frontier, German-American cultural enclave and romantic radical—in joining all these, that marriage provided Howells with a peculiar, and peculiarly American, mixed background. It was also a background and heritage from persons who were almost all out of the ordinary, all more or less "strange."

With dreams of publishing prosperity sunk, William Cooper took his new wife along on his printer's wanderings in August, 1831. He found a job for less than $300 a year on a newspaper in St. Clairsville, Ohio, where they lived in one room and took tranquil, romantic nature-walks. On September 1, 1832, Joseph Alexander, the first of their eight children, was born. Soon after, William Cooper took his family to Mt. Pleasant, the Quaker stronghold, to work on Elisha Bates's *Monthly Repository* and then back to Wheeling. In the spring of 1834, they moved again to what looked like real opportunity. In Chillicothe, the original state capital, one of the oldest and then one of the most cultivated of the Ohio towns, William Cooper's brother Thomas found him a place. A brilliant amateur with strong anti-Jacksonian political ambitions, Dr. B. O. Carpenter, had bought out the *Scioto Gazette,* which was a small but influential paper. He needed a foreman-editor to run it, and brother Thomas landed the job for William Cooper.

This year in Chillicothe, before the erratic Carpenter tired of his venture, was the final stage in William Cooper's basic education. Here, for the first time since the Wheeling radical days, he was something more than hired help, managing the paper with almost a free hand. And here also, for the first time since his marriage, he was exposed to fresh intellectual stimulation. Carpenter, a sparkling talker, was an "ultra" in politics and religion, an unabashed prose-lytizer for the anti-Jackson sentiment which would soon crystallize into the Whig Party, and for the New Church, the religion of Emanuel Swedenborg. He converted his editor to both.

William Cooper's adherence to the money-minded Whigs, which he maintained serenely in the face of overwhelmingly Jacksonian-Democratic sentiment in Southern Ohio until the Free Soil Schism in 1848, is not easy to explain. Radical Jacksonianism was often associated with Tom Paine free thought, and William Cooper's religious conversion may have seemed to call for a parallel political shift. Certainly the magic of Carpenter's tongue was an immediate cause. It is easier to comprehend the conversion to Swedenborg. His religion had deep appeal for seekers in that romantic age, and Emerson knew what he was doing when he named the Swedish seer one of his Representative Men in 1845. It was characteristic that, as Swedenborgian, William Cooper became what might accurately, if paradoxically, be called a Utopian Whig.

When Carpenter sold out, William Cooper was cast adrift. He farmed briefly in 1835. He tried to study medicine while supporting the family by typesetting in Cincinnati. He broke his health in the effort and developed a despairing conviction that further print-ing would sink him into the dreaded "consumption," the white plague of the frontier. Then John Dean came forward with a pro-posal. There was a new town building in the boom period of 1836 across the river from Wheeling at Martinsville (later Martins Ferry). Why should William Cooper not move his family back to Wheeling, take one of the plentiful house-painting jobs open in the new town, and build himself a house on one of the "easy-term" lots there? All this he did, restoring his own health with outdoor work as he painted houses and built, in the long evenings of the summer of 1836, a two-room brick house with a lean-to kitchen. There, on March 1, 1837, William Dean Howells was born, the second child and second son of an extraordinary son of the frontier.

A BOY IN A COUNTRY TOWN

IN THE LITTLE MARTINSVILLE HOUSE, LIFE WAS GOOD DURING 1836 and 1837. The homesick Mary was close to the robust affections of her family in Wheeling. She had a home of her own for the first time. Money was easy, and William Cooper seems to have accumulated a little in the boom which surged on locally until the panic of 1837 reached Ohio in 1838. Even when the bust had come and the fantastic financial system of the time had collapsed completely, the family seems to have stayed happy. In July, 1838 came the first girl, Victoria, and the family began to come into balance, Howells acquiring his closest sibling.

Domestic felicity, however, could not change the fact that there was no living to be made in a boom town gone bust, and William Cooper began to look around. His own family was gathering in Hamilton, Ohio, where his brother Joseph, a physician, had opened the town's first drugstore and brought his father in to run it. Another brother had a house-painting contract there and needed help. Just then, in the fall of 1838, Peter Dock, Mary Howells' Pennsylvania uncle, came driving his two-horse carriage on a tour through Ohio. William Cooper went along to Hamilton with him, painted the house, discovered that the local Whig newspaper was for sale, made a deal, and plunged into the Harrison presidential campaign with delight. He was his own master in his own game, and his career was fixed. And so Will Howells, aged three, came to his Boy's Town in the spring of 1840.

After his style, Howells had as his greatest artistic asset a tenacious and vivid memory. One of his boyhood friends discovered that with astonishment when he took him on a tour of Hamilton in 1905. George T. Earhart had never left town, and he found that Howells could flash back to 1845, pick out all the houses and stores

11

which survived, name their old occupants, and even locate the positions of houses since torn down, all unerringly. For Howells, going back to his youth was no delight; it cost him genuine pain. But something drove him to relive his childhood imaginatively in six autobiographical volumes and four works of fiction, not to mention various small pieces. The most permanently valuable of the autobiographies seems to be the telling of his life in Martins Ferry and Hamilton, *A Boy's Town*.

The American boy-story, which has never been properly studied as a literary phenomenon, was more or less founded by Thomas Bailey Aldrich and consolidated by Mark Twain, with Howells to help him clarify what he was doing. It is distinct from the "story for boys," though ordinarily sold to editors and librarians as such, in that it contains a depth level at which an imaginative exploration of the nature and predicament of the man-child is carried out. The importance to American literature and to American cultural self-awareness of the body of writing in this genre has never been fully realized. To name only some principal practitioners: Aldrich, Twain, Howells, James, Garland, William Allen White, Crane, Tarkington, Dreiser, and Sherwood Anderson all participated. They divided the form into two conventions, the ostensibly fictional and the ostensibly factual or autobiographic. In fiction the classic model is *The Adventures of Huckleberry Finn*. In autobiography there is as yet none in this genre, but it ought to be *A Boy's Town*. Its picture of the boy in the life of his time, its density, vividness, and completeness call out from the reader's imagination a structure near perfection both as cultural history and as formal experience. From the point of view of the present, its inescapable ignorance of post-Freudian psychology is of course a disadvantage. Nevertheless, there can be no question of the richness and depth-revealing suggestiveness of the psychic record it recounts, deliberately but quietly.

I

Looking back at Martins Ferry, Howells was sure of two significant memories from his third year. Both are connected with and were probably burned into his memory by the experience of his mother's moving the family to join the father in Hamilton. The first, the earliest, was of waking in the morning to see a peach tree gorgeously and delicately in bloom outside his window. The peach, which grew with unparalleled vigor and profusion on the Ohio frontier, was undoubtedly a symbol of civilization, abundance, and hope of success to frontier people like his parents. What intimate meaning it had for Howells one cannot say, except that to him its fecund blossoms always stood for the exultation of beauty. In old age he told the designers of what was to have been the monumental Library Edition of all his work (it was aborted by publishers' quarrels over copyright) that their motif should be peach blossoms. "Excepting my mother's face," he said to them, "the very earliest thing I can remember is peach blossoms." And finally, "To me there is no blossom more pathetic or impassioned."

The paired memory was also from the frontier and stood for the menace of nature and death. He remembered kneeling in the window seat of the ladies' cabin at the stern of an Ohio River steamboat. The boat was stopped, and he was watching raindrops dance on the surface of the yellow water. Then he saw that the yawl was bringing out from shore a one-legged man who stood in the boat with a crutch under one arm and a cane in his other hand. When they reached the ship's side, the man tried to step aboard, missed, and slid silently into the muddy river with, in the boy's memory, the same meaningless finality as the splash of the rain. Beauty and terror, clothed in vivid imagery, were paired at the threshold of his memory.

Out of the largely unrecoverable Martins Ferry years, and experience with the tributary Great Miami at Hamilton, and a number of free trips with the glamorous steamboating Dean uncles, and perhaps vicariously through brother Joe's failure to make good as a pilot, Howells knew the river and river life well. It was one of those points of contact that made his later intimacy with Mark Twain, and his ability to support Twain's work, possible. River knowledge was also part of his affectionate understanding of the Midwest. "The Pilot's Story," an antislavery narrative poem of 1860, has lyric descriptions of the river and steamboats which anticipate passages from *Life on the Mississippi*. There is also a late autobiographic tale of the river called "The Pearl," and river materials can be found scatteringly in many of his works.

II

In spite of being the village printer and steadily increasing in personal difference from the community norms, William Cooper had ten of the best years of his life in Hamilton. With 1,140 inhabitants in 1840, the little town throbbed with enterprise in the dawn of Midwestern industrialism. Already it had erected a "noble" covered bridge across the Great Miami River to ensure the continued dominance of its market in corn-rich Butler County. It was completing an elaborate "hydraulic system" to provide industrial water-power as a by-product of its place on the canal which tied it to Dayton at the north and, more important, at the south to the "Queen City," the "Athens of the West," or "Porkopolis": Cincinnati, twenty-two miles away. With his $1000–$1200 a year from the *Intelligencer*, William Cooper was much more prosperous than he had ever been before, and in the newspaper editor's fashion a weighty citizen in the town. Mary Howells gave birth to an entire new family in Hamilton: Samuel Dean in 1840, Aurelia in 1842, Annie in 1844, and John in 1846.

On February 20, 1840, the editorial page of the *Hamilton Intelligencer* announced that with its next number Mr. Howells would "commence his labors as the conductor of the Intelligencer." The retiring editor urged upon the local Whigs that "Mr. Howells is a practical Printer and a ready writer. He has cast his lot among you as a stranger, expecting to get his living in the true Democratic style, by the sweat of his brow. Will you withhold it? Though you are in a minority, the reading portion of you can easily support your *printer.*" On the following week, the page one masthead carried the emblem of the new Whig champion in Hamilton: "W. C. Howells, Editor and Proprietor." Page two carried an address "To Our Patrons" which aimed to "State the principles" of the new editor. These were, first, "a consistent attachment to the *true* doctrines of Democracy"—which meant Whiggism and a vote for Harrison. The editor proposed to use no personalities but promised a fearless advocacy of truth. He would select and reprint "useful and interesting articles," including scientific discussions, "occasionally mixing the sweet with the useful." He made it clear that tolerance in religious matters would rule his pages but that he thought Owenism and Fanny Wright Locofocoism, or radical Jacksonian democracy, to be forms of "political folly . . . grown from the seeds of infidelity." Therefore, he proposed to "venerate Religion" in a spirit of peace.

The new editor's handling of his paper showed that his doggedness in pushing into journalism had not been foolish. He ran it sensitively and it prospered. He was helped by a rousing presidential campaign, which rallied the local Whigs to their national victory regardless of the fact that they were snowed under locally, as usual. Apparently, his readers liked the literature and the scientific articles with which he supplemented their diet of political partisanship. His advertising prospered, covering all the back and half of the front of his four pages, mostly with "boilerplate" patent medicine ads. And he was careful to explain from the beginning that those headed "For sale at the Drug Store of J. Howells" had been paid for by the drug company. He added an agriculture department to the paper, and he was wise enough to wait for pork-killing season to make his drive for subscription payments. With all this he began to reap the rewards of good editors. His advertising grew bigger and better, he bought types, and he improved his format.

All these things were good for the proprietor. The paper also provided an outlet for many of the ideas and interests of the editor. He wrote in favor of temperance and against gambling and, without committing himself on abolition, defended the antislavery wing of his party. Never dreaming how it would one day recoil against him, he ran a sporadic horror campaign against hydrophobia, advocating the elimination of stray dogs—or perhaps all dogs. But the gospel he had to pass on to his readers, the center of his thinking and the source of his politics, was the idea which had been declared in his first statement of principles and which he renewed periodically. In an editorial headed "Mobocracy" on October 9, 1840, for instance, he attacked the delusions of the extremist Democrats. "We speak knowingly on this point," he said, "having in our youth been drawn away by the profession of equal rights, and the name of the working men's party." But now he saw that this was really only "Jacobinism revived . . . by Owen, Wright and others under the deceptive name of the working man's party. It unites the responsibility taking spirit of Jacksonism with the disorganizing spirit of infidelity to both religion and civil government." Their true slogan, he suggested, might be "infidelity . . . the foundation of locofocoism."

These notes of sincere conversion and of a religious objection to radicalism must have been comforting and reassuring to the Whig readers of the *Intelligencer*. Taken with the editor's able advocacy of Whig measures and candidates, they doubtless went far to convince them that here was a true, conservative Whig and that they must support their printer. Consequently, it must have been a shock to find on April 13, 1844, that the paper had been sold to Cornelius V. Duggins and to read on May 14 a bland "Valedictory" in which their editor explained that, while thoroughly satisfied with his paper and grateful for its prosperity, he felt called to higher things. Soon they were being asked to subscribe for a religious newspaper with a queer title, *The Retina*. Their printer had gone wildcatting off to risk his livelihood on a paper for that strange, socialistically inclined sect, the Swedenborgians.

III

Inhabitants of Hamilton must, of course, have been aware that William Cooper was a Swedenborgian. The print shop was traditionally the seat of a free-for-all village symposium on politics and religion. And William Cooper's shops, reflecting that passion for conversation which had best educated him, were always lively. With his frankness and Lincolnian ability to use his sense of humor for self-protection, he had never concealed his faith. As early as 1840 he had tried hard to get a Swedenborgian principal for the Hamilton Academy. The community may have been helped to overlook this crotchet in their apparently "safe" Whig editor by the fact that in Cincinnati the New Church was well-established. There was the second oldest Swedenborgian society in the United States, and it enrolled an impressive list of leading citizens. The Howells children were baptized by the Swedenborgian minister from Cincinnati in 1841. Such respectability tended to cover over the taint of extreme minority status, the incomprehensibility of its doctrines, the slight odor of blasphemy which rose from its founder's claims to divine inspiration and mystic visions, and the increasing intimacy between Swedenborgians and Fourierite Communitarians.

The Retina had begun quietly on July 1, 1843, as a side product of the *Intelligencer* shop. It was padded out with matter from what William Cooper began to call "my political paper" but proposed to meet the call of the Western New Church Convention of 1842 for "a general religious newspaper for the New Church in the West." It would print "gay flowers of Poesy and Belles Lettres" as well as "Science, Literature, Philosophy, and Theology" but in everything be "guided by that science of Universal Theology taught by the New Jerusalem Church" because that provides "all that pertains to human improvement and happiness, in the natural as well as the spiritual world."

Hoping to move to Cincinnati and the bosom of the church there, William Cooper strained his resources to keep *The Retina* afloat. On September 1, 1843, he bragged of "pecuniary prospects . . . nearly what will support it—quite, if it is all collected": quite, that is, if one considered only the costs of production, not compensation for the editor. Swedenborgian manuscripts began to flow in, often letting the editor pay postage. Sad to say, many were bitter polemics about church government. In the name of Christian tolerance and charity William Cooper refused to print "controversy," and found himself angrily charged with thought-control. By the end of 1843 he was trying to recoup by offering the rest of the year plus all available back numbers for half price to any subscriber who wished to give it away, presumably as a tract. Nevertheless, on April 19, 1844, he called on the approaching Swedenborgian convention to adopt *The Retina* and announced that its "pecuniary support" would maintain it. On May 3 he rejoiced that in one week "we shall be free from the political yoke," that the religious paper was now on a full-time basis, and that "if it is continued beyond the present volume, it will be printed in Cincinnati." The issue of July 5, 1844, is the latest discoverable. In September William Cooper was back, under contract, in charge of the "editorial and mechanical departments" of the *Intelligencer*. *The Retina* was blacked out.

William Cooper Howells' adventure of faith in laying *The Retina* on the altar of the New Church is representative of the man, his temperament and depth of conviction. The content of the paper is revealing. No equally objective source of evidence exists concerning the intellectual, moral, metaphysical, and emotional climate in which his children were brought up. Full title and subtitle of the paper were: *The Retina*, "The Tablet Whereon Truth's Rays Impress the Images of Thought."

The first issue ran a summary of the Swedenborgian religion in condensed form. It required faith in God as "essential" love, wisdom, goodness, and truth and accepted the doctrines of the Trinity and Incarnation. Christ, it said, had prepared the way for a New Church, founded on charity, and all men who live according to the best light they enjoy will be saved. Then the special doctrines came in. The Bible is the "Word of God" and has a "literal" sense. But it also has a "celestial or spiritual" sense which can be known through the "science of correspondences," a science "lost to the world" until restored by the direct revelation of the Lord to Swedenborg. The Apocalypse, which has already occurred, was the destruction of Christianity "in the eighteenth century, when immorality and infidelity were at their height in Christendom." The Second Coming was really the advent of the New Church, and it is its "unacknowledged influence" which has brought about the "revival" of religion. The Last Judgment "occurred in 1757 in the spiritual world."

Now the soul goes after physical death to a mid-world, where it comes for the first time to see itself as it really is, for what it has made itself. Then it goes voluntarily to join either the good or evil spirits. God, who is perfect love, does not judge, reward, or punish. He does not need to; the soul naturally and freely judges itself. In this present world man exists in "spiritual equilibrium between heaven and hell," enjoying entire free will in spiritual things. Every man is constantly solicited by the Devil to evils which destroy "the capacity to enjoy the happiness of heaven" but is forever steered by God's Providence toward events which are designed "to contribute to his final benefit and advantage."

A survey of *The Life and Writings of the Hon. Emanuel Swedenborg* runs through many numbers of *The Retina*. Before treating his doctrines it analyzes his scientific career in detail. And the editor is faithful to the Swedenborgian acceptance of science in reprinting a number of scientific articles. The idea, of course, was that of Emerson's proposition in *Nature:* "Natural facts are signs of spiritual facts." The usage of this idea of correspondence lay behind the name of William Cooper's paper. *"The Retina,"* he said, "is the expression of the optic nerve . . . and its use is to convey to the mind the images of objects in the material world. . . . It is thus we wish to use our RETINA . . . to impress upon it the forms of things within the soul's vision. . . ." Besides science, intellectual and literary matters entered the field of vision. The names of Coleridge, Pusey, Carlyle, and Barrow appear. These are poems of Schiller, Hood's "Song of the Shirt" and Freneau's "On Swedenborg's Theology"; and, of course, often the magic name of Fourier.

It seems clear that at bottom Swedenborgianism was ethical rather than mystical for William Cooper. It had its emotional side, its "metaphysical pathos" for him; but the deepest issues were those of conduct. On October 28, 1843, he wrote on "The Moral Heart of the World," explaining that "the highest hope" of the Christian and philanthropist lay in the "innate principle of right in man, a high and holy essence which . . . is capable of being made subservient to good no matter what his sphere or condition of life."

In discussing "Universalism" on April 26, 1844, he said, "Evil does exist. It cannot emanate from God . . . it is from the perversion of the faculties of man." Since there is absolute moral free will, "Man's highest happiness consists in reciprocating the love of God *directly* toward the Divine and *indirectly* through his fellow creatures, particularly the latter." The love of God will lead man to heaven; but love of self must lead to hell. Thus he refuted the Universalists: "If man directs his love wholly to himself he immediately demands the love and submission of others to him; and seeks to render them subservient to his wishes and gratifications. To this we know there is no bounds, and from it must grow contentions, oppositions, wars and fightings of every kind; in short, from this rock of self-love springs all moral evil. . . . It is man, then, that introduces evil, by the abuse of the freedom that is given him in order that he may enjoy heaven."

Forty, fifty, and sixty years later William Dean Howells was to be writing important novels based on precisely the same moral and psychological wisdom. But now he was, at six and seven years of age, beginning to haunt the print shop from choice and by request. William Cooper practiced the precepts of a bit he reprinted on September 30, 1843, "The Necessity of Work for Children." At work they are shielded from vicious idleness and come to know the world as it is, said *The Bangor Whig*. So Will Howells began by folding papers and later could remember when he could not read but not when he could not set type. Whether he could read or not, he felt the weight of *The Retina*'s child psychology.

On October 7, 1843, William Cooper started a "Youth's Department." Heaven, he said, is nearer to children, "let us seek to store their memories with those truths that will direct their affections to proper objects." Therefore, he wrote a little children's sermon for the November 18, 1843, issue on "Mistakes in Printing." Errors in life, like those in print, can be repented but not erased from the record. We must avoid them by doing our duty "the first time." But when we have made them, "our great care should be that we

do not *love* them; and call them *good* and *right,* for when we do
this, we can never be saved from them. . . . Then we shall put
evil for good and darkness for light, and our evils will most certainly
destroy us."

For son as for father this was most Howellsian. Whether it
helped a boy going on seven and struggling with the beasts in his
inner jungle, or whether it only deepened his feelings of guilt, is
problematical. Certainly the child's story of December 29, 1843,
made a deep impression with its Swedenborgian vision of a celestial
tug-of-war between two angels and two devils over each soul.
Howells remembered it in his memoirs. There was another set of
lasting impressions from the parental attitude which lay behind
December twenty-second's tale. Its punch-line was a father's prayer
for his son, "may heaven preserve you from being a merchant."

In *The Retina* period socialism came flooding back upon the Whig
printer. In spite of Owen's explicit materialism, Swedenborgians
had been the most numerous sect at New Harmony. After the
publication of Brisbane's volume in 1840, *The Social Destiny of
Man,* they had found a new star of hope in Fourier. The French
Utopian's notions of social solidarity and of man's essential innocence may have made a marriage of the two movements easy. But
if one looks at Fourier's vision of the communal Phalanx and then
at Swedenborg's accounts of the structure of spiritual society in the
next world, striking coincidences of pattern appear. In a sense
Fourier had transplanted one of Swedenborg's central myths to the
here and now. At any rate, the name of Fourier, the discussion
of his movement, and eventually a full-scale "investigation," since
William Cooper debarred "controversy," of the relations between
Fourieristic Associationism and the New Church were printed with
increasing frequency in *The Retina.* There are at least a dozen
articles, pro and con, with special attention to the Leraysville, Pennsylvania, Phalanx.

William Cooper, himself, was cautiously responsive to the appeal
of Association. Its details, he commented, "are pleasant to contemplate . . . though they may excite some ridicule in the unreflecting."
On January 12, 1844, with the discussion warming up, he took a
stand. "That a system of Industrial Association, in its general
features, like that of Fourier, is practicable we have long believed,"
he said. The New Church ought to make a "trial" of it. But on
March 15, following two long pro-Fourier articles, he dragged his

feet. He applauded Leraysville as an experiment. But the use of Fourier is "secular," he warned. He cannot be allowed to corrupt Swedenborg, and, "We must not by any means permit the opinion to go forth that Fourierism and the New Church are in entire harmony."

Nevertheless, his own social conscience was reawakened in *The Retina*. He printed two letters from Lydia Maria Child, one on pacifism and one protesting the destitution and the slum-exploitation of the poor in New York City. To Hood's "Song of the Shirt" he added the comment, "These social evils are the offspring of a corrupt church." And he contributed an able dialectic refutation of a college professor from nearby Miami University. Understood in its "celestial" meanings, he showed, "The Case of Hagar" did not support slavery at all. And, indeed, nothing in the Bible did support it.

No matter what antagonisms Howells may have felt toward his father, he was all his life acutely aware of William Cooper's beauty of spirit and mind. Since all his education up to about fourteen years of age was from or through his father, the father's ideas, attitudes, and methods were strongly impressed on his mind. He had the notion later that the father had never tried to proselyte his sons for the New Church. He had wished to acquaint them with the religion but to win them to a morality. Moral absolutism, joined with intellectual pluralism and relativity, is the key to the Swedenborgian aphorisms called "Materials for Moral Culture" in the September 30, 1843, *Retina*. Howells was to combine them all his mature life. The conviction that spiritual love and good works save —where self-concern and love of this world damn—he never escaped. The doctrine of correspondence, natural facts as the key to moral and spiritual truth, made it possible for Howells to be realist and moralist at once. Metaphor, said a Swedenborgian writer in the December 15, 1843, *Retina*, connects the natural; but correspondence connects the natural to the spiritual, the object to the subject, the form to the essence.

A thorough agnostic most of his life, Howells was to feel cut off from the Swedenborgian reach upward to spiritual intuition or reliable mystical experience—which made his this-worldly moral concerns the more intense. Many of the men who became "robber barons" and nature-wasters in Howells' generation came from small-town and farm-boy poverty like his. He became a social critic loosely allied to the pioneers of Christian Socialism and the social gospel. Much more important, he became the first major American novelist whose imagination dealt seriously with the problems of the business mind—and primarily because his father's social conscience was of the sensitivity revealed in *The Retina*.

IV

When Howells said, as he did repeatedly, "I am a Buckeye," he was thinking of back-country towns like Hamilton, Dayton, and Jefferson, especially Hamilton. All his life, when he tried a new pen, he wrote his name and then "Hamilton, Butler County, Ohio." There he was an energetic, blue-eyed towhead, always humiliatingly small for his age. In boys' games he had skill and won full acceptance, even apparently some ascendancy in boy-society. If the fighting got too rugged, he had Joe, muscular, aggressive, and four years older, to protect him.

With Joe, Will's relations were those normal between brothers that far apart in age. Will tagged after Joe in desperate admiration and rebelled against him in more or less equally desperate competition and aggressiveness. As boys, both tried to evade and ignore the girls and the rising population of family toddlers. Forbidden to use violence by the family regimen of conscience, Joe used moral strategies to discipline and repress Will. He successfully set himself up as the voice of the parents, as a sterling example of obedience, faithfulness to duty, and righteousness.

A great deal about the quality of the family life under the father's regimen as well as the relations between the brothers is revealed in Howells' account of their reading "The Trippings of Tom Pepper," a moralistic newspaper tale against lying. Having read how fibs destroyed Tom's career, Joe persuaded Will to enter into a covenant with him to tell nothing but the truth forever. They struggled painfully for weeks and finally dissolved the convention. For imaginative and endlessly introspective Will, this sort of struggle became the material for childish self-torture until he listed two anguished battles with conscience under the heading "Fantasies and Superstitions," in *A Boy's Town*. Though his warfare came to a neurotic rather than a metaphysical crisis in the end, he could look back on a long experience when he came in manhood to write some of his most effective satire against moral quixotism.

Such experiences were not, unfortunately, the sum of his troubles in the boy's town. He always insisted that the home was thoroughly happy, "serenely bright with a father's reason and warm with a mother's love." But his books make it clear that his childhood was haunted by terror. He had a trick of ending chapters of *A Boy's Town* with reference to fear. His friend, the novelist and most distinguished American pre-Freudian psychologist, S. Weir Mitchell, wrote to him immediately after reading the book, inquiring about the extraordinary melancholy. "The terrors of that boyhood shiver Langdon [his son] and me with interest," he said. He, himself, had no such recollections and found that his son had not of his boyhood.

Howells replied that it would indeed be fascinating if anyone dared lay bare the whole truth about boyhood; but who would dare? All his memoirs are loaded with notations of fear, "shapes of doom and horror." The extraordinary intensity of his boyish guilts and frights other boys caught on to and learned to have fun with. Earhart, his old Hamilton friend, recalled his technique for getting past the tombstone cutter's: "He was accustomed to approach the dreaded locality cautiously and on the other side of the street; then, when he was as near as he dared go, he would make a sudden dash and pass at full run, never slacking his pace until he felt the security of safe distance." Howells himself tells repeatedly how the same reaction attached itself to every association with madness, death, and the destruction of the flesh. Equally ample testimony reveals his pervasive and paralyzing fear of ghosts.

The most enduring symbol and channel of his malaise, however, was death by hydrophobia. At the age of nine or ten he convinced himself one ghostly moonlit night that he was going to die when he was sixteen, and worked himself into a near frenzy about it after that birthday. The special death was to have been hydrophobia. One reason for his fixation on that horrible disease, about which there was endless superstition in the days before Pasteur, was his father's obsession with it. In the *Intelligencer* on March 26, 1840, William Cooper urged the destruction of every suspected dog at once and stressed the "horror" of "the terrible effects of madness."

In the summer of 1841, when Will was four and a half, William Cooper let his pen run wild in a four-column description, detail by detail, of the death of a local Mr. Bowers. The neighbor's fear of water, sensation of smothering and smelling smoke, his spasms, fits, and delusions, his calling in Joseph Howells for religious comfort, and making his peace with God before death were chronicled in vivid detail. "Some two months since he was bitten by a dog (of his own), and appeared to enjoy good health, until Saturday last," wrote the editor. And then, "It is far from being certain that a dog will not communicate hydrophobia by biting at any time when he is enraged though he may never have been bitten." Someone, probably Joe, must have read the account to Will.

The Howells boys were pet-lovers who had a coon, rabbits, a goat, a pony, and especially a huge dog Whiggishly named Tip, for "Tippecanoe." Will, who loved Tip and played with him daily, nevertheless spent one afternoon of horror, when the family was away, crouched in the woodshed with Tip, convinced the dog was going mad. Some time in Hamilton, apparently, he was bitten by a dog, though he still kept a young Newfoundland when the family moved to Columbus in 1851. In Columbus, however, he was daily terrorized by a snarling neighborhood cur. After that the dog became a symbol of terror for him.

The malaria, or "ague," which everyone in Hamilton and almost everyone in Ohio contracted, undoubtedly affected Howells. He had it, of course, and his sister Victoria was to die in 1886 from a recurrence. The disease and the treatment for it, often with opium, could account for some of his experiences of horror. Nevertheless it seems fairly certain that his troubles were really psychic in origin and cannot now be clearly elucidated. Although amateur psychoanalysis of dead writers can easily lead one astray, it is clear that this child of vivid and constant terrors was suffering psychically.

Of course not all his experience was fearful, not more than a minor fraction could have been. Most of his experience must have been, as with all men, undifferentiated and more or less neutral. And some of it was packed with the personal magic of beauty and profound inward meaning. Allowing for the basic grayness ordinary to human experience, it may be said that his two earliest memories stand as cardinal symbols for the experience which his unusual memory, his sensibility, and his imagination enforced upon Will Howells. There was the mutilated man casually drowned; but there was the magic of the flowering peach tree. The village and its characters his memory registered affectionately; nature moved in rhythm through the year and framed intensely interesting animals, countryside, and waterways for him. Parades, elections, musters, holidays, circuses, market-days, travel on the canal, all the corporate life made the boy wonder and exult. It is this side of *A Boy's Town* which gives the book its greatest strength.

His schooling was not much, perhaps in all a total of sixteen or eighteen months in random doses during the Hamilton years, perhaps less. Its chief gift to him was to let him make an independent discovery of the rules of prosody in the back of his grammar and so begin to make his own verse at what must have been the age of seven or eight. His real school was the printing shop next door to the family dwelling. There even the family toddlers were welcome, so that, as Howells said in 1893:

'The office was in my childish consciousness some years before the paper was; the compositors rhythmically swaying before their cases of type; the pressman flinging himself back on the bar that made the impression, with a swirl of his long hair; the apprentice rolling the forms, and the foreman bending over the imposing-stone, were familiar to me when I could not grasp the notion of any effect from their labors.'

Each child in turn served his apprenticeship at folding newspapers and then "graduated to the type case." Will was something of a child prodigy. He could set type at six, was a useful hand at nine, and when he was eleven he could set five thousand ems per day, a man's work. Almost any print shop, the poor boy's college, as Lincoln said, would have given a better education than the district schools. With its owner's keen attention to literature and ideas, William Cooper's shop gave an excellent one, especially when coupled with his nightly readings of fiction and poetry at home.

The father recognized early that he had something out of the ordinary in his second son. He put books in his hands and discussed them seriously and sympathetically when they had been read. Will began to read with the absorption that makes *My Literary Passions* so apt a title for his autobiography as reader. He learned something of classicism early in Goldsmith's histories of Greece and Rome and in the *Gesta Romanorum*. The father's telling of Cervantes and Don Quixote one night and then putting Jervas' translation in his hands touched off a lifelong passion for the Don and his creator, the form and method of the book, Spain, and the Spanish language. His father bought him an English-Spanish grammar from a returned Mexican War veteran in 1848 and he set out, slowly, on the most unusual of his self-education projects: the study of foreign languages, beginning with Spanish. More important, he was writing at something or other most of the time and was encouraged by his father.

His first literary effort was an essay on the vanity of human existence "written" by setting it in type, a method he used for prose all through his print shop years, sometime "in my sixth or seventh year." Always a frank, confiding child, he announced his discovery of prosody at home by producing an attempt at verse. But he began to be more cautious about sharing his gift with other boys after writing a love letter in rhyme for one of them only to see the guileless recipient burst into tears after reading so strange an address. He also learned that such things were thought slightly sissy in the world of swimming and "soakball." Nevertheless, he wrote a tragedy modeled after *The Lady of the Lake* against a tyrannical schoolteacher, and almost succeeded in getting the gang of boys to put it on. He also tried to write a historical romance after Irving's *Conquest of Granada*, another root of his Hispanic passion. In Hamilton, where it did not dare to call itself the theater, he made his first contact with another lifelong passion, the drama. The editor's family got free tickets, of course.

Fortunately for William Cooper Howells, his successor with the *Intelligencer* did not prosper. He lost money through extravagant printing and not having William Cooper's ability to run a family newspaper—with his own family, that is. And on May 29, 1845, William Cooper took over again: "I now *own* the concern, and . . . I shall continue the business as a permanent one." The Whigs seemed, on the whole, grateful to have their printer back. Columbus and Cincinnati papers congratulated the party on his return. Apparently, no one was much upset when, for instance, he took pains to welcome the "Integral Phalanx of Butler County" to nearby Enoch's Mills on June 5, 1845. It was to be different when the Mexican War and the developing Free Soil movement convulsed the party in the following "year of decision."

With the events of 1846–48 more and more Americans were coming to the time when, as with James Russell Lowell, the slave would not let them sleep, or when, like Thoreau or John Brown, they felt driven to civil or uncivil disobedience. The antislavery movement in Ohio, of which Joseph Howells had been one of the pioneers and the Quaker center at Mt. Pleasant the nursery, was now a force poised to tear apart the political fabric of the state. In an atmosphere of suppression and mob violence, dramatic incidents like the Lane Seminary migration to Oberlin in 1834–35 had made converts by thousands. By 1836, Ohio had thirty per cent of the nation's antislavery societies.

Short of immediate total abolitionism, sensitive men like Abraham Lincoln and William Cooper Howells were becoming Free Soilers— believing that slavery would perish naturally in the South as it had in the North if it could be kept out of the territories. The Democrats, with their Southern support, could ignore and then defy antislavery sentiment. The Whigs were forced into more and more uneasy compromises to conciliate Free Soilers. But the people of Southern Ohio, mostly descended from Southern families and closely tied to the South through the river traffic on which their prosperity had traditionally rested, were overwhelmingly Democratic. They inhabited a free state but bitterly resisted the growing community of freedmen who seeped across the Ohio from the South. Except that there were no slaves there, slavery sentiment in Howells' *A Boy's Town* was not significantly different from that in Huck Finn's St. Petersburg.

With all that and patriotic expansionism in the air too, William Cooper Howells needed both his Quaker conscientiousness and Swedenborgian serenity when he decided to fight the annexation of Texas and the declaration of hostilities with Mexico as aggression and unjust war. For all his peaceableness, he became a telling controversialist in the local phase of the battle, a long skirmish against editor Franklin Stokes of the Democratic *Hamilton Telegraph*. But however often he scored on Stokes and his allies, the opposition had the leverage of local public opinion on its side. As early as June 11, 1846, William Cooper was defending himself, at first with scorn, against the irrational, irrelevant sort of personal attack which counts heavily in such warfare. They seized on his proud Welshness: "Weller called us a Tory, and said we had not American blood."

Therefore he preached the necessity of supporting the war, once the country was in it while he continued to deplore its basic immorality. He pilloried Stokes for warmongering but not volunteering. Therefore, with the war won and a presidential campaign in the offing, Stokes apparently went out to "get" him, and did. On January 27, 1848, the *Intelligencer* editorial page carried the heading " 'Tories.' " "In the last Telegraph appears an article under the above caption," wrote the editor, "which for vindictiveness,

malignity and scurrility surpasses anything we have ever seen. . . .
For daring to express our opinions upon this nefarious war, and
the causes which led to it, we are characterized as a 'Miserable
tool,' a 'despicable wretch'—and a 'traitor.'" Furthermore, he
added, "For the past three weeks the columns of the Telegraph
. . . have literally teemed with such expressions." Such McCar-
thyite tactics were, of course, viciously unfair; but apparently they
were victorious. The Whig editor was very nearly destroyed by them.

All that was needed now was the final alienation of the loyal
Whig readership. And that happened almost immediately upon
the Party's nomination of Zachary Taylor for president, by which
the Whigs won a presidency and lost their party forever. Led by
Tom Corwin, the golden-tongued Wagon Boy and elder statesman
of the party in Ohio, antislavery Whigs repudiated Taylor and
drifted toward the Free Soil Party. It was inevitable that William
Cooper should join them, together with almost none of the Whigs in
Butler County. On July 6 and 13 he was trying desperately to
round up Free Soil support and activity, proposing a club and a
publication, filling the *Intelligencer* with verbal blows at the opposition in both parties and with items encouraging a Free Soil grass-
roots uprising. His stand was no support of Taylor on the grounds
that he was not a Whig but a tinsel hero who symbolized the
aggressiveness of the slave power. He proposed to support the State
candidates and fight the "Locofocos," and in August he was printing
"the Free Soil Banner" for "the Free Soil Club of this place."

On November 9, however, he announced that, "Ever since the
nomination of General Taylor . . . we have had a standing proposition to sell out this paper to any Whig . . . who would support
the nomination" and that the offer had been taken. His "Valedictory" on November 16 correctly predicted the disintegration of
the Whig party and trumpeted a last defense of the Corwin Whigs
who could not "bow to the worship of mere military heroism." The
next week John P. Charles, the new editor, proclaimed himself a
solid Taylor man and called the Free Soilers back to the party. The
Hamilton decade was over, and William Cooper had only his conscience and his honor intact.

V

The collapse of his affairs at Hamilton must have hurt William
Cooper Howells, but he had the heroic superiority to mere events and

shifts of fortune which was in keeping with his religion and his temperament as idealist. In that passionate generation many editors experienced personal violence. Even the sedate William Cullen Bryant horsewhipped a man in the streets of New York. In William Cooper Howells' post-frontier time and place much more serious violence was commonplace. Cow-hidings, thrashings, shootings, tar-and-featherings came readily to offenders against public sentiment. As an antislavery sympathizer and anti-patriot William Cooper offended deeply, and was apparently as little impressed by his danger as by his economic loss. Such things were important, but were well risked in the interests of truth and public morality.

For Mary Howells, on the other hand, such heroism was harder. To be increasingly alienated from the community, especially the small-town ladies' gatherings, and then to know real fear for her serene husband's physical integrity dismayed her. Before long she had to face the entire loss of their Hamilton position, loss of home, loss of security for herself and her seven children. Her anxieties were deep and all too well founded. She might now be forced back to the hand-to-mouth wander years of her early married life. Perhaps the family might even drop out of the respectable classes into the hired hand or tenant farmer group. Since starvation or real destitution were unlikely with so many relatives to come to the rescue, this last was the basis of a fear which was to haunt her most of the rest of her life. She went down the grade with her husband and hoped, largely beyond his really caring except for her sake, to mount up the other side and into respectability again. She suffered deeply, but it is clear that she also loved her man deeply and endured whatever she had to with him as cheerfully as she could. But she began to organize her family to combat his nonchalance.

At first the family stayed on in Hamilton; there was really no place else to go. Joe and Will earned money as printers. There was a flurry of optimism about manufacturing paper from milkweed pods, or something like that. Finding Taylor much less proslavery than he had feared, William Cooper made what peace he could with the Whig party. Again, there was nowhere else to go if he wished to stay in the newspaper business. Religious journalism was closed, and in Ohio the Free Soil Party as such hardly existed. For the present he would have to try to make do with the Whigs.

After a winter of casting about, William Cooper found a Whig paper available and "bought" the *Dayton Transcript* in May, 1849. Then he put his family aboard a narrow canalboat and moved them all through the lovely spring weather to a new start in a place that was not to be a pleasantly intimate boy's town but a tartarus of youth, especially for Joe and Will. William Cooper Howells had still to learn that economic survival in the "political newspaper" demanded either essential harmony between editor and readers or else editorial hypocrisy. On the *Dayton Transcript* the whole family paid dearly for his second lesson.

The move to Dayton marked the end of Howells' boyhood. He had followed the family tradition by developing to the edge of adolescence as a decidedly "different" boy. His reverie life was at least as pervasive as that of other boys, certainly richer in its content of beauty, romance, and terror. His talent for language and his ability to care for literature were decidedly out of the ordinary. His talent, his lisping in numbers, his drive to create, and his absorption in writing and reading suggested genius. In some ways it was good for such a boy to belong to the Howells family. Differentness was no shock there. He met with sympathy and guidance. There was ample stimulation.

On the other hand, there were penalties and dangers. The father's adventures, however admirable morally, deprived the boy of the formal education which might, even short of college, have meant much. In Dayton there was to be real physical suffering. The family was too much turned in upon itself, too isolated from the rest of the world, especially in the last Hamilton and the coming Dayton-Eureka Mills-Columbus periods, which coincided with Will's crucial twelfth, thirteenth, fourteenth, fifteenth years. The usual adolescent difficulties in making terms with the outside world were intensified. And the tension within the family was the more racking when there was nothing to go toward outside.

In Dayton, William Cooper again made arrangements by which he put down a small first payment and tried to amortize his paper out of income. To hold the old rural and small-town subscribers while also catering to the new tastes of a robust little city, he put out a daily, a tri-weekly, and a weekly paper—something for everyone. When he failed, it was not because of shiftlessness or laziness. Simply as a business idea the multiple editions were probably sound; and, to try to still Mary Howells' anxieties, the father worked himself and his boys spartanly. Will shuddered to recollect how, aged twelve, he used to toil until eleven at night under flaring, leaky gas fixtures to set the proud "telegraphic despatches" for the morning daily and then was routed out, six days a week, between four and five o'clock in the morning to deliver the papers. William Cooper and Joe, who worked later and harder, were always up to wake him.

Failure on such terms would have crushed many men but, for William Cooper, the desperate labor only made it sure that the source of failure was again a matter of principle. The flood-damaged files of the *Transcript* show William Cooper Howells as editor and publisher on January 15, 1850, in mid-course. He is running a great deal of advertising, less than twenty-five per cent of his space given to editorial content. Some of the gaudiest patent medicine ads are for Sands' Sarsaparilla, guaranteed to cure ulcers, cancer, arthritis, consumption, and female complaints. They list I. F. Howells—another druggist brother, Israel—as "sole agent." There is also steady advertising for "The New York Circuit Co.," paid for in free admissions which were giving a future dramatist his first full taste of the glamor of the stage. As was usual with William Cooper's papers, much of the slim "editorial" content is given over to literature—mostly melodramatic fiction like "Judith the Egyptian: or the Fate of the Heir of Rimon," of the sort of which Joe kept a bulging scrapbook.

The specifically political content of the paper is firmly Conscience Whig. From its tone one infers that the editor's quarrel with the other local Whig newspaper has already begun. The *Transcript* is against Clay and against the Compromise of 1850, which it calls "base, servile, and degrading." Its reaction on March 8 to "Mr. Webster's Speech" is frigid. Webster's, it says, is "that dead conservatism that all stand ready to bury and forget." On May 1 it frankly attacks the slave-holding arrogance of "The South." On June 6 it flies in the face of the Know-Nothing branch of Whiggism by heading the editorial column with praise of the new academy founded by the Sisters of Notre Dame. And all along the advertising falls off in quantity and especially in quality. Items become shorter, more trivial, and obviously cheaper. After all, Dayton was only a few miles north of Hamilton. On July 30 the paper is "Edited and published by W. C. Howells and J. B. Underwood." Antislavery remarks disappear, and there is more deliberate appeal to regular

Whigs and to farmers. On Tuesday, August 21, the name of William Cooper Howells appears for the last time. Perhaps it was on Wednesday, but Joe Howells liked to tell the story that, on the day of his final failure in Dayton, William Cooper came home early and gaily took his hard-worked boys for a swim in the canal.

VI

For Howells the eighteen months in Dayton were inevitably unhappy for the most part. Before the *Transcript* became a daily, and the exhausting battle to keep it alive began, Will did have the chance to feed his theatrical passion on a real, if provincial, stage. He had to be suppressed in a desire to become an actor by his father who could not, however, suppress his own composition and the brief production of a historical melodrama about the War of 1812 by the same company. Here began Howells' long passion for Shakespeare, which eventuated in an almost uncanny ability to quote him and at last in Howells' coming to hold the record for most titles of books taken from the bard. Of course, like most record holders, he had, with the one hundred-odd volumes he had to name, more chances than most competitors. His first experience with art came when Dubufe's "Adam and Eve" was exhibited with special lighting and optical effects. It was probably also an experience with sex since, the mores of the time being what they were, "Eve" was the first nude female figure he had ever seen.

He tells, too, in *Years of My Youth* about another and revealing experience with sexual problems. With their Swedenborgian devotion to Christian charity, the Howellses employed as a seamstress, and made a point of befriending, the sort of poor girl only too common in that age of the rampant double standard. She had been seduced and abandoned by a prominent local citizen and of course become a pariah. When she came into the family, Will, about thirteen years old, took it upon himself to stage a Pharisaical persecution of her. He refused to speak to her, take a dish at table from her or to hand her one; he pointedly left the room when she entered; until she burst into tears one day. Then he had to explain himself to his mother, and she put him to shame. The episode could be taken as one more example of the conscientiousness which Howells as autobiographer customarily labeled fantastic. Or it could be taken as a stage in his adolescent sex education.

Since Swedenborg had a good deal to say about sex, it is not probable that William Cooper Howells neglected to educate his sons in it. Questions of sex and sex in literature remained of central importance to Howells all his life, and it is worth noting what the sexual ideals were in which he was trained. Swedenborg himself handled his basic notion almost everywhere in his religious writings, but his most careful elucidation is given in a book which carries the English title *Conjugial Love*. He recognized the three branches of love which are distinguished with difficulty in our limited English vocabulary—but with ease in the Greek terms of *agapé, philé, eroté:* spiritual love, personal or perhaps intellectual love, and sexual love, what Emerson called, in his poem, "Initial, Demonic, and Celestial Love." But Swedenborg was inclined to think of the ultimate unity of all love and to insist on the spiritual importance of different ways of taking it. Love might be grasping, self-gratifying, arrogant, destructive, and therefore diabolic. Or it might be humble, generous, joyfully self-sacrificing, creative, and therefore divine. Sexually, the true love was "conjugial." It must be essentially, though to never-married Swedenborg not necessarily legally, monogamous. Conjugial love was the most beautiful and harmonious of human experiences, a type in the doctrine of correspondence of the perfect, self-forgetful heavenly state, and one of the surest paths to goodness and God. Its opposite was correspondingly already a state of hell on earth and the sure road to that stinking existence as one of the devils which Swedenborg knew how to depict with Swiftian images of nauseating filth.

Some Swedenborgians, not the Howellses, were attracted toward the Utopianisms of "Free Love" which scandalized the era. It is reasonable to suppose that the basic excellence of the marriages of both William Cooper and later Howells himself owed something to *Conjugial Love*. But, also, the aura of dirty disgust with which Swedenborg surrounded selfish, lustful sex must at least in part account for the reaction Will experienced then and always to it, whether in life or literature.

VII

William Cooper Howells was not alone in his alienation from the world of Southern Ohio. If there had been no one else, there were always the other sons of Joseph Howells. William Cooper and Israel grew very close during the terrible Dayton year. Waiting for inspiration after the *Transcript* crash, the unemployed editor put the boys into printing and store-clerking jobs, even in a German language print shop for a while. At the same time he was maturing a dream into a plan with three of his brothers: Israel in Dayton, Joseph the doctor, and Henry the druggist in Hamilton. For more than twenty years he had been dreaming of Utopian communities in one form or another, and apparently he could now fire his younger brothers with his vision. Their plan was calculated to avoid the errors of New Harmony and other Utopias which had been smashed by the practical difficulties of personal adjustment among members in the first months. Theirs would start out as a family Utopia. Once established, it would slowly assimilate others and grow.

They wanted a "mill privilege" with standing buildings and a dam, which could be converted from gristmill into a paper mill. Presumably, there is some connection between their choice of an industry and Hamilton's present stature as a major paper manufacturing center. Apparently, no one was at first troubled by their complete inexperience with paper-making. They searched the countryside and found what they wanted in the grist and sawmill at Eureka Mills, auspicious name ! The brothers put up the capital, Israel probably most of it, and bought the mills. William Cooper found a log cabin inhabited by a shiftless poor-white couple, came out with the older boys to patch it up, and then moved his family from Dayton. As they came out in October weather which had changed from cold and rainy to the blazing perfection of Indian Summer, William Cooper was exuberant with release and enterprise. Returning to the land and to the surroundings of his frontier youth seemed romantic. And he was the advance agent of a social adventure which would liberate him from the spiteful ways of a world which had just inflicted two defeats upon him for righteousness' sake.

For Mary Howells, who saw her own frontier past through no veil of glamor, and who thirsted for the comforts, the securities, and the domestic symbols of respectability in town, the golden scenery must have seemed cold and empty. She was moving her seven children into a tiny, dilapidated cabin. To be sure, a new house was promised, but she had come far down in the world with only vague prospects of coming up again. All she could do was to fight to keep from breaking down and reinforce her resolve to lift the family back to respectability whenever the chance came.

The episode intrigued Howells all his life. His first bit of autobiography was *My Year in a Log Cabin* in 1887 (magazine publication). The time figures vividly in *My Literary Passions* and *Years of My Youth*, and when he finished his fictional treatment of it, *New Leaf Mills*, in 1911, he told Henry James that he had been meditating it for fifty years. Part of its impressiveness no doubt came from the burst of freedom, of boyish leisure to play and read, of contact with nature, and of romance in the situation which was part of his escape from the purgatory in Dayton. Part, also, was in the thrill of coming to know his father on new terms.

William Cooper also had leisure, and in it he took pains to reconcile and cultivate the boys he had worked so hard. He read to them, directed their own reading, and discussed it with them. He made them feel and see the countryside and its past as he did. He taught them the trick of his command of the oral tradition of frontier humor, with its power to deflate pretentiousness and pomp. He taught them to value as well as enjoy laughter. His serenity and compassion, his morality of Christian charity, his radicalism he communicated along with his rich set of romantic attitudes.

At the same time, the family drama was, however subconsciously, communicated. The spectacle of the anguished mother torn between her love—and even her worship—of the father and her rebellion against the position he had brought her to, this sight and the memory of it sank deep, especially into the older children. For the strain of worry, overwork, and failure in Dayton told heavily on the family in spite of the father's buoyancy. The mother's unhappiness stiffened the reaction of Joe and Will, who announced symbolically that they were through with printing and through with cities. The romance of a log cabin and the intoxication of renewed boyhood in the country reconciled the boys to Eureka Mills. But nothing could reconcile their mother to squalor and defeat. Her unhappiness and rebellion deepened, and of course the older children felt it as they had in Dayton. Howells was to dramatize it vividly in *New Leaf Mills*, sixty years after.

At the same time, Will's reading began again and with it an exhilarating new comradeship with his father, who now had ample leisure to make amends and take up the education of his prodigy again. The record of the reading here, as almost always, needs no elaboration from *My Literary Passions*. Scott and frontier tales, especially from Howe's *History of Ohio*, were incorporated into active, imaginative games. The Spanish passion continued and was reinforced by the discovery of Longfellow.

The new intimacy with his father in that back-country setting gave Will an accurate notion of living on the frontier. The father revived the old skills of log cabin living. He walked out with the family and made them feel and see the countryside both as it was and as it had been earlier. His stories and the reading to which he guided them taught them vicariously what living and doing could no longer call back. This sense of the frontier became one of the deep roots of Howells' imagination and especially of his grasp upon American life and character. But the most important effect of their new comradeship was the real understanding of his father's personality Will received. With him he came even to one night of poetic beauty while walking through the moonlit woods in which there was no terror, no dread of ghosts.

As Will came closer to his father, however, his psychological problems grew more intense, not easier. Perhaps it was because the mother was moving away from her husband in revolt against their status and drawing Joe with her. At any rate, ghosts lurked horribly all in and around Eureka Mills. He was paralyzed by attacks of homesickness at even the prospect of leaving her. These did not begin at the Mills; he had returned in despair even to the hell of Dayton after one night of a visit at his grandfather's in beloved Hamilton. But now his susceptibility to nostalgia reached crisis stage and stayed there for years. In the second fall at Eureka, when money was badly needed at home, he was offered a week's emergency job in the print shop at nearby Xenia. Anguished at leaving home and terrified of the laughing girls at the boardinghouse, he tried to go home again the night he arrived. Only his father's coming made it possible for him to stay. Later he went to Dayton on a similar job and was housed by his favorite uncle Israel. There he woke in tears every morning and got through his meals only by gulping down huge amounts of water between bites to suppress his sobs, although at almost fifteen he was really too big a boy for such behavior. His homesickness, a real disease, was always a longing for his mother. And when he came home from Dayton she made him "company" for the day and let him know that, in spite of herself, she was glad of his defeat.

In three autobiographies and a novelette, Howells has so luminously told the Eureka Mills story that there is no need to retell it further. After living in the new house a few months, the family left on a snowy morning late in the fall of 1851 to go to Columbus. The Howells brothers had decided not to risk Utopia, and the enterprise was to be liquidated. But William Cooper's martyrdom had not gone unnoticed by the Free Soilers of Ohio. He found a chance to report the proceedings of the Legislature verbatim for *The Ohio State Journal,* a Whig paper soon to become Republican. He could move to the state capital, where there would be economic opportunities for the boys. The way up and out began to open for Mary Howells also.

Chapter Three

A COUNTRY EDITOR'S LOT

To come to Columbus was to return to the world again, but on different terms. When the Howellses moved to Columbus they took a train at Xenia, a few miles to the east of Eureka Mills, and were traveling on a through line that connected Cincinnati on the Ohio River with Cleveland on Lake Erie— and so joined a net of mechanized transport which linked New Orleans to New York via the Erie Canal or the railroads. Hamilton had been an ambitious pre-industrial village, Dayton a personal hell, Eureka Mills a retreat toward the backwaters of the frontier. Columbus, however newly, was a part of the great world. After the Dayton experience the older sons firmly intended to secede from printing forever. But Joe went off to try to become an Ohio River pilot with the Dean uncles; and before Joe came invalided home with a river illness, Will let himself be enticed into work as a compositor for his father's paper. William Cooper made ten dollars a week, Will four, and Joe, when he returned, three as a grocery clerk. On their combined seventeen dollars a week the family of nine lived comfortably in a ten-dollar-a-month house on a back street. Mary Howells added the tenth and final member, Henry Israel, on March 30, 1852.

The security of seventeen dollars a week in Columbus, and the fresh opportunities for acquiring knowledge and sophistication for the children, would doubtless have made the Howellses glad to stay. But William Cooper's job was good only for the duration of the session, and he carefully used the contacts he made in the Legislature to find a new chance.

There was, he discovered, one part of Ohio where eccentricities of religion and idealism were not unusual and antislavery convictions were welcome. This was in the northeast corner, along Lake

Erie, where the Western Reserve had been settled by Yankee emi-
grants—men and women who were as often the siftings of romantic-
transcendental New England as their forefathers had been of Puritan England. They were readers of Horace Greeley, and no form
of Yankee radical dissent was entirely foreign to them. And in the
very heart of this, Ashtabula County, which had sent Joshua Giddings to Congress as the most stalwart and provocative foe of slavery there, they needed a printer-editor to conduct the *Ashtabula
Sentinel*, "the Voice of Giddings." Obviously, the opportunity and
the man had met. When the legislature went home in the spring of
1852, William Cooper prepared to take his family into a part of Ohio
so different from what he had hitherto known that it might have
been another country.

I

In *Years of My Youth* Howells wrote with considerable freshness
about that winter in Columbus. He confused the chronology, tending to think of himself as younger than he really was,* but he used
his rediscovered diary of the period to excellent advantage in ana-
lyzing the writing he was then doing. His father was reading Dickens and Thomson to the family. But Will was disciplining himself
doggedly to write in the heroic couplets of Alexander Pope, con-
structing unfinishable enameled pastorals and a backyard fence
mock-epic entitled *The Cat Fight*. His father took him on guided
tours of the wonders of the city: the Insane Asylum, the grand new
capitol then being built, the penitentiary. And then, at first shock-
ingly, he pushed him into print.

In the generalized mode of the nature poetry of his time, Will

* On page 70 he makes himself "thirteen" and on page 79 puts himself with young J. J. Piatt in the book-room of the *Ohio State Journal*
aged "thirteen or fourteen" in the spring of "1850." Actually, of course,
he is correct on page 71 when he makes it the winter of "1851–52." He
was fifteen years old on March 1, 1852, before he left Columbus (see "In
an Old-Time State Capital," *Harper's Monthly*, Sept. 1914, 595, where
he recalls that he dug a garden, in what must have been at least April
in Columbus before he left) ; he was apparently still in Columbus when
his second poem appeared in print on June 3, 1852. Cf. *Years of My
Youth*, p. 74; Gibson and Arms, *A Bibliography of W. D. Howells*, item
52–3, p. 74.

had done a little piece inspired by a premature March warm spell, and his father, without warning him, had it printed in the *Ohio State Journal* for March 23, 1852:

> Old Winter, loose thy hold on us
>   And let the Spring come forth;
> And take thy frost and ice and snow
>   Back to the frozen North.
>
> The gentle, warm, and blooming Spring,
>   We thought had come at last;
> And thou with all thy cold and woe,
>   Wast for a season past;—
>
> The blackbird on his glossy wing,
>   Was soaring in the sky;
> And pretty red breast robin, too,
>   Was caroling on high. . . .

Though this is thoroughly conventional "newspaper" verse, it is good of its kind. The rhymes all rhyme; there are no lame feet or sawdust lines, and it says something. It is not poetry, but when we know the author's age it hints that he might someday have genuine literary powers. As newspaper verse this maiden had a small, deserved success. A New York paper picked it up for reprinting, as did the *Cincinnati Gazette,* which commented, "The following lines from the Columbus journal are just in time. All our people cordially join in the regrets and desires of the poet." At which the poet, masking delight in Dutch comic dialect, confided to his diary, "Just think of that—called me a 'poet.' I swan it peats all." But he had a bad case of jitters as well as joy, when he had to face the consequences of this publicity attendant on authorship. He rebelled, but only briefly, and managed to live through the scene when a jocular fellow printer seized him on the publication of his next poem, "The Emigrant's Last Meal in the House." Patting him on the head from his superior adult height, the wag quoted his lines,

> And pats the good old house dog
> Who is lying on the floor.

Will bore up and got through a humiliation which would have almost slain him could he have anticipated it. And no doubt began to acquire a little badly needed callus on his ego.

The flat, water-stained exercise book which he used as a diary and journal from 1852 through several years afterward reveals more about Willie Howells in the spring during which he became fifteen than America's most distinguished man of letters thought it necessary to tell when writing his autobiography sixty-odd years later. Willie worked long and hard hours in the print shop, yet often had fun doing it. He looked forward eagerly to holidays, but was bored rigid if for some reason he had no work for a couple of days. His confidences to his diary and impressions of daily life are most "lit'ry"—the highly articulate, self-conscious, skillful, and naive writing of a prodigy. "Conundrum," he announced:

> Why is an idea like a pig?
> Because if you want to keep it you must *pen* it.

At the same time he was thoroughly a boy. As the spring weather improved he spent evenings and Sundays out of doors, and entries in his journal tapered off toward zero. With a fellow apprentice he made and flew a huge kite and scored an "indescribable triumph" in the boy-world, being courted and waited upon by mobs of small fry. A rare Saturday off was spent in a mode more appropriate to Penrod Schofield than a budding Tennyson. It was a day, the journalist recorded, of "a little writing, a little eating of sugar cakes, a little of playing marbles, a little of ball, and a little of everything else." Nevertheless, there was that "little writing," and the day clearly ended as it had begun—in the journal.

When he left with his family for Ashtabula in July, he was a published author who had been given the greatest possible encouragement by the editor of *The Ohio Farmer* on the publication of a third poem, "The First Blue Violet." Though "yet a mere lad," said the editor, "if riper years do not cheat the promise of his youth, he will make his mark among the . . . writers of the nineteenth century." He went on tinkering with Popean pastorals. He wept over *Uncle Tom's Cabin* and shuddered over Ossian while fearfully resolute not to look up from the page and see a ghost after the family had gone to bed. He went on studying Spanish. But it was all with a new seriousness and hope of finding himself somehow in literature. An almost desperate determination came to possess the adolescent boy who looked up from small-town and back-woods obscurity to the peaks of glory occupied by the literary demigods of the intensely literary nineteenth century.

II

After six months in Ashtabula, the *Sentinel* was moved down to the county seat at Jefferson on January 1, 1853, at which time "J. A. Oliver & Co.," publishers, announced William Cooper Howells' editorship "since May last." This brought it directly into Giddings' stronghold, a village even more than Hamilton part of the preindustrial, handicraft and agriculture civilization so soon to disappear. Its extraordinary feature was the population of literate, radical, tough-minded if not somewhat crabbed Yankees. Among only seven hundred of them, the village already had resident a United States Senator and a Congressman, a State Senator and Representative, and of course the usual complement of county officers. About life in general, and politics and religion in particular, they were far more earnest than Southern Ohioans. Ideas mattered seriously to them. "I imagine," said Howells much later, "they tested more religions and new patents than have been ever heard of in less inquiring communities." At the moment, they were intent upon spiritualism, "and they were ready for any sort of millennium, religious or industrial, that should arrive, while they looked very wisely after the main chance in the meanwhile." In the New England fashion, they took the mind hard.

The Western Reserve, latest settled of the old sections of Ohio, was still not very far from the frontier days in which almost all its leading citizens had taken part. The combination of Yankee radicalism with the frontier hang-over made its people informal and egalitarian. Home for the summer from baiting Southern aristocrats in Congress, Giddings walked around the village streets barefoot and in his shirt sleeves, with old brown linen pants and a worn straw hat. He was the best and most enthusiastic baseball player in town and loved to show off his immense strength with homely stunts. Giddings was the most popular man in the whole region, its political fulcrum.

The paper which was known as his "voice," partly because he contributed a Washington letter to it and partly because it was controlled by his backers, was the most powerful organ of the antislavery movement in Ohio. Except for those who also took a farm paper or Horace Greeley's "Trybune," it was the chief source of mental life for the isolated country farmers. And the new editor took his responsibilities seriously. The literary tone which had characterized his periodicals since *The Gleaner* was deepened in the *Sentinel.* For its front page Will selected poetry and Joe fiction, usually, with their father primarily responsible for the following political pages. With his Ashtabula County readership William Cooper could be as radical as he liked. Often the readers were ahead of him.

In this happy new situation the only major change in his ideas seems to have been a natural growth in his defiance of slavery, the slaveholder, and especially the Fugitive Slave law. The note of gaiety in a typical comment from the period shows how delightful he found it to be at ease in his editorial Zion. "The days of catching runaway negroes," he wrote, "are pretty well over in this part of Ohio. Nothing would delight the boys here, more than to rescue half a dozen or so of them. It would be a very unhealthy enterprise for a Kentuckian to visit this county, for fugitives, unless he desired a footrace, and a good one at that."

As a matter of course the region was criss-crossed by Underground Railway routes. Soon there would be a local fraternity called The Black String, organized to aid and abet John Brown and his sons to commit armed rebellion against the United States Government and then to shield fugitives from the consequences of that treasonable act. Local legend has it that when a U.S. Marshal came to Jefferson to arrest one of Brown's sons, he called on William Cooper Howells to guide him out to the man's farm. The printer-editor politely begged to be allowed to finish locking up the form he was working at, stepped out the back door a moment to pass the alarm, took half an hour to finish, drove the Marshal to his destination, and was surprised to learn that Mr. Brown was not at home.

When Mary Howells died in 1868, her will disposed of the substance and symbols of the respectability and security she had fought fiercely to insure her family in Jefferson. With a sympathetic audience, her husband's talents and ideals reversed the Dayton fiasco into prosperity. But he could never be persuaded to care about money. To make sure of her opportunity Mary Howells worked demoniacally, worked herself into the grave, Howells thought. She enlisted Joe, twenty-one years old in 1853, as eldest child and son a chief sufferer from his idealistic father's economic lapses, and eager to begin his own life, to care for her dream and fight for it as she did. The property was held half in Mary Howells' name and half in Joe's for reasons probably divided between justice and expedience. And when Mary Howells died she left behind her "Homestead," a half interest in the printing office and its lot, and her stock in "J. A. Howells & Co." She had cared for her household and children without outside help, and taken in the journeymen from the shop as boarders to save on their dollar-a-day wages. She had borrowed money from her brothers. She had channeled all her emotional force into overwork, anxiety, and pressure to save and produce. The psychological price was high for the whole family. But she died in her own house with the family status and finances secure.

By 1856 it is safe to say that her battle was really won. William Cooper Howells was rewarded for services and sufferings by election to the office of Clerk of the State House of Representatives. He went to Columbus, leaving Joe in charge of the business and Will of the editorial page. The next year he took Will with him to break into journalism with legislative letters to the big city papers, and Victoria for company. The family was maturing and threatening to scatter, though of course Mary Howells' Hamilton brood was just entering adolescence, and she still had a baby.

Henry, the last in a baby-loving household, brought heartbreak to Mary Howells. As was revealed by X-ray long years after it was too late to correct the condition by newly invented methods of surgery, a childhood fall from a swing caused the development of a bone spur which grew into his brain. He became a magnificent-appearing man without developing mentally out of childhood. In manhood he was the walking tragedy which many a nineteenth-century rural family knew: a household idiot. His sister Aurelia's life was devoted to his care, and there was a barred room in the house in which Henry had periodically to be locked up, raving and beating the bars, in crises which were apparently sexually based. Mary Howells did not live to see this or Aurelia's becoming, as one old Jefferson resident puts it, "the most beautiful and most terrible example of self-sacrifice I have ever known." But she could guess enough about the future to leave a special plea for Henry in her will. And of course, in the absence of sure knowledge of the mechanical cause of his madness, "poor Henry" became a worrisome part of the background of the rest of the children.

With the rise of Republican power in Ohio, the editor of the "voice of Giddings" became a weighty figure. After the Civil War he reaped the rewards of prophets belatedly recognized which went to many of the surviving antislavery martyrs. In 1864 he was elected to the State Senate by a record majority. Tendered the honor of introducing the Thirteenth Amendment to the Constitution for ratification by Ohio, he took the occasion to note that he did so "as a life-long slavery-abolitionist." In 1867 the Cleveland *Leader* noted a brief boom for him as candidate for the lieutenant-governorship of the state. When one newspaper doubted his ability to "do well on the stump," he took a characteristic mode of withdrawing by observing that he shared that doubt but had no doubt that "a goodly number would be stumped."

Toward the last, with almost automatic political power at his penpoint, William Cooper Howells made his contribution to national politics. He helped groom for Congress, advise, support, advance, and mature a boy from the Reserve: James A. Garfield. The Garfield papers have a long series of letters between them, many from Garfield marked "Confidential," which have apparently never been sufficiently explored. Garfield became a friend of the family, his wife especially close to Victoria Howells. He got Joe the Jefferson post office in 1869. After Mary Howells' death, when home began to pall on a bereaved husband, Garfield pressed until Grant awarded the consulship at Quebec to William Cooper in 1874. In 1877 it was Garfield again who got Hayes to move him to more attractive Toronto. The consular years were happy ones. He has been credited, somewhat improbably, with founding Swedenborgianism in Canada; his daughter Annie married the Canadian poet-politician Achille Fréchette. William Cooper Howells' life ended tranquilly in Jefferson on August 29, 1894.

"Will is so much a continuation and development of my own aspirations and efforts that he seems almost myself," William Cooper wrote proudly on May 2, 1862, of the son who was then American consul in Venice. And it is true that Howells was in significant ways a continuation of his father. The deep love for literature and ideas, the passion for nature, the humor, and the sensitive but homely ability to get on well with most people all went from father to son. Howells' sense of the ethos and meaning of the Ohio frontier, and the understanding of the American common people which always underlay his sensibility and his work, came from education by his father. William Cooper's Swedenborgian-radical alienation from the normal patterns of this world, combined with his faith in the efficacy of deep dreams and moral absolutes, colored Howells' mind all his life. There were, of course, ambivalences and rebellions. Howells was, after all, a son. But even some of these melted away when, in the middle way of life, he suddenly found that the father's social and moral passion for a religion of the Good Community no longer seemed queer, impractical, or impossible. When he discovered Tolstoi with something like the shock of a conversion experience, he liked to think that he had come upon something startlingly new. But a detailed analysis of the two influences would show that everything essential to Howells in Tolstoi he might have learned from his father at Hamilton, Eureka Mills, and Jefferson, Ohio.

III

Jefferson was richly pregnant with opportunity for the Howellses. The chances to win security and status again, and to achieve self-expression and influence in a favoring milieu, galvanized the whole family. With his new hopes and sense of maturity, Will was stimulated, too. For the first time since Hamilton, and the first time out of childhood, he could have a coherent social life. Young people flocked gaily into the cold "office" above a machine shop in a flimsy wooden building to make an occasion of folding and addressing papers on publication day. They had parties, sleighrides, serenades, and sparking. Will fell in love, first with Mary Ellen McAdams and then with Julia Van Hook.

In the new situation his father's humor sparkled out and made a happy shop for the day's stint of typesetting. Quips, poems, practical jokes and horseplay, stories in the full tradition of American oral, "frontier" humor flashed about all day. Journeymen and apprentices boarded at home and became almost members of the family. Long, colorful discussions of literature—Shakespeare, Dickens, Holmes, Poe, Irving, Byron and Macaulay—and of politics went on through the day among men who were engaged in a skilled handicraft and knew how to make the ten-hour working day humane. The family "homestead" was bargained for, and the family came to live in town, a block west of the court house square and only a block and a half from the shop.

The humor which greased the ways of daily labor in William Cooper's printing shop was, given the character of the proprietor, undoubtedly "clean." The stories were part of the back-country, or "frontier" tradition, sharp-eyed to ridicule personal eccentricity or puncture swell-headed pretentiousness in other folks. They liked to tell courtin' stories: of the country suitor who, at once lazy and desperate, decided to sit up on the fence rail and wait for a prospective wife to come by. The first female to pass he challenged, abruptly, "You married?" When she blurted out a scared and nettled, "Yes, indeed!" he silently swung over backwards and let himself vanish behind the wayside weeds on the ground, defeated. Or, a bit indelicately in a pre-plumbing age, they told of the school marm surprised out in the blackberry patch, who almost kept her poise successfully. She had just come out, she said evenly, to gather a handful of berries for tea-hee-hee-hee!

The favorite stories were like the one Howells thought most representative of American humor: the time the vacationing banker took a shine to the farmer's horse. "How much is your horse worth?"

"Five hundred dollars."

"I'll give you fifty."

After hard bargaining they settled for eighty-five dollars, and the banker took the horse, knowing how small was the farmer's total worth and that he'd made a profitable sale.

"Say, if you were going to sell this horse for eighty-five dollars, why'd you tell me he was worth five hundred?"

"Well, you looked to me like the kind of fellow that'd *want* a five-hundred dollar horse."

Much of the quality of the father-son relationship as well as the essence of the family humor lies in the quip with which Howells almost forty years after smoothed over a difficult moment in family financial arrangements at a time when his contributions largely supported his father's home. How should potentially embarrassing adjustments be worked out? "I feel like saying, with the easy-going Quaker," replied Howells, " 'Just as thee damn pleases.' "

Amid all this, Will struggled on with his fight to earn a place in the sun by studying and writing. He was able to do a man's work at typesetting between seven in the morning and two in the afternoon. Still slender and short, he was regarded as "too frail" for the heavy press work. And his father, though unable to free him for the schooling at a local academy for which he longed, was willing to give him what chance he could to progress on his own. Walking home across the dusty streets and down the gravel paths at two, he slid into a cubbyhole study under the stairs to read, write, or plug away at languages. He could now handle Spanish with some facility, and his first publication in Jefferson was a translation of a piece on "Don Pedro II, Emperor of Brazil" which he sent to the *Casket* (of gems, no doubt) published by the nearby Kingsville Academy and printed at the *Sentinel* office. He signed it modestly "W." and was rewarded, if he tried to impress the academics, by an editorial note that he was a self-taught Spanish student "only about sixteen years old" who was henceforth invited to contribute whenever he wished. He gave them "Beauties of Mythology" in September and a narrative poem, "A Christmas Story" for December. Then the *Casket* ceased to publish.

Using an omnibus "sixteen-bladed" grammar of the Romance languages, he went on to try to master Latin and French, pounding away. He sent to New York for imported volumes, developed a passion for *Lazarillo de Tormes,* and read plays of Lope de Vega and of Cervantes. In these years 1853–54–55 came passionate immersions in Shakespeare, Dickens, Ik Marvel the sentimentalist, Chaucer, Macaulay, Lowell, Longfellow, Curtis, and Thackeray, among others, a large mixed bag. And he was writing a good deal. 1854 was a particularly productive year, with eight separate publications, including three poems (two rather good), a clever parody of Shakespeare (Pistol, Bardolph and Nym discoursing on August, "O, 'tis the most hottest weather") and four bits of fiction, one an attempt at a serialized novel. He signed two of the poems with one of the more interesting of his several pseudonyms of the period, "Will Narlie." In Ohio speech a "gnarly" man is, like a gnarled limb on the chopping block, complicated and knotted, hard to understand— not gratuitously mean like an "ornery" man—but difficult. In 1855 there were eleven items, but almost all are either translations or reviews and all are short. 1856 is sparser still. There were only two review-pieces and a few editorials in the *Sentinel* during the five weeks or so in February and March when his father left him in charge of the paper; he published nothing creative.

The fiction of the good years is particularly interesting. The poetry improves steadily, shows some lyric strength, but is mostly in the vein of the nature poetry of the time familiar, for instance, in the early work of James Russell Lowell. Howells' first published fiction, "A Tale of Love and Politics, Adventures of a Printer Boy," in the *Sentinel* for September 1, 1853, was written when Horatio Alger was still at Harvard Divinity School, but it belongs to Alger now. It was an obvious daydream, composed in type as fast as in the printer boy's head. Adopted by the local Judge after a generous patriotic act on the Fourth of July, an orphaned printer boy later saves his daughter Ida from drowning but is still denied the right to love her. He founds his own newspaper, and soon anonymous articles elect the Judge to Congress: "Ably written articles . . . addressed to all classes—farmers, mechanics, and laborers. The original and vigorous style, clear and convincing arguments, deep and profound reasoning—invariably carried conviction." On election night the victorious Judge and Ida dropped in on "George Wentworth," and the Judge's last prejudice was melted when he found the boy fast asleep over his desk with his head on "a freshly written article, with the mysterious 'stars' attached." Shallowly conventional in plot, the tale was interesting for the freshness of its newspaper and print shop setting.

His most important literary production of the Jefferson years was a fiasco so painful he remembered it all his life. Imitating Dickens, Thackeray, and the popular American sentimentalist Ik Marvel, seventeen-year-old Will Howells began on November 23, 1854, to print in the *Sentinel*'s literary place of honor (top of the left-hand column on page one) a full-scale serialized novel called *The Independent Candidate*. Its start was free-flowing and bold. But it was over-plotted and over-populated with the eccentric Dickens characters the novice author introduced in successive installments instead of developing his plots. Though at least technically anonymous, he was in the excruciatingly embarrassing position of presenting installments to the public before he had seen his way clear to the actual development of fleshing out his scheme. It looked so easy when the professionals did it! Once he tried the Thackeray trick of digressing into the light essay while stalling for ideas. He even skipped one weekly installment. At last, in desperation, he pulled everything together, killed off some characters, drove others mad, ignored still more, and hurled the whole enterprise toward a huddled close which forgot almost entirely to be scenic or even descriptive. It degenerated into a bald revelation of plot outline. His chagrin, no doubt little spared by the shop jokesters, was profound. It would be years before he dared try, even cautiously, to spread his wings in full fictional flight again.

Yet his writing was often excellent—smooth and colorful, if sometimes lush. He could observe and record sharply the forms of life about him and communicate, even sentimentally like Ik Marvel, his feelings about it:

'An after-supper listlessness pervades the whole village. The heat and bustle of the day are over, and Oldbury gives itself up to the enjoyment of twilight. Little boys, in scattered groups, are launching dust rockets into the air, and assailing the buggies as they rattle to and fro along the streets. Here and there an easy smoker may be seen sauntering toward his evening haunt in the post-office, or pausing to hold a moment's chat with a friend on the queer turn politics have taken. On the tavern stoop several urchins just verging into loaf-hood, are seated in the chairs which are always filled, an hour later by a choice coterie of thorough-bred loungers. —A bevy of serene office holders linger about the court-house steps, and talk together in idle clumps: and laugh uproariously at jokes which reach the sidewalk only in hoarse, indistinct whispers. It is yet too early for moon lighting, and no merry two and two strollers are abroad to crowd one from the pave. Quiet home folk, standing near front gates, gaze and guess at passersby; and some, whose indoor toil ended at five, are refreshing themselves with hoe and spade among the thrifty garden beds which flank the white houses.

Twilight is to day and night what those weeks of mellow sunniness which hale the going-out of October are to fall and winter. The garish beauty of summer day melts into the more pensive loveliness of evening, and night with dreamy stealth dusks the valley and the hill, and seems half-mournfully to hover near the little realm of light on the plain: the rich season of red and yellow fields and woods fades slowly away behind soft veils of purple and amethyst, and winter calms his blustering gales until she breathes her last amid the bliss and plenty she had strewn around. In the gentle suings with which they fill the year, the Twilight and Indian Summer have kin as well. The same quiet blending of light and shade, and the same muffling of sound with melancholy stillness, invite to revelry in both; and the forgetfulness of earth-life that one tastes in the twilight of the day, is drunken with a sweeter and deeper draught in the twilight of the year. If angels ever journey on errands of peace and mercy to this world, they fly nearest at such times.'

At the same time, something most interesting was going on in his mind, something which would develop until one day he would despise the like of Ik Marvel, raise disturbing questions about the artistic intelligence and integrity of Dickens and Thackeray, and emerge as the American captain of the movement toward realism in fiction.

Already young Will Howells was in revolt against some of the popular romanticisms of the day. His passion for Cervantes—and perhaps a revulsion against brother Joe's fondness for sentimental-sensational trash like "Lilly Bell: or Why Uncle Harry Was a Bachelor" which had to be set in type for the *Sentinel's* front pages —led Will to his first groping assertion of antiromanticism. The digressive and "Rather-Didactical" Chapter Four of *The Independent Candidate* opens with a quotation from the prologue of *Don Quixote* and continues:

'. . . I would like to make the most beautiful, lively and discreet story that was ever penned. If I do not, [the reader] will please remember that my failure was not from lack of willingness to do better. Let him remember, moreover, that I have not the high-topping quaintness of Lippard, not the gory skill of Emerson Bennett, nor Lieut. Murray, and that I shall not even attempt to imitate these masters; but shall content myself with the following, at goodly distance, the less dazzling authors of *Pendennis* and *Bleak House.* Let him, I say, who is wont to regale himself with the literary blood-puddings of the great western novelist, or to gloat over the faithful pictures of sea-life which the man of pen and sword has furnished us, remember that I can offer him nothing of the kind. Unfortunately, I have neither Indians nor Pirates to deal with, and it is such a very serious thing to kill off a Christian, that I cannot find it in my heart to slaughter so much as a single character, as yet. It is true that I might have Merla fall sick of ague, or have Walter hang him with his neckcloth; I could make an end of Mr. Gilky by means of *delirium tremens,* or could drown the heir of the house of Trooze in a tub of rainwater with a mere stroke of the pen; but I fain would have these children of thought play at foot-ball with chance for a while; and I cannot but think some kind heart would be pained to see them brought low.'

This was not the doctrinaire realism of later days. The mature critic found Dickens and Thackeray only less sorry models than the "Blood-pudding" group. It did not take arms against the coincidence-laden, saccharine romances which inundated the country, but it did assert a young writer's self-taught conviction that material treated simply and honestly made better fiction than that ephemerally inflated with the hot-air of romance.

In spite of the crusty old farmer who almost broke Will's heart by announcing at the office one day when *The Independent Candidate* was in midstream that he would be glad when that there continued story was through, Jefferson was a hospitable place for a young literary aspirant. At the general store's nightly colloquium the hot-stove leaguers deliberated and decided that Will Howells would be nowhere in a hoss-trade. But that did not keep them from respecting him. It was easy to find friends to literature at the drug-and-book-store's gathering where Goodrich, the eccentric English organ-builder and Dickens cultist, wrangled with the Yankee Jack-of-all-trades and Macaulay disciple who ran the machine shop beneath the *Sentinel* Office. United States Senator Benjamin Wade was literate and willing to bestow the accolade of his approval on Will, even though his short month's trial at studying Blackstone in Wade's office in May, 1855 had proved a failure. In village homes the student and aspiring poet was caressed with encouragement, one neighbor throwing him into a spasm of embarrassment by pointing to the works of Irving along the shelf and predicting, scantingly as it turned out, that his published works would one day fill a shelf like those. A bookish Scotch farmer offered to head a group of local men who would subscribe to send him to Harvard, since the family could not educate him.

Much more important, though, was the friend of his own age who came to work on the paper and board at the Howells home. Jim Williams was lively, extraverted, and much better socialized than Will; but he was also intellectually ambitious and eager to fit himself eventually for a college professorship somewhere in the West. He read with Will and sympathized with his literary dreams; he set him to try to study Greek and, best of all, to learning German. Howells took on the language slowly and with difficulty, working with Jim Williams and then, the summer of 1857, with a lonely, sensitive German refugee of 1848 named Limbeck, who made his living in the village as a bookbinder. And Howells acquired a literary passion to match Cervantes for permanence and for depth of influence. This was the German romantic-ironist, poet and travel writer, Heinrich Heine.

So imbued with Heine did young Howells' imagination eventually become that it amounted almost to identification. Lowell was to keep the first poem Howells submitted to the *Atlantic Monthly* for months. He had to be sure "Andenken" was not a mere plagiarism in translation before accepting it. Later he told Howells he would have to sweat the Heine out of his bones the way one did after a course of treatment with mercury. And it was to be many years before the Heinesque tricks and quirks ceased to appear in Howells' writing, if they ever did disappear completely. The part of Heine which hit young Howells hardest were the poems called "Young Sorrows," which came first in Heine's *Buch der Lieder*. Something out of the depths of Howells' own troubles seemed to answer to the wry and often self-mocking or self-reproachful melancholia expressed in the poems of Heine's obsession with his lost Amalie.

There was another and much healthier side to the influence of Heine on Howells, who could have learned the tricks of *Weltschmerz* and Byronistic posturing from a thousand sources in the decadent Romantic Era of his youth. For Heine was the greatest of the romantic ironists. He could not only entrap his reader in vivid romantic emotions, he could also, with brilliant comic and satiric effect, snatch away the veil of illusion, lay bare the machinery of artifice which had entrapped him, and unite reader with writer in a hearty, self-cleansing laugh at authors and readers who indulge in such claptrap. The methods used and the effects obtained by the romantic ironist are complex. They exercise one's wits. They harden one's mind against sentimentality and emotional sloppiness, and against intellectual irresponsibility of every kind. They sharpen one's sense of irony—and Will Howells had already had his sense of the ironic in life awakened and fed both by Cervantes and by his own father.

Heine's sense of incongruity, of antithesis and bathos, his power to belittle romantic pretense and find sources of literary power in common, nearby objects were important literary lessons for a future realist. And Heine's *Pictures of Travel* were, in the long run, more important to the future novelist than any of his poems. Howells' ideal of style was made more natural and colloquial by reading Heine.

Most important, in Howells' adolescence his passion for Heine was an intensely civilizing experience. It helped him to live imaginatively in a realm, far from the mentally simple post-frontier world about him, where wit, irony, detachment, and the elusively rich rewards of complexity in intellectual life were a recompense for suffering. It is possible that Heine helped save his sanity.

IV

His Jefferson experiences, with their strong overtones of growth and success, should have made Howells happy and hopeful. In a sense they did, yet all his life he looked back on Jefferson with a profound ambivalence in which hatred predominated until he had become an old man.

There were two principal sources of his negative feeling. By 1856 he had begun to develop that artist's revolt against the village, the "small-town virus," which some of the writers born two generations after him supposed they had invented. Worse than that, he suffered in Jefferson a neurotic crisis which left him psychically invalided for several years and forever obliged to stay on guard against the threat of recurrence. Coming as it did as a climax to his adolescence, this was a crowning misfortune. It doomed a life almost ideal in its outward serenity and progressive success to permanent inward anxiety. The famously magnanimous, sympathetic, humorous, and winning personality Howells achieved in maturity was a structure built with endless courage against the howling winds of a psychic storm. Only courage and his father's gift of moral sensibility made it possible.

What with the ghosts and the terrors and all the over-intense fantasies and superstitions, it is clear that Will Howells had suffered from some sort of psychic malaise throughout his childhood. In adolescence, even amid all the absorbing activities and concerns of the Jefferson years, these symptoms did not abate. They increased until he suffered a neurotic breakdown. Howells himself made a frank record of the experience in *My Literary Passions* and *Years of My Youth,* apparently recognizing some compulsion behind his confession. The form which the crisis took was what Howells called "hypochondria," that is, the illusion of having a disease. Not surprisingly in view of his background, the imaginary disease was hydrophobia.

Ever since the afternoon he had spent cowering in the woodshed at Hamilton, convincing himself that his huge dog Tip was going mad, hydrophobia had served to symbolize his psychic turbulence. The dog-bite his family chose to minimize in Hamilton and the terrorism of curs in Columbus, recorded in the 1852 diary as making him "desperate," had been added to the original effect of his father's emotionality over the horribly mysterious, deadly malady in the *Intelligencer* and the family dramatics over the death of poor Mr. Bowers in Hamilton. In the *Ashtabula Sentinel* for May 18, 1854, Will published a suspenseful, and in spots very funny, story called "How I Lost a Wife," a clever blend of Ik Marvel and Western humor in which a shy bachelor leaves his fiancee's home in a tempest of embarrassment because a Newfoundland dog stole his pants while he was taking an early morning dip. "I am 'down' on dogs . . . I detest the whole canine race," the author makes his bachelor say at the beginning. "I am in favor of the formation of a Dog Exterminating Association. I'll invest my pile in it."

Beginning with an intuition on a weird moonlit night in Hamilton, Will had been obsessed with the notion that he would die when he was sixteen. After his sixteenth birthday on March 1, 1853, he was in a frenzy of fear which was only partly dispelled by a neat verbalism of his father's: he wasn't sixteen now because it was his seventeenth year; it was too late to die at sixteen.

Sometime early in 1856 he heard the doctor in Jefferson speculating ignorantly about hydrophobia. "Works round in your system for seven years or more, and then it breaks out and kills you." It was seven years since Will had left Hamilton, and when the heat of summer, always depressing to him, came that year* he "had" hydrophobia. He fought to experience Mr. Bowers' early symptoms, especially convulsions following the threat of splashing water, and the odor of stifling smoke which was both a Bowers symptom and one of Swedenborg's ways to detect evil spirits. He lived in an ecstasy of terror, forcing himself against reason toward dread and toward a hysterical experience of the sensations he feared. He was unable to work either at the printing office or in his study all summer, though in reading he could escape into the strong plots of Dickens and into identification with the soul-sick heroes of Tennyson, who was always able to move Howells profoundly.

His wise father, having had his own troubles in youth, helped with empirical techniques of mental hygiene: long walks into the

* My reason for giving 1856 as the date is Howells' connecting his purchase of Tennyson's *Poems* in 1856 with the "same summer" as the breakdown (*My Literary Passions*, p. 118; cp. 114–115). This is reinforced by the total absence of publication by Howells between April 3, 1856, and Jan. 6, 1857 (Gibson and Arms, p. 76).

woods with a gun or berry-basket for physical fatigue and nature-therapy, day-long drives with him on errands through the country, and incisive counsel. The trouble was psychological and not physical, he told his son; the mind could be dealt with on mental terms; the most important fact was to understand that the trouble was subjective. By fall, with the heat gone, Will had conquered hydrophobia and won the crucial, though not by any means the last, battle.

There is nothing intrinsically important about the hydrophobia delusion as such in Howells' life, of course. What is important to an understanding both of his life and of some qualities of his work is the fact of which his "hydrophobia" must have been only symptomatic, the fact of his profound psychic turbulence. It is not probable that the nature of that disturbance can be identified exactly from the evidence available (or from any set of data not clinically gathered by a medically trained observer). Only the existence of the fact itself and its reasonably inferrible consequences are usable. There are several points from which it might be guessed that Howells' disturbance took its origin. Among others, there were the Howells pattern of estrangement from the norms of the culture; Will's personal intellectualism; and a family psychological conflict.

The tribal pattern of alienation from society was intense for the family from 1847 through 1851 and hardly relaxed much during the brief stay in Columbus. Once they reached the haven of Ashtabula County, ideological differences disappeared in the political sympathy and the agnostic tolerance of local thought. But in speech, manners, customs, adjustment to climate and a dozen other things, the Howellses were newly alien in the Western Reserve. They were Southern Ohioans with a blend of Middle States and Virginia in their background. And of course they went on feeling Welsh.

It is also true that Will was the kind of person denoted by the term "intellectual" in its non-pejorative sense. That is, he had the sort of mind which is dominated by symbolic experience (ideas, and non-discursive symbolic structures) rather than by sensory or social experience. He had the ambition to control this world, the absorption in it and consequent estrangement from non-intellectuals, and the drive to excel, impress, and win his way back to affection by intellectual means which make up the ordinary pattern of intellectualism. He was thus doubly isolated and estranged from local society, and by his intellectualism somewhat alienated from his own family, even, defiantly, from his mother. Whatever isolates damns, said Hawthorne, and this is perhaps generally true in psychological terms, if no other, and was specifically true for young Will Howells.

There was no hope of help for him from religion. His father's Swedenborgianism never became personally real for Will, though he was long interested in its ideas and always in its ethics. Perhaps to clear away his superstitions, perhaps in an effort to help Will travel the way he himself had gone, the father systematically destroyed the possibility of his accepting orthodox Christianity by reading George Eliot's translation of Strauss's *Life of Jesus* with him. Jefferson was a largely agnostic town, except for dabblings in a spiritualism which was more harmful than otherwise for Will. Insofar as Howells was ever religious as distinct from simply moral, it is safe to say that religion made as many difficulties for him as it solved.

As a third choice, it is also possible to construct a "psychoanalytic explanation" of Howells' neurosis. As the second child between a brother four and a half years older and a sister only sixteen months younger, followed quickly by many other babies, he was inevitably forced into desperate sibling competition for his mother's attention. Her rich affective nature made that prize the more desirable. This competition betrayed him into an Oedipal situation, which led to his patterns of terror as guilt and punishment projections. These were made more "real" because his father was a generous man whom he also loved. He was drawn toward his mother and away from his father by the Dayton experience and by the mother's rebellion which was a part of that. This was then complicated by the Eureka Mills year when the father's new leisure brought them very close together while the mother pulled more strongly the other way and drew Joe completely with her. The homesickness crises at separation from her might have been motivated by the fear of "losing" her.

In Jefferson the grand crisis came because, perhaps, in the father's political and business absorption and the mother's obsession with economic anxiety and household cares, he felt completely deserted. Or also because the development of his own ambition and devotion to writing and study isolated him and made him feel that he was deserted in retaliation. This is at best a plausible theory sharply limited in its usefulness as well as in the probability of its representing more than a part of the truth.

Nevertheless, there is a good deal of evidence which points toward conflict for Will within his family. Mary Howells' overanxiety about money and security is several times hinted in *Years of My Youth* and made explicit in a letter Howells wrote in 1910 to a Mrs. Upton. The depth of his anxiety about her is indicated when he says there that his unbearable homesickness was always longing for her and in his continuing to say that he often dreamt of her thirty years after her death. This is illuminated by the *Years of My Youth* accounts of his quarrels with his elder brother. Joe, fully responsive to his mother's drive for security, resented Will's freedom to study and tried to act as taskmaster. Money could be found to support Will to read law in Wade's office, but not to send him to the academy for mere general and literary education—and Joe was to feel guilty about it all his life. Joe was his mother's favorite.

With these facts against the background of our scant knowledge of her personality and Will's feeling for her, it is almost impossible not to read Mary Howells in as the heroine of the following poem. Howells published it in *The Ohio Farmer* for September 18, 1858, after his third invalidism in two years. Although it is at least as good a poem, in its rather repulsive mood, as some of those he collected into volumes, he never took it up again from its obscure place.

THE DREAM

By Will Narlie

I dreamed one Monday morning—
   In the morning, ere daylight,
(And they say that what you dream then,
   Comes true before Saturday night.)

I dreamed I saw my darling,
   All sad and heavy-eyed—
A beautiful, languid phantom—
   Come sit down by my side.

She turned her sad eyes on me,
   Thrilling me through and through—
She twined her white arms around me—
   O dream that will never come true !

She twined her white arms around me,
   And kissed me lip and eye

With wild, delicious love-kisses,
  And sobbed with a passionate cry,

That she loved me, loved me, loved me !
  Then brake away in tears,
And faded upon the darkness.
  Since I dreamed it is many years.

I may live to see her children
  Grow men and women and wed—
I may wait in my heart sick longing
  Till both of us are dead.

The years may pass as the days pass—
  My dream, it will never come true;
Never, never, even in heaven—
  O dream, that will never come true !

Howells' own explanation of the breakdown was that it was caused by overwork. He was setting an ordinary full day's stint of type between seven in the morning and noon, wolfing his dinner to get back in time to correct his proofs by two, and laboring in his study until long past the family bedtime. Then he lay awake to count the feverish pounding of his heartbeats and hear the deathwatch ticking in the wall. No doubt he did overwork desperately and help to speed on the crisis that way. But was that not a symptom as well as any of the others? The emotional climate of one branch of the popular literature, with its fixation, dominated by De Quincey and Poe, on the post-Byronic cult of the scorched heart and the guilt-maddened mind, damaged him too. Much of that, including some of what Will Howells wrote, was in the conventions so deliciously satirized in Huck Finn's accounts of the art of Emmaline Grangerford, who didn't even have to stop to think. In young Howells' case the mood was not *ersatz;* but the conventions of melancholia tempted him to play with them and then turned and hurt him deeply. His passion for Heine—who knew how to slash back with his irony—and even more the beginnings of his realistic revolt, were perhaps partially motivated by those experiences with the literature of terror and sentimentality.

What is more important than any speculation, however, is the fact of this profound crisis in the development of Howells' psyche.

In 1868 he put his own understanding of it in the precisest terms
to his mother: "I have not a shadow of hypochondria [now] upon
me. But I must always be a different man from that I could have
been but for that dreadful year."

V

In 1856 William Cooper Howells returned to Columbus in minor triumph as an official clerk to the Legislature for which he had been a
job-seeking, impermanent reporter in 1852. It was an excellent sign of
his having arrived at prestige and security in his new place. When
he returned to the post for the session which began with the new
year, 1857, he brought Will and his sister Victoria with him. Will
had just been through his crisis; he was obviously unhappy at home,
and then there was the problem of fledging him for a career. Vic
came along to keep him company and to be provided with a look at
the great world too. The war-between-the-sexes of early adolescence
outgrown, Will and Vic had come together over their books and
been drawn into comradeship by a mutual discovery. Both had been
infected by the small-town virus, both were members of that movement which has since inspired dozens of novels, tales, plays, and
poems. Will had begun to feel "frozen" in "the meanness and hol-
lowness of that wretched little village life," as he told his favorite
"Sissy." Together they "comforted each other in our hard task of
making bricks without straw for those Jefferson Egyptians." Some
day the mood which they expressed so early will be closely studied in
a book of pivotal importance to American cultural history, the best
title for which might be, "I *Gotta* Get Out of This Town !"

Chapter Four

DREAMS OF THE GREAT WORLD

THE NINETEEN-YEAR-OLD YOUTH WHO PUT UP AT THE GOODALE House in Columbus with his father and sister just before the Ohio legislature convened for the 1857 session was both well and badly equipped to start his career. He was worried about his age, and the comfort he took in the notion that he looked three or four years older than he was is not supported by his daguerreotype taken earlier that year. Posed with two friends, presumably the pundits of the drugstore symposium, Goodrich and the machinist, is a carefully dressed young dandy with thick, glossy dark hair worn stylishly long and carefully brushed. He is short (Howells never grew taller than five feet four inches) and slight, with the sloping shoulders typical of his family. The face is extraordinary: the longitudinal halves unusually symmetrical, the forehead high and square, the long chin rather heavy, the nose straight and firm, the mouth a shade large and sensuously curved. The blue eyes are deep and either dreamy or haunted. The slant of the head suggests shyness, but the eyes are searching. It is a face one would look at twice, and then again, yet not a comfortable one.

Besides his age, the poet in the picture was worried about his health when he came to Columbus. He seems not to have been troubled about his ability to succeed in the exacting, decidedly unpoetic job he had come to do. Although the new Republican party had shown its power in Ohio by capturing the legislature and electing Salmon P. Chase governor in 1855, it was struggling for its existence in the period of wild political flux which followed the demise of the Whigs. In the fall there would be another state election, and the Republicans were already fighting the impending political reaction which would snatch control of the legislature from them and return Chase to office by only 1,281 votes.

61

William Cooper Howells saw that Republican newspapers might be glad to have a partisan view of the activities of the legislature and sold his idea to the *Daily Cincinnati Gazette,* a Republican journal embattled in the Democratic stronghold of the state. His idea was that he might begin the "Letter from Columbus" with Will's assistance and then gradually turn the job over to him, hoping he could do it well enough to reconcile the *Gazette* to his youth. Since Joe, married the previous June, could run the *Sentinel,* the extra money from the two additional salaries in Columbus would contribute handsomely toward retiring debts on the house and newspaper in Jefferson. And Will might be launched in the great world. As it turned out, Will took the column over, along with his father's signature "Jeffersonian," coolly and efficiently almost from the start. He quickly won the newspaper's consent and went on to score a shining success.

I

Life in the *Sentinel* office, contrary to Howells' later autobiographical accounts, had prepared him beautifully for his task. As *The Independent Candidate* showed, he had grown up understanding the workings of American "practical politics." His brief editorship of the Jefferson paper in 1856 had been politically mature and effective. And he had given himself a careful training in the methods and tone of the gossipy personal writing which is still the key to popularity in American journalism.

The Columbus letter gave *Gazette* readers a smooth blend of human interest, legislative drama, and sophisticated political effects. On January 7, for instance, he built up their anticipation of the opening of the new State House. Touching their taxpayer's tenderness with ironic references to the "over-ornate ginger-breadishness" of the fixtures on which the Democrats had fed their graft, he noted that the Republicans had *"forty thousand dollars"* surplus in the treasury. But at the same time he made his readers feel the glamor of the capitol's newness and greatness:

'In the cavernous depths, where the six huge boilers forever perspire to heat the innumerable apartments above, and where the fires are as undying as the flames of vestal lamps, and subterranean Irishmen flit about like gnomes in the uncertain light, the foundations of the massive pile are as firmly laid as those of the State Houses which Cheops built for his dead.'

The readers, none of whom had central heating, could feel at once proud, fascinated, and personally superior. It was excellent journalism.

The next day's story on "The State House Warming at Columbus" was his masterpiece of the year. Factual, politically astute, full of human interest, humor, and consolation for the stay-at-homes, it was superb reporting. The *Gazette* gave it two twenty-seven-inch columns in a good spot with a display head and subheadings by way of showing its appreciation.

It was a great occasion but not easy or decorous, Howells told his readers. A huge, impatient mob fought to get in, and the ladies' hoops suffered—"Crack, crack, crack, crack went the whalebone as the crowd closed in." Party clothes showed the marks of battle: "Collars that had been standing once, now dangling about the wearers' necks—stove-pipe hats, with the crown knocked down or a big dent in the side. But ah, the ladies—who could describe them? —dishevelled hair, broken combs—one ringlet straightened and entirely out . . . flounces in tatters—plaits ripped at the waists from having been trodden on, and pink ribbons torn off the gay blue dresses."

Inside it was so hot that perspiration made streaks in the ladies' powder. The crowd consumed "24 barrels of milk, 300 turkies, 1,000 gallons of oysters, and 125 hams." But "your reporter" heard in the midst of the feast "the invectives of those who happened to have a dish of oyster soup spilled on them." He was respectful to the Prayer, gave a long account of Governor Chase's "Remarks" and noted that "hearty and prolonged applause followed." Finally, mindful of his principles, he pointed out that "all ranks and classes came . . . The rough country-man with his rough stogy boots (trousers legs tucked in), . . . hands in his breeches pockets and his old, summer straw hat on his head," strode about "perfectly at home" among the "delicate ladies" who danced all night "till broad daylight."

After that he worked with easy confidence. He knew how to exploit conflict in the ranks of the Democrats, making drama of their clashes in debate and a *cause célèbre* when one Cincinnati Democrat struck another and was expelled from the House. When lethargy or frivolity seized the lawmakers he held them up to contempt without fear, as for example when they descended to horseplay over a bill to protect birds: "the member from Auglaize, a region of great moisture, where even wit is watered," he said, "moved to amend it by adding *frogs* to the protected list." Then there were gay motions to prefix "bull" before "frog" and "green" before "bull"—"while another justified the motion on the ground that the frog was a kind of bird, or at least more like a bird than a fish."

He praised Republicans like the radical Unitarian Rev. Moncure D. Conway of Cincinnati, when he lectured in Columbus, or Mr. Monroe, who made a plea for the enfranchisement of the Negro in Ohio so "masterly" Howells despaired of doing it justice. And on March 18 he pilloried Mr. Hutcheson, a Democratic champion, for the "vicious imagination" he showed in ridiculing Negroes. Hutcheson's progress was reported with irony: "Quitting, then, this continent, he betook himself to Europe, and gave it to the Holy Alliance and the Republican Party with merciless savagery . . . his speech bore the evidence of great research into cyclopedias . . . miserably contrived . . . of incongruous elements; but expressed in 'the largest and handsomest words in the dictionary.'" Altogether, "The boot and the thumb-screw, compared to this speech, were pleasing and amiable contrivances."

II

Obviously, a young man who could do such things on his maiden run had a valuable talent for Western journalism. Personally, he was in his element, circulating about the State House as if he owned it and becoming *persona grata* with Republican politicos. If he spent much of his time reading books out of the State Library and was rumored to write poetry, that was all to the good; it explained his power with words. If he bored people a bit by reading or quoting Tennyson or De Quincey at them, nobody minded too much; he was young. No one imagined that both authors were therapeutically helping him to project and control terrors which kept rising up into his imagination from somewhere below. And it was nobody else's business. Sometime in March, Edmund B. Babb of the *Cincinnati Gazette* offered the young man, then just turned twenty, a glittering journalistic prize, the city editorship of the paper at the then munificent salary of one thousand dollars a year.

The *Gazette* carried no "Letter from Columbus" on March 30, 1857, and only a short paragraph reporting that there was "really nothing to report" on March 31. It resumed next day, April 1, in the no-nonsense style of William Cooper Howells who continued it through the legislative adjournment on April 20. It is safe to guess that on March 30 or 31 Will Howells stepped off the train at Cincinnati into the waiting arms of opportunity. At almost exactly the same time a slender, drawling, journeyman printer two years older than he, a flaming redhead named Sam Clemens, left Cincinnati for New Orleans, determined to sail for fame and fortune on the Amazon, but actually destined to begin his famous education as a river pilot that spring. To this point their lives had been in many ways parallel, but they were now to diverge radically before they would cross, delightfully for both, in Boston in 1869. Nevertheless, the trip to Cincinnati was as much an Odyssey in prospect for Howells as Clemens' to New Orleans was for him.

Will was welcomed to the *Gazette* by his sponsor, Babb, an owlish little man, even shorter than Will, who lived entirely in his intense devotion to the newspaper. He took Will in to room with him in his dusty, cluttered bachelor diggings, and undertook to train him both in his own ideal of journalism and in the background to the city editorship (local news) which had been offered him. Howells' first reaction to his big chance was a determined enthusiasm. He fought down the familiar homesickness which immediately attacked him and went to work.

In a letter to Joe of April 10, he first congratulated him cordially and playfully on the birth of a first son, who was named William Dean Howells, II for reasons which are not easy to guess. Then he went on to color his situation gaily. Helping Babb in the news department, he was writing "items" and finding, rather superiorly, that he had to correct "the Mss. of the present incumbent" of the job he was preparing to take over. "I am grown fond of this big, bustling city," with all its rush, he said. He was putting in his free time strolling about alone, taking it in and speculating on the people he watched. Nearly every day he went down to the waterfront to see if one of the Dean uncles was in with his river boat. It all seemed fine, and yet he was to remember the Cincinnati episode with shame as a time of suffering and tormented failure.

A week or so after the letter to Joe, Howells went out on the street with the city reporters to learn their job. He began to contribute to a column of news and comment called "City Intelligence," doing a long review of a lecture by Senator Benton on April 20, typical of his writing in its tone and apt quotations from *Tristram*

Shandy. The tone was heavier and uncertain in treating of Police Court news on April 22. It was more normal in its account of a concert at the Mt. Auburn Female Seminary on May 1 and determinedly professional and ironic the same day in its handling of a Police Court scene headlined "Marriage and Misery."

The story gave the record of what had followed after the elopement of a girl who had been booked and interviewed, raving drunk, the night before: "a brief period of bliss . . . was put an end to by the bride coming home in a state of intoxication . . . and 'cutting up shines' on Wednesday, declaring she had taken lodgings at a disreputable house, and would go there. She was fined, but having no money, was sent to jail." This sounds stylistically like Howells under stress; it was journalistically excellent for a Victorian newspaper. But the inward tension the episode caused Howells was more than his precarious nerves could stand.

He was further shaken when he sat up most of the night with Babb and other editors to hear a prominent local citizen and his lawyer argue that the news of his affair with a married woman should be suppressed. Babb argued the moral responsibility of the paper to expose vice. The man pleaded the future of his family and the woman, and the *Gazette* was merciful. In the morning the rival paper carried the full story.

With Howells' extraordinary moral sensibility and empathic imagination, and against the background of his own history of guilts and terrors, he simply could not make himself tough enough to take such experiences. His breakdown had exhausted his psychic resilience. What suffering and vice meant to him, especially when it was connected with sex, we have seen. He had to tell Babb that he could not go on. Babb tried to place him on the city desk, but he couldn't even handle the stories now. He tried bringing him back to the news department, and on May 4 Howells published one half-hearted example of a column idea and title with which, later and elsewhere, he scored a success: "News and Humors of the Mail." But now nothing could save him. His homesickness drowned him like a wave, and he walked out on the great opportunity, disconsolately rattling three hundred miles diagonally across Ohio on a train back to Jefferson, a thorough failure. The Odyssey had ended in another psychic shipwreck.

If there had been any real personal chance of his making good, it could be said that Will had thrown away a great deal more than a thousand dollars a year and a post of large prestige for one so young. The Ohio Period in American politics was about to dawn, as the center of national power which rested there in the 1870's came close. In on the ground floor earlier than any, an influential young Ohio Republican newspaperman might have risen, like Whitelaw Reid or John Hay, to almost any height of political power and influence. But he would not have been Will Howells had he been prepared to follow the lines which led to Washington and politics instead of to Venice, Cambridge, and the novel. As it was, he made some friends in Cincinnati, and at least one enemy on the *Gazette*. He learned a lot about urban journalism, and he kept a still viable reputation for great promise as a newspaperman. Psychologically, however, it was agony to drag back to the emprisoning small town, to return to typesetting beneath the unspoken disappointment of his father, to wonder if he should ever be able to right himself, to escape, to succeed. When hot weather came he was invalided for weeks with "rheumatic fever," a disease notoriously hard to diagnose, the apparent symptoms of which are often psychosomatic in origin.

When the legislature convened again for 1858, the Howellses were on hand in Columbus in spite of the father's having lost his clerkship in a house narrowly ruled by Democrats. Will had a contract to do the "Letter from Columbus" for the *Gazette* again and a similar one with the Cleveland *Herald*. The *Gazette* letters he signed with a fine Spanish picaresque name, "Chispa," taken from Longfellow's *The Spanish Student*, which he had loved at Eureka Mills. The *Herald* letters he rewrote conscientiously and labeled, from the other linguistic passion, "Genug." His *Gazette* contract was for five hundred dollars, and it may be supposed that the *Herald* paid little or no less, so he had nearly recouped the lost salary, in a job he had done brilliantly the year before and in surroundings he liked.

Nevertheless, by January 20 he had come down with inexplicable vertigo; everything reeled and circled around and under him. Rest and even a trip back to Hamilton failed to help. He struggled and relapsed, and finally crawled home to Jefferson and the resumption of his nature cure. Tiring himself out physically and keeping his mind vacant by lugging a silent gun through the thawing spring forests of Ashtabula County eventually did the trick. The vertigo left, and in August he began to print translations, a poem by Heine and an eccentric sketch from the French, in the *Sentinel*. Somewhere in this period, probably, he wrote "The Dream." In keeping with his own literosity and the psychic nature of his troubles, he discovered, in a minor German romance borrowed from his language teacher, a therapeutic symbol. Theodore Mügge's *Afraja* pictured the hero sailing wildly through the fiords of Norway. Apparently trapped again and again by great walls of rock, he kept finding a new escape channel at each last moment and pressing on. The image took Howells' imagination, spoke decisively to his condition, and remained permanently with him as an instrument of self-healing and hope.

After his recovery in 1858, Howells never quite broke down again for fifty years. Until his marriage in 1862 he suffered more or less continuously from neurotic symptoms of one sort or another, homesickness, melancholia, fringe reactions to hydrophobia and dogs, but he could control them. Yet, even after his marriage, which restored him immeasurably, danger remained definitely there beneath the surface, always to be reckoned with.

III

Newly stable and increasingly fit, he went into the autumn of 1858, aged twenty-one, in much the same position as that he had occupied while trying to write *The Independent Candidate* in 1854 at seventeen. To set type and study in the old Jefferson pattern was still to be agonizingly imprisoned in boyhood. The only observable difference was that the poems he wrote were better. He tried desperately to get legislative correspondence to do; he even proposed writing a column of gossipy notes to be called "Desultoria" for the deadly earnest abolition newspaper, *The National Era*.

Then came one of those turns of fortune which always seem miraculous to the beneficiary. *The Ohio State Journal,* in beloved Columbus, was reorganized to become the Republican standard-bearer for the state. They wanted fresh, young talent and they offered Will the same job, city editor, he'd had in Cincinnati, though at five hundred dollars, half the old salary. But he jumped at the chance. He was remembered! The Republicans welcomed him back to journalism: "He is a gentleman of fine literary taste, studious and talented," said the Cleveland *Leader,* congratulating the *State Journal* on getting him. Fate, Will felt, had rescued him from obscurity and heartbreak and given him the great chance once more. He took care for the rest of his life not to need to be rescued again.

In Columbus Howells was welcomed enthusiastically, primarily for his proved Republican zeal and journalistic prowess, of course. The fortunes of the antislavery party, to which Governor Chase and his backers were tied, had been materially advanced by "the Voice of Giddings." To the *Sentinel,* and even more to the revitalized *Ohio State Journal,* Chase's forces looked for vital support in the election of 1859. Much was involved in bringing Henry D. Cooke, the political specialist among the rapidly rising Cooke brothers, down from the Sandusky *Register* as editor-in-chief. If Cooke knew how to make the *State Journal* the "most readable paper in the State" by recruiting Will Howells with Samuel Reed as one of "two brilliant young editors," that was wise journalism. The first aim of the new investors in the paper was Republican victory, and they were happy to have young Howells on hand as a member of what was for the moment a little journalistic dynasty in the service of the party.

Cooke, for all the historical notoriety his later collaboration with his brother Jay won him, impressed Howells very favorably. He was elegant and gentlemanly. Best of all, he spent his time in politics and let Reed and Howells run the show in their own cooperative and imaginative fashion, steadfast to the political faith but striving always to use their command of wit and irony in the humor tradition of the West rather than the fading conventions of Daniel Websterian rhetoric.

Shifted quickly from the city desk, Howells could give his talents full play. He revived "News and Humors of the Mail," clipping interesting items from "the exchanges" (other papers) and putting facetious tags on them in something like modern *New Yorker* fashion. Tales of the pursuit of runaway slaves, for example, he headed ironically—"Sylvan Sports." He translated from French, German, and Spanish papers, giving his page a cosmopolitan and somewhat pedantic air. His printer friends on the *Journal* joshed him for his pedantry ("We translate from the Spanish of *La Cronica*") and for his poetic posturing (he had done a rather condescending allegory called "The Poet's Friends") in a fine staff-joke parody:

THE POET'S FRIENDS

An owl sat perched on the limb of a tree
   Dismally tooting up at the moon:
The stupid cattle all hastened to see
   What in thunder could mean such a tune.

The owl screeched out, " 'Tis a beautiful song,
   But asses cannot appreciate it."
"Your song," quoth they, "is in some heathenish tongue:
   Why the devil don't you *translate* it?"

The *Ohio State Journal* position filled Howells with the joy of achievement as well as escape. It made him feel like a newspaper-man for the rest of his life. Reed, with whom he joked and shared ideas all through the long working day, was a devotee of Shakespeare and Dickens. An agnostic with a natively ironic mind, he cared as little for poetry as for the church. But he made an almost ideal partner for the long walks which had now, after his cure, become a lifelong need for Howells. The poetic side of his mind Howells could satisfy with his roommate in the old "haunted" medical college which had terrified him in 1852 but was now Columbus' *de luxe* boardinghouse. Fullerton, a law student, read Heine, worshiped Browning, and very early published poems in the *Atlantic*, to Will's envious despair. Another boarder was the Western sculptor, John Quincy Adams Ward. With James M. Comly, also a literate law student and Howells' friend for life, they formed around the generous table of their $3.50 per week boardinghouse the kind of ambitious but lighthearted and masculine society Will Howells badly needed. They let him be at home with them yet be himself, and almost nothing could have done him more good.

Threatened often by homesickness, Will was able to keep his head above water this time. When his "hypochondria" returned with hot weather in 1859, he managed with the help of a wise and friendly local doctor to beat it off, partly by learning to refer to it lightly as "my hippo."

Working on the paper all day and then often out socially in the early evening, he was ready to cultivate his moods and try to write, mostly poetry, late at night. The late hours came partly from a youthful conviction that he could compose better at night, but they were dictated, too, by demands on his time, by economics, and by ambition. With his new prestige and maturer powers, he could now sell things. The *Odd-Fellow's Casket* paid him two dollars a page for at least thirteen pages in 1859. The *Saturday Press*, put out by the Bohemians of Pfaff's Cellar in New York, paid nothing but reached a national audience of people who liked brash young wit. They printed nine items for Howells that year. In emulation of Fullerton, he also sent one of his imitations of Heine, "Andenken," off to the *Atlantic*, where Lowell agonizingly kept it for months, checking Heine to be sure it was no plagiarism.

Worldly sophistication came slowly to a small-town poet. It became one of the cherished legends of the old medical school boardinghouse that when the *Atlantic's* twenty-five-dollar check finally came in payment for "Andenken," Howells was at a loss to know what to do with it. "I don't want to spend the money. What should I do?" he asked Comly. "Why, put it in the bank," was the obvious answer. Some weeks later Comly was visited in the evening by a Howells full of aimless conversation. After an hour or so, he got up to leave, observably dissatisfied. He walked out, closed the door, and then popped his head in again to ask, with rueful embarrassment: "Say, Jim, when you have put money in the bank, *how* do you get it out again?"

As time went by on the job at the *State Journal*, Howells did increasingly literary things. He wrote reviews and literary comment. He developed his eye for "material," for usable incident and detail, and began to write little sketches really striking in their blend of humor, topicality, full-rounded form, and quick penetration into the human significance of situations. His prose began to carry a striking power that his verse seldom shared. "Dick Dowdy," a Dickensian piece on what would now be called a drugstore cowboy, is crisp and acid. Another good bit of local color, "Bobby, Study of a Boy," foreshadows *A Boy's Town* and was widely republished. One more step toward realism had been taken.

Meanwhile, the political work went forward toward a Republican landslide which took over the legislature solidly, elected a new governor, and sent Chase to the United States Senate, a second Ohio abolitionist to sit with Wade of Jefferson. And if this was all in the day's work to Howells, another political event that fall was not. On October 16 John Brown raided the U.S. arsenal at Harper's Ferry in the hope of launching a major slave insurrection in the

South. Then followed a great national drama, as Brown's huge dignity and imperturbability, the romantic grandeur of his calm, ideological fanaticism, were communicated to the country in his examination, trial, and execution. Northern abolitionists with a Puritan hang-over were reminded of Foxe's *Book of Martyrs.* Romantics (and who in 1859 was not somehow romantic?) thought of *Representative Men,* of Prometheus, Socrates, even Jesus. Will Howells was swept off his feet by an idea as never before in his life.

By early November Brown had become an obsession, and Will was seized with a fit of genuine radicalism. He wrote to his father, sending Wendell Phillips' speech to be given to young John Brown on a farm outside Jefferson, and hinting reproach that the *Sentinel* was not violent enough. He even wondered if Giddings were falling by the wayside, and he quoted Thoreau (correctly identified as the author of *Walden*) against what seemed to be Giddings' moderation. On November 15 he published a poem on Gerritt Smith, the upstate New York philanthropist who had wisely had himself committed to an insane asylum with a "broken" mind after Harper's Ferry, a good out for a man who might have been tried for treason against the United States for having helped finance Brown's raid. But Will took it with deadly seriousness:

> . . . I honor all my race
>   In homage to the darkened soul
>   Once luminous,—yet so sweet and whole
> So perfect in remembered grace.

His father duly reprinted it in a John Brown issue of the *Sentinel* for December 1, the day before the hanging.

About November 25 he was moved to final poetic statement on "Old Brown." In a two-part poem of forty-four lines, he devoted the first half to a meditation on the relative fates of "Success" and "Unsuccess" in history: the one "goes royal crown'd"; the other dies amid sneers and scorn, while history, "in the waning light," comes to write "the failure into infamy." Nevertheless, there one day comes a man with the eye

> To read the secret will of good,
>   (Dead hope, and trodden into earth,)
>   That beat the breast of strife for birth,
> And died birth-choked, in parent blood.

Then he turned to apostrophize Brown in the only call for violence he wrote until World War I:

> Old lion! tangled in the net,
>   Baffled and spent, and wounded sore,
>   Bound, thou who ne'er knew bonds before—
> A captive, but a lion yet.
>
> Death kills not, in a later time,
>   (Oh! slow, but all-accomplishing.)
>   Thy shouted name abroad shall ring,
> Wherever right makes war sublime:
>
> When in the perfect scheme of God,
>   It shall not be a crime for deeds
>   To quicken liberating creeds,
> And men shall rise where slaves have trod;
>
> Then he, the peerless future Man,
>   Shall wash the blot and stain away,
>   We fix upon thy name to-day,
> Thou hero of the noblest plan.
>
> Oh! patience! Felon of the hour!
>   Over thy ghastly gallows tree
>   Shall climb the vine of Liberty,
> With ripened fruit and fragrant flower.

IV

In Columbus journalistic success and the friendship of masculine peers fulfilled some of Howells' dreams of the great world. But his sister Vic and he had discovered their mutual longing to get out of the small town by daydreaming aloud over the picture of "high society" people on the cover of a folder of sheet music. And almost at once in Columbus he was invited to the Governor's home for a New England Thanksgiving dinner—a custom not yet general in Ohio. There he met Kate Chase, soon to become the ravishing belle of Civil War Washington, and intoxicatingly found himself accepted into her group. Other leading Republicans followed the Governor's lead. Will was invited by the celebrated Judge Swan, whose drawing room was the pinnacle of social recognition in Columbus. He was taken up, almost adopted, by a distinguished local physician, Dr. Samuel M. Smith and his family.

The entree won through Will Howells' political potency was confirmed by his looks, especially the eyes, and by his drollery. In a parlor he could step to the bookcase, take down the latest Dickens or Thackeray, scan a few pages, and begin to toss off gay ironies which kept a whole room entertained. With women, the gracious hostesses rather Southern in style, and the buoyant Midwestern girls, he found himself a sparkling success. As a poet and conversationalist, as a quietly pleasant personality with a substratum of melancholy which called forth maternal sympathies, and as a rising, already influential young man who would one of these days be eminently marriageable, he was a prospect in whose education they delighted. He was invited to all the dances and parties that winter and heartily welcomed wherever he called by women who were eager to initiate him into the social game and happy to find him teachable. Howells in turn found them fascinating.

His recollections of their drawing rooms and conservatories in *Years of My Youth* is almost a hymn to the ladyhood he learned to worship in Columbus. In later life he became disenchanted of almost all his other romanticisms. But he never entirely sloughed off his worship of the lady, though by means of it he gained deep insights into the nature of the civilized woman.

Looking back from 1895 on a life already rich in fame, friendships with genius, and prosperity, Howells judged that "those two happy winters in Columbus . . . were the heyday of life for me. There has been no time like them since, though there have been smiling and prosperous times aplenty. . . ."

The year 1860, indeed, was to be packed for him, not only with a young man's seeing of glorious visions for an ambitious future, but also with the unmatchable thrills of a young man's "firsts." It began a little early, at Christmas time in 1859, when his first book, *Poems of Two Friends* in collaboration with J. J. Piatt, was issued by a Columbus publisher. It had in prospect his first volume of prose, a campaign biography of Lincoln, and then his marvelous pilgrimage to the East to gaze at and touch hands with the literary giants of Boston and New York. But the greatest event of a young man's first *annus mirabilis* was that in the winter of 1860 he met the girl who was to be his wife for almost fifty years of an unusually good marriage.

One of the girls who came often to the dances given by the gay bachelors at the old medical college was Laura Platt, who afterward married John G. Mitchell, one of the boarders. And that winter Laura brought her visiting cousin from Brattleboro, Vermont, Elinor Gertrude Mead, to the dances. Apparently Elinor had come to Columbus feeling rather like a Yankee sophisticate out on the edge of civilization. For when she saw her favorite magazine lying on the Platts' parlor table, she shrieked in maidenly wonder, "Why, have you got the *Atlantic* out here?" And Laura Platt could answer proudly: "There are several *contributors* to the *Atlantic* in Columbus." Actually, there was only one left in town, and nothing could have made Elinor more anxious to meet him. Newly glamorous in thin, low-cut sideburns and a filmy mustache, he was eventually introduced. And when at a dance she drew a funny cartoon on her fan of the sculptor J. Q. A. Ward clumsily galloping about the dance floor, convulsing the brethren of the boardinghouse by flashing and then concealing it in the folds of her fan, humor-loving Howells was enchanted. By summertime he and she were courting seriously on the basis of an "understanding," if not an engagement.

Elinor Mead was as nearly perfect for Howells as it is humanly reasonable to hope a prospective wife can be. Exactly two months younger than he, petite, sudden and graceful in movement, and with the Yankee combination of fair coloring and light brown hair, she was attractive in person. But she was extraordinary in mind and character. Connected through both parents with the Brahmin caste, the "intellectual aristocracy" of New England as Dr. Holmes was just then calling them, she had the sharp intelligence, the intuitiveness, the inward biting conscientiousness, the personal force and vividness, and the good taste tending toward hyperesthesia which were cropping out in that last true generation of the Brahmins.

Elinor's father, a lawyer, fulfilled the Brahmin function of intellectual and social leadership in a Vermont village so well as to have won the popular accolade of "Squire" Mead. He did his duties manfully, fathering nine children, Brattleboro's first town library, and its first bank.

Elinor's mother, Mary Noyes Mead, was a sister of the fabulous John Humphrey Noyes, founder of a Utopian community in nearby Putney and then of the Oneida Community which his prophetic forcefulness and charm and his mental brilliance made the most significant and enduring of all the experiments in communalism of the romantic era. Mary was one of the only two of his siblings able to resist being pulled into his orbit. She eventually led the family opposition to the prophet, but radical ideas must have been as familiarly known, if otherwise received, in the Brattleboro home as in the cabin at Eureka Mills. At any rate, something of the Noyes intensity and vividness appeared in her children.

The rupture with her brother and the others who went with him must have come hard to Mary Noyes Mead, because both she and her husband were strongly family-minded, constantly visiting and being visited by far-flung but affectionate relatives. One of these, a nephew of the Polly Hayes who was Mary Noyes Mead's mother, was young Rutherford Birchard Hayes of Delaware, Ohio. Left fatherless early, Hayes visited Brattleboro and Putney in 1834, when he was twelve, and again in 1847 and 1852. He always had a good time, taking the goings on at Putney equably and enjoying the swarms of kinfolk. From the 1852 visit he reported home that, "We had a jolly gay time at Brattleboro. The Meads are a happy family and have the gift of making others happy. I love them all." Nine-year-old Joanna loved to romp, he said. "Eleanor (*sic*) is older, more cultivated . . . but witty, chatty, and capital company. Mary Birchard thinks her 'sarcastic,' but as she is not ill-natured in her satire, I like it." The Mead joy in wit was not less than the Howellses'. Their gift for affection tempered with humor made them good company. "Never yet saw a Mead that I didn't like," wrote John Fiske to his wife in 1874. "The same streak of brightness, sweetness, and simplicity runs through the whole family."

Though Elinor Mead struck some Ohio folks as hyperintellectual and thus raised the Victorian specter of the "advanced" woman in their minds, her active brain was just what Howells wanted. In after years her absence on vacation left a great emptiness in his day, as he complained, for it was she "who keeps all the talk going." When from Venice he first revealed her identity to his family by announcing his intention of marrying her, there was brief family demurral based on a negative report from a Columbus woman. And Howells wasted no time in setting the family straight about Elinor. "She's not violently intellectual, by any means," he said, to lay that specter. "She has artistic genius, and a great deal of taste, and she admires my poetry immensely. *I* think she's good-looking and rather suppose she was picked out for me from the beginning of the world. . . . She's good as well as smart—and in fine I love her very much."

There was indeed artistic talent in the Mead children. Of Elinor's brothers, Larkin became one of the ranking sculptors of his day, and William Rutherford Mead was of the firm of McKim, Mead, and White, who dominated American architecture for a generation or more. At home, bright colors stood on the sitting room table ready for any sudden impulse to paint, and exact communication among the children was often carried out in sketches. Brattleboro had some contact with the great world through its being a small spa and eventually a popular summering place.

Family affection and the wish to let Elinor get away from Brattleboro conspired in 1860 to bring her to the prosperous home of Rutherford Hayes, a rising Republican lawyer and politician in Cincinnati, to "stay the winter." Whether she met Will Howells there at Miss Nourse's before, or, as seems more likely, at Platt's after she went to Columbus, sometime before spring she was visiting in the home of Hayes's sister Fanny as the companion of her daughter, Laura Platt. Her Ohio stay was long enough to make a courtship effective; it seems to have lasted into the summer.

V

Second only to his one great love affair—how merely normal a life, to have been thoroughly in love with just one woman for fifty years ! —Howells' great thrill was, of course, the publication of his first book. Even if he had to share the joy with a collaborator, it was a bid for fame, and a book of poems. The little Preface to *Poems of Two Friends,* even behind its mask of Heinesque irony, shows clearly how tremulous the authors' hopes for it were:
                                                     'It may be that
the Tenderness which cannot leave these poor children of the Heart to generous Oblivion, is not wise. There is the Doubt.

Gracious Reader ! (approached with the reverent Affection due to the Reader of a first Book), solve us the Doubt.'

But when the public verdict was in, the best that could be said for the authors was that the Doubt had not been solved. Like most first volumes of verse, *Poems of Two Friends* sold practically not at all. The publisher was left with almost the entire printing on his hands, and so much of it was pulped that the little book is now a collector's item. Not even Howells himself had a copy when, by request, he tried years later to present the State Library of Ohio with his complete writings. And despite certain other parallels between this book and *Lyrical Ballads,* no one could say that the public was wrong. There is no great poetry in *Poems of Two Friends* and no clear promise of great poetry to come.

Piatt, with whom Will Howells had tussled and skylarked in the composing room during his 1852 experience in Columbus, was a derivative nature-poet, at his best in Western genre pieces where rather thin sentiment was reinforced by his power to observe Midwestern customs and farm details and bring them naturally into his picture. Howells, who could do the same sort of thing about as well as Piatt, had the other, Heinesque string to his bow. Both suffered from not having enough in their portfolios and having to pad their slim volume out with second-best productions. Piatt, sticking to verse, remained a semi-obscure regional writer all his life. There is not much reason to suppose that Howells would have risen higher as an author had he confined himself to poetry.

Yet there were compensations for Howells in the critical reception of *Poems of Two Friends*. He had the bitter-sweet joy of reading his first reviews. The mercurial Henry Clapp, editor of *The Saturday Press,* New York's ill-fated periodical challenge to the cultural supremacy of the *Atlantic Monthly,* disparaged Piatt but said that Howells, whose poems he had been accepting regularly, was a "man of genius . . . not, indeed of the highest order; but . . . genius," and predicted for him "what Shakespeare, or somebody, calls a 'brilliant future.'" And following two more of Howells' poems in the April *Atlantic* came Lowell's tempered but friendly judgment. The volume he thought "very agreeable," especially for its "thoroughly Western flavor" in spots. In conclusion, he noted signs of "fresh and authentic power" in the authors. It did not matter so much then that Lowell also underscored the Emersonian critique of Moncure D. Conway in the transcendentalist Cincinnati *Dial* that Howells was, though admirably cultivated and very promising, not original enough. Conway even scented "a certain fear of himself" and a need to amputate "all classes and models."

On balance, Will Howells had occasion to feel that things were going pretty well. And, what with love and a celebrity which loomed very large in Columbus, he came to feel more secure and expansive than at any time since his boyhood. He began to go out with the newspaper and boardinghouse boys after the girls had been taken home for the night at eleven and enjoy good fellowship over Swiss cheese sandwiches and the excellent Rhine wine of Ohio. When Conway became his friend that year he found the poet personally impressive. His antislavery sentiments were impeccable, and he had "read everything." But to a devotee of Emerson, what he *was* personally (or what he seemed to be) was most important. What Conway found about him was "a sincerity and simplicity, a repose of manner along with a maturity of strength, surprising in a countenance so young—and, I must add, beautiful, that I knew perfectly well my new friend had a great career before him." Obviously, Howells had been winning important victories in the battle of his psyche.

Consequently, he was not too upset when sometime that spring, probably late in March, Cooke regretfully informed his two brilliant young editors, to whom he already owed a good deal of back salary, that the paper could no longer support them except as free-lance contributors. With the State campaign triumphantly over and Republican politics in a muddle nationally, his financial backing had dwindled. Reed took a new job in Cincinnati, and Howells was left to cast about. The event made him feel that perhaps he was professionally outgrowing Columbus. The town seemed to have "contracted" for him, and he began to dream of a "wider field of action," perhaps in New York, though he felt it wise to assure his father that he would never "be seduced by Bohemianism" if he went there.

For the time being, however, he found that Follett and Foster, the publishers of *Poems of Two Friends*, would give him a job as reader and book doctor. For them he collected biographical details and wrote brief introductions for some of the figures included in William T. Coggeshall's pioneering book, *The Poets and Poetry of the West*. He reworked and in part rewrote *Three Years in Chili*, "By a lady of Ohio." Late in May, however, Follett and Foster thought of a really good way to use their bright young employee. They had scored a lucrative publishing success with the *Lincoln-Douglas Debates*, and now the once obscure Illinois lawyer had been nominated for the Presidency by the Republican party. What could be more fitting, or potentially more profitable, than that an able

Western writer should do a campaign biography of him for a Western publisher? They proposed that Will Howells should hop a train for Springfield and get the facts.

Neatly missing the opportunity for an intimate brush with history (as he explained patiently long after, no one could have known), Howells decided to stay home and write poetry. He had never been an interviewer, and a young law-student friend named John Quay Howard was going to Springfield anyhow. He let Howard talk to Lincoln.

Of what Howard brought back, however, he was able to make much better use than Howard himself, who at once went into competition. Remembering his own year in a log cabin, he discovered a vein of wilderness poetry in the materials Howard picked up from Lincoln's Springfield friends, especially from George Close, who had split rails with Lincoln in Marion County, and from the files of the *Sangamon Journal*. With these sources and Follett and Foster's *Debates*, Howells went to work on a rush job. His years of literary discipline and his reporter's facility stood him in good stead. In little more than a week he had turned in to the publisher an astute and glowing judgment, seventy-seven pages long, of Lincoln's career. It took Howard a month longer (by which time he was competitively out of the market) to do a much worse book.

In spite of his speed, Howells wrote better than his later modesty recalled. It was not hack work but warm and perceptive. The Cincinnati *Commercial* was not wrong in calling it "spirited, flowing, and graceful." He slipped a Heinesque touch into the introduction, saying, "When one has written a hurried book, one likes to dwell upon the fact, that if the time had not been wanting one could have made it a great deal better. This fact is of the greatest comfort to the author, and of not the slightest consequence to anybody else. It is perfectly reasonable, therefore, that every writer should urge it." His political strategy was unobtrusive but, on the whole, effective. Usually it was less literary, but he got in one telling blow, with a trick learned from Hawthorne, while discussing the famous debates:

'Douglas was full of words. . . . The banner of popular sovereignty smote pleasantly upon the sight. When Lincoln reversed it, and men read the true inscription, they saw that it was the signal of discord, oppression, and violence. There were old stains upon that gay piece of bunting; stains of blood from the cabin hearths of Kansas, and from the marble floor of the Senate hall; and a marvelous ill odor of cruelty hung about it, as if it were, in fact, no better than the flag of a slave-ship. Where its shadow fell across the future of a State, civilization and humanity seemed to shrink back, and a race of bondmen and their masters thinly peopled a barren land that would have "laughed in harvests" in the light of freedom.'

What was most cared for at the time, of course, was the political effect of the book. But now the impressive fact is that Howells, who had not troubled to go to see Lincoln, was able to grasp and express, in an extremely early form, the majestic Lincoln myth. It was because he too had gone to school very little and had seen the frontier partly through his own and partly through his father's eyes. And perhaps it was because he was a poet. He quoted the old backwoodsman, Close, "God never made a finer man," and continued:

'No admirer, who speaks in his praise, must pause to conceal a stain upon his good name. No true man falters in his affection at the remembrance of any mean action or littleness in the life of Lincoln.

The purity of his reputation, the greatness and dignity of his ambition, ennoble every incident of his career, and give significance to all the events of his past.

It is true that simply to have mauled rails, and commanded a flat-boat, is not to have performed splendid actions. But the fact that Lincoln has done these things, and has risen above them by his own force, confers a dignity upon them; and the rustic boy, who is to be President in 1900, may well be consoled and encouraged in his labors when he recalls these incidents in the history of one whose future once wore no brighter aspect than his own wears now.

The emigrant, at the head of the slow oxen that drag his household goods toward the setting sun—toward some Illinois yet further west—will take heart and hope when he remembers that Lincoln made no prouder entrance into the State of which he is now the first citizen.

The young student, climbing unaided up the steep ascent—he who has begun the journey after the best hours of the morning are lost forever —shall not be without encouragement when he finds the footprints of another in the most toilsome windings of his path.

Lincoln's future success or unsuccess can affect nothing in the past. The grandeur of his triumph over all the obstacles of fortune, will remain the same. Office can not confer honors brighter than those he has already achieved; it is the Presidency, not a great man, that is elevated, if such be chosen chief magistrate.'

Howells also knew how to retail some of Old Abe's funny stories with the transparency of familiar skill and understanding.

His book eventually took on unique value as an association piece, because at the request of a friend Lincoln annotated it carefully. The corrections he had to make are surprisingly few in the light of the circumstances under which it was done, and apparently Lincoln himself liked it, or at least found it interesting. He withdrew it from the Library of Congress on May 4, 1863, and returned it on May 31. On March 22, 1865, he took it out again, and it was in the White House when he died. Howells himself was too apologetic about it in later years. For one thing, his self-concept after middle life dictated that his early political activities must be minimized or ignored. His failure to go and meet Lincoln was an embarrassing blunder. His profiting under the spoils system to the extent of the Venetian consulate looked different in the years after Civil Service Reform than it had before. It was easier to gloss the whole matter over with deprecation and remember that it was only one of a dozen campaign biographies of Lincoln and that, in spite of good sales in the West, it had, as he told an interviewer in the early nineties, netted him only $199.

VI

Whatever it looked like in the perspective of later affluence, that much money in addition to Howells' salary was a bonanza in 1860, his first. Cannily he made arrangements to invest it in a project which would be educational, pleasurable, and perhaps productive of fresh opportunity: a trip to New York via the St. Lawrence waterway, Quebec, and Boston. He meant to see the country, meet literary celebrities, and perhaps visit Brattleboro, Vermont. He arranged with the Cincinnati *Gazette* and the *Ohio State Journal* to publish his travel letters. Follett and Foster enabled him to stay on their staff by proposing research for a book on the principal industries of the states he was to visit. Early in July he arrived in Jefferson "to lounge beneath the dark maples that shadow the home threshhold" for a while before he went to Ashtabula on the first leg of his trip. He was moved to romantic attitudinizing by blue

Lake Erie and to Heineisms on the hack drivers at Buffalo, from which he sent his first travel letter dated July 16.

At Niagara Falls he was guided to choice view points by Godfrey Frankenstein, a painter who specialized in the Falls, watched the famous tight-rope walker Blondin, mocked rhetorical sublimity about the scenery and then tried it anyway, and commented on the honeymooners: "Happy people ! . . . Happy, indeed, if you could walk here forever, and not become Mr. and Mrs. Jones, and be old and fat." He went on to Toronto, Montreal, and Quebec, squeezing the last drop of exoticism out of them for his newspaper letters. Comparison between this writing and the expert handling of the travel writing which made him internationally famous a few years later is revelatory. The Howells touch in the mature books is in the under-writing. There the tone is subdued, and he never warbles or tries for picturesque sensations—*effectisms,* the prophet of realism would someday call them. In the 1860 letters these temptations are never resisted. They are pumped up vigorously from Catholicism in Montreal, the antiquity of Quebec, or Longfellow associations in Portland, where he arrived on July 28 for his first sight of salt water. On July 30 he left by train for Boston, stopping overnight at Haverhill to fail in the effort to investigate shoe manufacturing. On August 1 he arrived in a smokeless, preindustrial Boston with the Hancock house still standing: for him, of course, it was Mecca, the holy city of American literature.

The story of his adventures with the prophets of his shrine—which he was surprised to find centered in Cambridge and Concord rather than Boston—Howells has told in one of the few classics among American literary memoirs, *Literary Friends and Acquaintances.* He tried hard to see them all, missing only Whittier, Longfellow, and Harriet Prescott Spofford because they were too far away from Boston. The rest he saw: Fields, Lowell, Holmes, Hawthorne, Thoreau, and Emerson, in something like that order. He got along better with the first four than with the transcendentalists. But the intensity of his worshipfulness made his insight into each of them penetrating. The quality of Thoreau's social relations which made Emerson say you would as soon think of taking the branch of an elm as Henry's arm comes out clearly in Howells' account of their meeting. He had admired *Walden* in 1858 and felt himself fighting shoulder to shoulder with Thoreau for John Brown. Now he was seated clear across the room from orphic phrases about a

John Brown principle and found the altitude simply too high for his lungs.

At Emerson's he was invited to dinner but baffled by the great man's plain speaking: Hawthorne was a magnificent man but *The Marble Faun* was "mush"; the West was the hope of America; poetry, and by inference literary art, was properly only a pastime. Yet he recorded Emerson's fundamental reaction to the difference between the theory of literature at the head of which he stands and the only other one there really is in America, that headed historically by Edgar Allan Poe. Howells mentioned Poe. Poe? "Oh," cried Emerson after struggling to remember, "you mean the *jingle man!*"

The high point of his days (August 9–11) in Concord was a slow talk with the shy Hawthorne, of whom Howells retained a much more human impression than that familiarly retailed by Hawthorne's Saturday Club associates. Hawthorne had never seen a woman he thought entirely beautiful; Yankees were slowly freezing to death spiritually; and he had hopes for the West, he told Howells. He would like to see a part of the world where the damned shadow of Europe had not fallen. But after all, it was Boston, where the celebrities knew how to enjoy their eminence and the literary cult had its temples, which most impressed a youthful pilgrim. In the *Atlantic* office Fields let him read the proofs for "The Pilot's Story," being made ready for the September issue, and Ticknor ceremonially counted out and paid him five five-dollar gold pieces for it.

Lowell gave him good advice in his study in Cambridge, and he sat with Lowell, Fields, and Holmes at dinner at the Parker House, listening to the talk from two in the afternoon until dusk. The talk was brilliant, but what intoxicated him was Holmes's saying mischievously to Lowell, "Well, James, this is something like the apostolic succession; this is the laying on of hands." They gave him the "full treatment" for visiting literati. He went to a breakfast at Fields's, complete with the latest anecdotes of Tennyson and a tour through the rich collection of literary mementos. Holmes had him to tea and coaxed him into a recital of all his neurotic experiences, sympathetically received—Holmes loved to collect *dossiers* on people. Holmes's son, then a Harvard senior, not yet Captain or Justice Holmes, wandered around Boston with him until two in the morning and they became friendly enough to begin a correspondence.

All this had its effect, of course. Will Howells' heart was won completely. An idealized Boston became (as it ceased to be almost at once when he later went to live in Cambridge) his spiritual home, the Great City of his dreams where the good life was lived, truth and beauty were served, and the keys to success were kept. No European experience ever moved him so profoundly.

Although in spite of his springtime pledge to his father he was at first worshipful when he went on down to New York, it was inevitable that the Bohemians there, mostly much nearer his own age, should make an impression of anticlimax on him. When he told Henry Clapp how Boston had pleased him, the "King of Bohemia" strode blasphemously up and down the office, cussing out Boston and listing all the violent things he would do if anyone accused *him* of respectability. In spite of the watchful delight of the local crowd, Howells was neither awed nor amused. He had listened to professional bad boys in newspaper offices before, and he was conscious that a deliberate effort was being made to shock him. Perhaps he wore a too-obvious halo fresh from his Boston experience. Perhaps his ambivalent article, which Clapp had printed on August 11 with the geographically inaccurate Menckenian title, "A Hoosier's Opinion of Walt Whitman," made them suspicious. At any rate, the Bohemians who had publicly called him a genius in January were hostile in August. Clapp put him down solidly, at last, by asking him about Hawthorne. Howells started to say that, well, Hawthorne was shy and *he* was shy, when Clapp squelched him by interjecting: "Oh, a couple of shysters !" The hangers-on roared, and Howells retreated into private irony.

That irony was fully operative when he dropped in at Pfaff's beer cellar to observe what Columbus would have been sure was a Bohemian orgy. What he saw was a tame if smoky session where the young men of the working press talked over steins of beer. The one fine experience of the evening was shaking hands with Whitman, who leaned back in his chair and gave the young Westerner the full benefit of his magnetism. The benignity and sweetness, the dignity and spiritual power of Whitman became a permanent memory for Howells, though nothing ever persuaded him to give unqualified approval to Walt's poetry. Altogether the New York visit was painful, especially in contrast to Boston. He had been as proud of his *Saturday Press* connection as his *Atlantic* one, and had responded to the energy in it so like that which characterized the "little magazine" of a later age. Fitz James O'Brien, Henry Arnold, Fitzhugh Ludlow the hashish eater, Aldrich, Stedman, William

Winter, and Clapp himself were naturally closer to him both as contemporaries and as journalists than the Bostonian demigods. But now it was all spoiled, and he cared no more for the *Saturday Press*.

Since Howells easily made his peace with the literary world of New York when he came to live there as a free lance in 1865–66, the unfortunate part of his clash with the *Saturday Press* Bohemians was that it deflected him from a growing fascination with Walt Whitman. As reader and contributor, he must have seen the *Saturday Press* publication of "Out of the Cradle Endlessly Rocking," one of Whitman's great poems and one peculiarly fitted to speak to Howells. Certainly Whitman's ideas, in many respects the same as his own father's ideas, struck young Howells as profoundly important. He quoted a "Poemet" in one of his *State Journal* columns and enthusiastically reviewed "Bardic Symbols" when it appeared in the April *Atlantic* along with his own poems. Finally he wrote the essay, by far his best early piece of literary criticism, which appeared in the *Saturday Press* as "A Hoosier's Opinion of Walt Whitman" on August 11, while Howells was in Concord.

Having read the 460 pages of the third edition of *Leaves of Grass,* Howells found himself both impressed and baffled. Whitman, he says, is much too important to be denied a hearing. Perhaps he is a "Bull in the China shop," but he has been pronounced "a splendid animal" by Emerson. The trouble is that "The Misses Nancy of criticism hastened to scramble over the fence, and on the other side, stood shaking their fans and parasols . . . and shrieking, 'Beast! Beast!'" Whitman violates all the canons of poetry and too often writes chaos, Howells thinks—and then there is his insistence on overt sex. The verse is "metreless, rhymeless, shaggy, coarse, sublime, disgusting, beautiful, tender, harsh, vile, elevated, foolish, wise, pure and nasty." It mixes passages "of profound and subtle significance and of rare beauty, with passages so gross and revolting." The trouble is that, "He has told too much . . . the secrets of the body should be decently hid." The reader "goes through his book, like one in an ill-conditioned dream, perfectly nude, with his clothes over his arm." He concludes that Whitman has so far been "both overrated and underrated. It will not do to condemn him altogether, nor to commend him altogether. You cannot apply to him the taste by which you are accustomed to discriminate in poetry." Only time could bring in the true verdict.

As criticism of the 1860 edition of *Leaves of Grass*, the third edition which lacked much of what was to be Whitman's best poetry, that is defensible as a judicious contemporary estimate. There is courage in the attack on the "Misses Nancy" and in the estimate of Whitman's importance. There is the intimation of a new appreciation dawning in the background when the critic theorizes that *Leaves of Grass* calls for new standards and discriminations. The reservations are not to be wondered at in a self-taught poet who had begun with Pope, or in a neurotic small-town boy become a provincial newspaperman.

After the New York fiasco, unfortunately, it would be decades before Howells came so close to Whitman again. As a member of the Dante Club and worshiper of Lowell in Howells' first decade in Cambridge, Howells was intimately associated with men who could see no good in Whitman. While he was editor of the *Atlantic*, Whitman was not published there. In the seventies, indeed, there was real hostility from Whitman and his followers toward Howells. He "needs a good critical cudgelling," John Burroughs said indignantly in 1876, "Someday I will send an arrow at him. . . ." But by the end of Howells' tenure on the *Atlantic*, the atmosphere had lightened. Coming to give the St. Botolph's Lincoln lectures in Boston in 1881, Whitman was charmed to find Howells personally attentive and publicly cordial. In 1887 Howells contributed to the Boston Cottage Fund for Whitman. And in the conversations recorded by Horace Traubel, especially in 1888 and 1889, Whitman was increasingly pleased by the Tolstoian, Christian Socialist Howells, approving Hamlin Garland's efforts to act as a go-between, and gratified by Howells' friendly review of *November Boughs*. In Whitman's last year, in fact, Burroughs symbolized this reconciliation by proclaiming the humanitarian, fighting realist Howells a true heir of Whitman and Emerson. If that was only a partly true statement, yet it rightly called attention to the broad spiral through which Howells' thought had swept from 1860 to 1890.

When Howells got back to Columbus, then, it was with his head full of Boston and sound words of advice from Lowell ringing in his ears: "Don't print too much and too soon; don't get married in a hurry; read what will make you *think*, not *dream*; hold yourself dear, and more power to your elbow ! God bless you !" But he had failed in his effort to escape from Columbus. Just before leaving Boston he had braced Fields for the job of assistant editor of the *Atlantic* only to be told good-naturedly that it had just been filled. Fields gave him a cordial note to John Bigelow of the New York *Post,* urging his fitness to do the paper's "literary work &c.," retailing his experience in the West, and ending "Lowell and Holmes put the poem 'The Pilots' Story' among the fine things of our day." Bigelow lived to regret that he was not impressed by the much experience in Ohio and thought the young man too literary. His dryness may have been another source of Howells' discontent with New York.

At any rate, he had a happy surprise waiting at Columbus. With the presidential campaign to fight, Cooke had acquired the sinews of war and was anxious to have at least one of his bright young men back again, even willing to hire him primarily as literary editor. He paid up Will's back salary and raised his wages. Price, the new partner Cooke found for him, became a close friend from the start, even to the point of calling him "Willie," as his mother did. Instead of going back to the medical college, he took a room and ate his meals in restaurants with Price. He stayed out of Columbus "society" for a while, giving himself to professional journalism more enthusiastically, and going out at night with Price and Whitelaw Reid, who had taken over his *Gazette* correspondence, to make oyster stews and drink claret punch. They entertained Artemus Ward, the *Cleveland Plain Dealer*'s humorist, in a typical riot of fun. Horace Greeley dropped in and lectured them owlishly on the *State Journal*'s defects.

VII

On the *State Journal* they fought through the election and got Lincoln in, and then, with all the rest of the country, found themselves caught in the slow, agonizing, uncontrollable drift of events toward the Civil War. Majority Ohio opinion, a product both of radical abolitionism in the Reserve and the southern Ohio commercial orientation, favored a compromise on peaceful secession; let the South go if it wished. The influential Greeley preached it from New York, and Chase's pessimism, unappeasable because he was not President, strongly affected the *Journal.* Howells and Price adopted the policy even a bit too wholeheartedly for Cooke, who had to tone them down. Then came Sumter, and Ohio was incredibly electrified. Gala volunteers in Garibaldi red shirts, singing careless songs, flooded into Columbus. Ohio alone could have met Lincoln's first call for 75,000 volunteers.

As a reporter, Howells was close to events and to the romantic boys who were soon camped out in Goodale Park. He wrote a series of letters for the New York *World*, "From Ohio," describing war preparations. In part this was another bid to get out of Columbus. Many of his friends were volunteering. Comly and John G. Mitchell, who was to marry Laura Platt, got commissions and were started on their way toward general's stars. The same was true of Elinor Mead's Cincinnati host and cousin, Rutherford Hayes.

For Will Howells, of course, military service was psychologically out of the question. He applied for a foreign consulate, preferably Munich, as a political reward for his campaign biography. While waiting for a decision he was half-seriously tempted to accept the offer of a lieutenancy in an Ohio company, but actually that was beyond serious thought. He could console himself with the idea that the consulate would at least be government service, and his political convictions of the moment allowed him to believe that war with the South was probably both wrong and impossible of success. But he was to have guilt feelings about the Civil War for the rest of his life.

As the spring of 1861 lengthened into a strained summer made tragic at Bull Run in July, Howells' personal affairs came to a kind of crisis. In May, Cooke, owing him about two hundred dollars in back salary again, announced that he was selling out the *Ohio State Journal* and going to Washington where his enterprising brother Jay saw a great opportunity for a trustworthy man who had the confidence of Chase, the new Secretary of the Treasury. While Cooke scraped up the money to pay him off, Will lacked the capital to carry out an *Atlantic* assignment to write a series of articles on Western cities and had to beg off. To make matters worse, James T. Fields, new editor of the *Atlantic,* was refusing the melancholy lyrics which Lowell had accepted, and was putting pressure on him to work in the vein of "The Pilot's Story." By September he had been goaded into writing Fields a cool note objecting to his policy and threatening not to send him any more poems at all. That he did not break down under all these pressures is another good measure of how far he had come psychologically since 1858.

Instead, Howells redoubled his effort to land a consulate. Ever since Washington Irving had been a successful ambassador to Spain, a tradition of appointing men of letters to diplomatic posts had been growing. Hawthorne had been given the most lucrative consulate at the State Department's disposal after writing a campaign biography of Pierce. And as soon as Lincoln was elected, Columbus friends urged on Howells the propriety of his being rewarded with some good consular post. Politically he was sophisticated enough to know beforehand, as he said in the hindsight of September and as Herman Melville's pathetic failure even to get an interview out of his effort to land a consulate at the same time demonstrates, that office, like kissing, goes by favor, and one needs a persistent and articulate friend at court.

In February he wrote to Chase, asking his backing for the Munich post. Chase was well disposed toward his Ohio supporters. He had put Piatt into the Treasury and found governmental jobs for the Ohio authors Kinney and Gallagher. He backed Howells and had him file recommendations from a bevy of Ohio politicians in April. Eventually he was awarded Rome, where there was no salary and, as Piatt found out for him at the Treasury, only five hundred dollars a year in fees. On June 10, stimulated by the news that the new owners of the *State Journal* had no place for him, he wrote again to Chase, still seeking Munich. On the same day he tried John Hay, one of Lincoln's secretaries, who as a river boy from Keokuk had been vocal in his admiration of "The Pilot's Story" and was eager to support Western authors. The political know-how and sophistication he put into the effort, by contrast with the literarily far more deserving Melville's naivete, is a sound index of the incorrectness of Howells' later conviction that in Columbus he had been a meek, flitting literary creature.

In September, having been paid off by Cooke, he staked his remaining capital on a plunge and went to New York. After failing to get a job or even to sell a poem there, he went on down to Washington to stay with the Piatts, and he won his gamble. Lincoln's other young Western secretary, Nicolay, found that Venice was open and, as a seaport, eligible for a wartime raise in salary status. He got it raised to $1500, saw that Lincoln signed a commission with Howells' name on it, and sent it to the State Department. Will saw Lincoln wearily drinking from a corridor water-cooler one day and was too awe-stricken to come forward and thank him. But after that the second Eastern trip turned into a celebration. In that mood, he charmed E. C. Stedman in Washington, who found him of "catholic taste and intellect," and later William O'Connor, the dashing Irish friend of Whitman. He went up to Boston for visits with Fields, Holmes, and Lowell and was reassured by their continuing friendship. He made a pilgrimage for a last visit to his old Welsh grandmother now in western Ohio, hung around Jefferson, went down to Columbus where kindly Dr. Smith loaned him $150 for his voyage, and made a second trip to Washington to be sure that his bond, once miscarried in the mails, arrived safely. On at least one of these trips he went up to Brattleboro for a thoroughly successful visit with the friendly Meads. Probably he made at least a private engagement with Elinor.

When you embark for Europe in November, said Howells in the inevitable "Letter from Europe" he sent back to the *State Journal* for the first few months, you "laugh and jest with friends who have come down to the steamer to see you off." When they are warned off the ship, you "stand at the foot of the gangway, to make the parting bow, and crack the farewell joke." Meanwhile the "weather weeps dismally." It was a last Heinesque touch as he sailed out of the country and out of the youthful part of his long and complex life on the S.S. *City of Glasgow* on November 9, 1861.

Chapter Five

"THAT VENICE FROM
WHICH I SHALL NEVER BE EXILED"

A S THE *City of Glasgow* FOUGHT HER WAY INTO THE OPEN November sea in 1861, a single sad-faced young man tried to pace her wet decks and fish within himself for poetic inspiration. "A dirty night," the captain observed in an effort to cheer him up. He agreed, and went still more sadly down to his cabin to be seasick. By the time he was convalescent and on deck again, there were icebergs to poeticize, and he could feel like a traveler in earnest. He could not know it, of course, but his journey was into an entirely new life as well as a far place. What he was leaving behind especially was his active citizenship in the West, though of course he never ceased to be a Westerner. All Howells' life he was frankly "a Buckeye," a boy from the Ohio frontier.

In his time there were, roughly speaking, three Ohios. River Ohio had Southern attitudes and amphibian customs. Richly agricultural central Ohio held the state in balance and was growing accustomed to the political power focused in Columbus. The Yankee Western Reserve, skirting Lake Erie, was culturally mature in the New England way long before it was anything but economically crude, and it throbbed with idealism and enterprise. Ohio was a state rich in character and in destiny, packed full of interest and instruction for the observing eye: a good training ground for an American novelist. And Howells had lived in all sections of it. If he became a regional novelist only incidentally, that was not because he denied or deplored his Westernism. It was because his imagination became intrigued with the comparative: West against East; America against Europe; individual against caste, class, or system. The "social liberty and equality" of Ohio he "long hoped . . . to paint as a phase of American civilization worthy the most literal fidelity of fiction." If he never quite satisfied himself in painting Ohio, it was not entirely for lack of trying. Seven of his books are clearly Ohioan, and Midwestern folks and themes people many other writings. Living, as he did, through the Ohio Period in American politics, he would not have been allowed to forget, and did not wish to, the parody which ran:

> Some are born great
> Some achieve greatness
> And some are born in Ohio.

But now he disengaged himself from Ohio and ceased to grow up with it. His detachment was partly just opportune: he had grasped an almost perfect opportunity to complete his self-education. It was also voluntary, however, because of his earnest revolt against the small town. In the spring he wrote back, with exactly the kind of excess acid which so many of the later participants in the anti-village revolution displayed, that the beauty of Trieste "even excited the wonder of one who had seen the plank sidewalks of Jefferson, and who could not forget the town pump there."

His revolt from the village also implied rejection of the romantic view of the West as the perfect place for the growth of an organic, national American literature. Hawthorne, Emerson, and Lowell had all tried to impress him with that view and failed. Lowell was to continue to try for years. Equally he rejected the Western argument that, since all the seers said the West should produce geniuses and since it had not, it must be that there was an Eastern conspiracy to rob the authors of the West of their just recognition. The time might come for a true Western literature, Howells thought, when "the poet shall cease to hunger amid the abundance of our sea-wide cornfields," and that was worth struggling for; but it was a long way off. Like Mark Twain, he sought a career in the East because that was where one could be found. Nevertheless, he remained a Westerner, as he discovered sharply when he came to live in Cambridge and Boston. There he neither felt Bostonian nor became "Boston-plated" like Thomas Bailey Aldrich. With the advantages of his Yankee wife's inside information, he had the greater advantage of seeing Boston from without. Still later, become a realist and a socialist, he developed a new ideal of his democratic, pre-industrial, and deeply known West. In this he also anticipated the outcome of the revolt against the village in the twentieth century.

Thus as a mature writer he would have the huge advantage of a bifocal, continental view of America, and always with a coloring which could have come only from Ohio.

I

His ship arrived in Liverpool on November 23, and Howells went on by train to London through a countryside he saw as lovely through the eyes of Tennyson and Dickens. London seemed all "vastness, hurry, struggle, murky splendor, skulking wretchedness and systematic gloom" to him as he put up at the Golden Cross Hotel because David Copperfield had stayed there. In his three London days he saw the sights, reacting in *Innocents Abroad* fashion eight years before Twain's book was published. The Poet's Corner and the Abbey seemed glamorous at first, but then it reminded him "how stupid, how cruel, how miserable" the past was; "the man who lives in the newest log-cabin in the far West, is happier than the mummies in the oldest pyramids of Egypt," he said. Part of his negative reaction to England was caused by the fact that his arrival coincided with the full blaze of the Mason and Slidell affair, which had occurred on November 8. He found Englishmen eager to impress their antagonism personally upon an available Yankee. With "chuckling delight," he wrote to the Ohio papers, "the English exult in our disaster, and would do anything to compass our ruin." No doubt the Welsh and Irish sentiment of his family had prepared him to dislike the English. And his repeated experiences during his Civil War residence abroad drove a bitter suspicion of Britain so deep into his emotions that nothing afterwards ever quite erased it.

Leaving London, he had a day in Paris and then went on the long all-rail route across Southern Germany to Vienna, across the Simmering Pass to Trieste, and so down to Venice on December 6. Stopovers with friendly American consuls, almost as new on the job as he, in Stuttgart and Vienna gave him little tourist adventures and let him see that fate had been kind in barring him from the German posts he had first coveted. Germany was dark and snow-filled, and Howells suffered from Alpine cold in the Pass. But coming down the other side into Italy was like a return to life.

Even the blackness of five o'clock of a December Saturday morning could not take the glamor out of his arrival in Venice. Lighted

to his gondola seat by a picturesque beggar, he forgot his chill and
his homesickness as he glided across the lagoon into a fantasy world
of stately palaces rescued from their decay by the starlight. "The
quick boat slid through old troubles of mine and unlooked-for
events gave it the impulse that carried it beyond, and safely around
sharp corners of life," Howells wrote of his thoughts at the moment, probably unconscious of the new form this gave to his therapeutic myth of the boat in the fiords. At the top of his mind he
played with conventional romanticisms about the danger of robbery
and assassination in a city traditionally given to secret wickedness,
and his reporter's eye registered the petty swindling of the hotel
portier with accustomed satiric sharpness. But very deeply for
Howells, and in a way which made a great difference in his future
life, psychic as well as intellectual and professional, Venice spoke
to his condition and fed a deep hunger which could probably not
have been satisfied anywhere in the America of that day.

For this was the period when an experience of Europe was somehow essential to the education of every sensitive American. In one
way or another that has been true for many, if not all, generations
before and since; but for Howells it was especially acute for reasons
which never have been really clearly explained, even by Henry
James. England and France were good for the purpose, but somehow Italy has been best of all in most generations. It was a sympathetic fate which brought Howells there. Yet for all that, the
use to him of the experience was not simple or unified, nor is it
easy to make a pattern of it. One of the best things living abroad
gives an American is leisure, psychic freedom from the pressures
to be busied of our business civilization, and freedom in the detachment of his days from the ordinary responsibilities of social and
community life because he is in a strange land. As it turned out,
Howells' leisure in Venice was ample, at times almost absolute, so
that he had to discipline himself to turn it to account in observation,
reading and language-study, thinking, and writing. His official
exequatur did not arrive until April, which gave him no duties at
all, and no salary. After that, with the fighting and commercial
concerns of the United States thundering far away from the
irrelevant Rialto, he found that his consular duties, even when
extended to the entertainment of visiting American celebrities,
could be done in a few hours a week.

With his leisure Howells did the obvious things. He began a

serious study of Italian, with daily lessons and earnest reading, which soon gave him idiomatic ease both in the literary language and Venetian dialect. His habitual long strolls carried him on a systematic exploration of the town, not so much to the Baedeker items as to the back streets and obscure courts where the life of the people went loudly on in the open. His appetite for mere experience, taking everything in and converting it to understanding, was insatiable. Venice was picturesque and exciting, but he began to find that he loved it most not for touristic reasons but because it displayed simple human life vividly, and the difference in the angle at which it struck his alien eye made it possible for him to penetrate into it as he could never have penetrated life at home. Something inside him did the rest. Socially he was at first acutely lonely, but significantly free of the old nostalgic illness. Gradually he began to go to the theater, the opera, and occasional balls. In the international set he found the inevitable Russians congenial and was further antagonized by the English.

Before long, Howells, with his gift for friendship, began to acquire Venetian friends who could open deeper perspectives into the life of the town for him. The first was Antonio Tortorini, a comfortably endowed bachelor of fifty-six with a minor title and little country-place to match. Tortorini, the "Old Venetian Friend" of whom Howells wrote as "Pastorelli," had the not uncommon Italian passion for English and met Howells because he was taking language lessons from his consular predecessor. Finding him *simpatico*, he gave the young American his friendship with the speed and the reservations which seem normal in such situations with Italian men, and became his companion, guide, and good angel through the first, difficult, late winter and spring. He introduced him properly to the life of the cafes and the Piazza. He helped him search for proper consular quarters and, when his money ran low because of the delay over the exequatur, lent him fifty florins in Austrian sovereigns of antique gold, specifying only that the loan, when repaid, should return in the same coinage.

Through Tortorini, Howells began to meet Venetians of good family and came to understand their opinions, especially the force of the Demonstration they were making against the Austrian occupation of Venice, their liking for America, and the necessity of keeping his own republican sympathies unmistakable if he were to maintain contact with them. Late in February he walked all day in the drizzle, sat up late reading a German translation of Euripides, and came down with a solid case of the grippe. Then it was Tortorini who came in to nurse him, sternly keep him out of the hands of the local doctors, prescribe for and medicate him, and see him back to health. As Howells wrote home to his father and, later, to Vic about it, the experience was a decisive one for him. He thought and dreamed about home, about being cared for in illness as a boy by his mother, but he recovered quickly and, in the old sense, was not homesick.

The second English-speaking Italian friend, Eugene Brunetta, if able to be of less immediate service than Tortorini, was a more congenial friend and in the end more important to Howells. Brunetta was young, about twenty, and preparing for matriculation at the University of Padua. And it was he who introduced Howells to Goldoni's plays and to contemporary Italian drama and poetry, all of which were to influence Will's future profoundly. Brunetta could also introduce him to other young Italians, even a young beauty, the Signorina Perissinotti, and to the maddening complexities and inhibitions of the Italian system of chaperonage. Though he enjoyed innocent promenades with the signorina, presided over by Brunetta and her uncle's secretary, and later made an excellent sketch out of the experience called "Tonelli's Marriage," Howells saw through to the sexual assumptions behind the system and was enraged. He came to think, as he wrote to his sister Vic, and as Henry James generally was to agree, that European society was tainted with guilt by comparison with American freedom and innocence. He also thought, where James could never agree, that American social life was more pleasant, satisfying, and even beautiful—because Europe's must either be guilty or rigid. Finally, he made the pleasant acquaintanceship of two priests: the lastingly *simpatico* Padre Giacomo Issaverdenz of the Armenian Convent on the island of San Lazzaro, and Padre Libera, who taught him Dante and in 1875 served as the model of Don Ippolito in *A Foregone Conclusion.*

II

Established in Venice with his $1500 a year and a pleasant standard of living, Howells was ready to make a very important move. Since he could not leave his post for the month or more a round trip to the States would have taken him, he proposed that Elinor Mead should meet him in England, marry him, and make the return to Venice via Paris her wedding trip. He wrote to his mother firmly asking her blessing for the project and, after some hesitation, got it. The idea could hardly have been new to Elinor, or even entirely so to the Meads. They liked Will Howells and respected Elinor's judgment. Also, to an artistic tribe, the lure of a residence of Venice for her was irresistible. This was the period when esthetic American circles were enthralled by Ruskin and *The Stones of Venice*. With sculptor brother Larkin to keep her company and stay in Italy to complete his own education, they sent her off to Liverpool almost precisely a year after Howells had taken the same route.

When her ship dropped anchor in the Mersey River at Liverpool, Elinor Mead could see Will coming out on the tender to meet her and take her ashore to a minister. She was carefully dressed in her combination bridal and traveling gown—brown dress and coat, a tight little bonnet with one wedding-rose, and new tan gloves, slightly large to facilitate slipping the left one off for the ring. Will's greeting was ecstatic, but his news was disappointing: Liverpool required a seven days' residence for matrimony and they had better go up to London. At London there were also difficulties. Very well, surely as a member of the diplomatic corps Howells could be married at the American legation, subject only to the laws of his own nation; and he went buoyantly to call on Minister Charles Francis Adams. At the legation, however, he failed to see either the Minister or his son and personal secretary, Henry Adams. He was sneeringly turned away by the official secretary, a bureaucratic snob named Moran, who cleared his skirts of the personal troubles of the consul at Venice and justified himself to his diary by observing that the suppliant seemed a "sleek, insipid sort of a fellow." The fellow's only recourse was to take his party off to the legation in Paris, where they were cordially received and married in the secretary's library by an Episcopalian minister on December 24. Elinor's new gloves were frayed and split out at the fingers before she came to remove them for her ring.

It was typical of the highly successful marriage there begun that they dashed off to spend the rest of the afternoon and have their dinner at the Louvre (Elinor denounced by Larkin for forgetting her muff at the legation and delaying them), and that the story of their tribulations became an elaborate family joke. Elinor loved to laugh as much as Will, and her satire was never more exquisite than when it was devastatingly applied to sentimentality, emotional pretense, hypocrisy or excess of any sort, or egotism. Simply as a wife she was far more than adequate for Howells, and he worshiped her. But her qualities of mind were also precisely what the circumstance of his "hypochondria" needed. His own humor, the "aëry playfulness" which Sir Edmund Gosse found the most attractive part of his personality, burgeoned. She entered into his work with energy and full sympathy and extended his horizons with entire comradeship. Through her Howells achieved his celebrated insight into what has been called "the feminine oversoul." As he said of one of his later characters, he himself "found his wife an inexhaustible source of mental refreshment. He prized beyond measure the feminine inadequacy and excess of her sayings; he had stored away such a variety of these that he was able to talk her personal parlance for an hour together." But the first stanza of one of Howells' Venetian poems tells the story of his debt to his wife much more adequately:

> I walked with her I love by the sea,
>   The deep came up with its chanting waves,
> Making a music so great and free
>   That the will and the faith, which were dead in me,
>   Awoke and rose from their graves.

Most significant of all, perhaps, was his note to his mother of April 18, 1862. He had never felt so well in his life and was putting on weight, he told her, and he could hardly remember that he had ever been ill or melancholy. Thus, Elinor helped him turn his drawn battle with the inward demons into a victory which made his next twenty years extraordinarily happy ones. Not at all surprisingly, the victory and its maintenance exacted from him the price of "forgetting" the struggle, of adopting forcibly what William James called the religion of healthy-mindedness by which "the slaughter-houses and indecencies without end on which our life is founded are huddled out of sight and never mentioned, so that the world we recognize officially in literature and society is a poetic fiction far handsomer and cleaner and better than the world that really is." Howells had every reason to know otherwise; the childhood image of the mutilated man drowned never left his deepest mind. But his imagination was constrained to focus on the flowering peach. Thus he made a leap of faith, aiming at psychic safety, which was possible only so long as experience should not rupture his "poetic fiction."

The Howellses' first housekeeping, with all the struggles attendant on solving the intricacies of Venetian service and supply, began in a furnished apartment in the Casa Falier, a decrepit palazzo with a fine view of the Grand Canal. Neither of them seems to have cared a great deal about housekeeping or the complexities of domestic elegance. They lived simply, devoted to his writing, her sketching, and their absorption in Venice and each other. When they could no longer be bothered to cope with Giovanna, the serving-woman who began as a "gem" and ended as a leech, they sent out for their meals and often watched from the balcony as dinner came majestically down the canal by gondola. It was their reversion to the same Bohemian simplicity after the children were grown and gone which prompted Henry James to comment pointedly on the horrors of their way of life and the "thinness" of Howells' existence. Elinor, who adored James and his work, took a feminine revenge in mocking the fussiness of James's Rye establishment and theorizing that James was so entrapped in material goods because he never had a proper home when he was young.

Married life in Venice became a kind of idyll. Friends dropped in often, and above lived the Signorina Marietta de Benvenuti with whom Larkin Mead fell in love, courted in the Venetian mode with Brunetta's help, and eventually married. Now both Venetians and visiting Americans could be entertained, and the Howellses made a number of interesting friends. Moncure D. Conway, in England as a paid abolition propagandist, and smarting from an ill-advised part in the *Trent* affair, got a consoling invitation in March, 1863:

'To tell you the truth, you and Mrs. Conway are two people whom we should very much like to see in Venice. The spring is coming on after "the slow, sweet" fashion of spring in southern lands; the Adriatic is warming up with the view of being bathed in; the sun is bringing out all that is brightest and loveliest in the city and embroidering the islands and the *terra firma* with flowers. Four weeks ago we gathered daisies on the Lido; and now the almond-trees are heavy with bloom and bees. Besides all this, we live in the old Palazzo Faliero (where Mario Faliero, according to all the gondoliers, was born) and we have a piano and a balcony on the Grand Canal, and the most delightful little breakfasts in Venice. You *will* come, won't you?

The *we* is not used editorially here. Of course you know that I am married and to whom. Though I've never heard directly from you, I used to hear a great deal about you, in letters from Cincinnati. You have an additional merit in my eyes because you met Elinor there.'

To Conway when he came that summer it seemed like "Avalon." Howells rose with the dawn and took him on a ramble through the town before returning to a long breakfast on the balcony overlooking the Canalazzo. Then he retired to his office to write, having formed in the leisure of Venice his lifelong habit of doing his creative work after a hearty breakfast, while his wife took Conway touring to churches and galleries. After dinner they sat in Florian's cafe on the Piazza, watching the promenaders, and came home early to hear Howells read the lines of a poetic novelette (eventually *No Love Lost*) which he had written during the day. The Howells love of laughter infected the normally solemn Conway, and he could hardly hold himself in when a lovely Italian countess came to breakfast one day and, discoursing passionately on the sufferings of Venice under the yoke of Austria, let her tears flow down on the big, black cigar she was smoking.

Unless they went to the theater, of which both were passionately fond, Howells' reading aloud to his wife was a regular feature of their evenings, a regular part of their intensely literary life together. And, for almost all the rest of her life, every major literary idea he had was discussed with her, every word read by her before it went to the printer—if not read aloud to her, the most searching possible test for style—and often the proofs read by her. In the kind of way which is only to be guessed at, not measured, by an outsider, Howells' career, like his daily life, was a partnership with his wife.

Living with Elinor also made a difference in the way Howells took his Venice. From the beginning the beauty of the place had affected him deeply, but he had tended to enjoy it vaguely as a part of the atmosphere. Elinor intended to master Venetian art. She put him to reading Ruskin, as well as histories and guidebooks in three languages, and early in 1863 she copied after his dictation an English translation of the handiest guide to the city, which happened to be in the German of Adalbert Müller. Will sold the text to a local printer and with the proceeds bought a gold watch from Switzerland which he wore until his death and left to his best-loved grandson in his will. Day after day they sallied out to find the treasures of Venice; and the terms of historical and critical analysis of painting, mosaic, sculpture, and architecture filled their talk. For Howells, of course, this was all new. Previously his experience of art had been literary, but now he was given a prolonged and intimate exposure to the plastic arts which developed all his esthetic responses. He learned to see the serious craftsmanship behind the work, and seeing it learned both the futility of romantic gush about art and the need to respect artistry in his own field as something else than posturing. He also learned to respect his own instinct to study people at first hand, living in the present, as right for him and the most important impulse of his mind.

III

Reviewing the meaning of Venice to Howells in a bit of criticism as perceptive as it was friendly, James Russell Lowell urged on his readers the necessity of using their imaginations to understand the circumstances. "Fancy," he begged them, "an imaginative young man from Ohio, where the log-hut was but yesterday turned to almost less enduring brick and mortar, set down in the midst of all this almost immemorial permanence of grandeur." What would happen to such a young man, a young poet? The "impression would be so strangely deep"; above all, his eyes would be "quickened by the constantly recurring shock of unfamiliar objects." And so it was for Howells, in a way which surprised him and altered the course of his literary development. After his fashion he had previously worked as a poet, a reporter, and a scholar-critic, in about that order of importance. He began in Venice to work again at all three, but it is safe to guess that he thought his exotic surroundings would stir the poet to new heights of achievement. On the contrary, by the time he was done with Venice the poet had almost dropped out of sight, the reporter had made a creative leap to a path which led up toward a dazzling future, and the scholar-critic had won the plaudits of the very Americans Howells thought most worth impressing.

Perhaps the best thing about living abroad is the fine perspective it gives on life at home. Howells' first Venetian stimulus produced one of his best long poems—on a Midwestern theme and neatly tailored to James T. Fields's wishes. Sitting on the front porch at

Jefferson in September, his father and mother had fallen to reminiscing about frontier camp meetings, and now the germ sprouted in Howells' imagination. He did a longish tale, modeled on *Evangeline* for sentiment and meter but freshly interesting in its use of Ohio settings, and called it "Louis Lebeau's Conversion." Fields printed it in the November, 1862, *Atlantic*. It was Howells' only literary publication of the year.

After that it became increasingly difficult for him to publish poetry at all. His account of the Civil War in *terza rima* no one would ever print, and *No Love Lost* had to wait, in spite of Elinor's illustrations, until 1868. Although *Harper's* featured his "St. Christopher" with a nice sketch by his wife in its 1863 Christmas number, on the whole his success with magazines was not so good as it had been from Columbus. Fields would take nothing more he sent. When *Commonwealth,* outlet for young transcendentalists, did print a few verses, he had the humiliation of having a strong-minded female poet reply to a melancholy bit called "Drifting" and tell him tartly to wake up and "paddle his own canoe."

In New York, his old publisher Foster, moved from Columbus, oscillated between confidence and despair for more than a year and finally discovered that he could not bring out *No Love Lost* (then called *Disillusion*), then told him plainly: ". . . poetry rarely pays anything in this country. Your efforts in prose will produce you more in 'greenbacks.' " In London, where Foster's excuse of wartime inflation and disruption did not apply, Conway had no better luck in placing the manuscript volume of verses he had brought back from Venice. He elicited a note from Browning approving "The Pilot's Story" and praising the "power and beauty" of Howells' poems, but no publisher was overawed. Howells the poet was given pause: had the Muse deserted him? Had his vocation as poet been a delusion? At any rate, a radical change occurred in his productivity. When he wrote to his friend Stoddard on November 25, 1864, he noted that he had not written a poem for two years. Thereafter his production of verse was to be occasional and sparse except for a brief flare-up twenty-five years later. He had, without of course being able at the time to know it, come to the end of the first (Poetic) period in his literary career and was launching out on the second period, which might best be called Experimental.

Thus the poet lost first place in Howells' ambition. The scholar kept steadily at work, exulting in Dante's great moments and plowing through what he found dry or irrelevant. He persevered with German, perfected his Italian, and took up French, all on the chance that if a literary career failed to materialize he might become a professor of modern languages at home. He began to collect materials toward a history of Venice, a life-long project forever left unfinished beside the life of Cervantes with which his dreams of scholarship had begun in Hamilton and Eureka Mills. Under Brunetta's guidance he mastered the contemporary literature of Italy, especially its drama, since that seemed to have more vitality than the scarce poetry, or the fiction which was mainly historical romance in the decaying modes of Scott and Cooper. The mills of punditry, however, ground too slowly. Significant production, salable and prestigious, was sooner promised by the reporter's eye at work in Venice.

To the reporter the whole European opportunity seemed golden indeed. After Washington Irving, travel literature had achieved new stature as a literary *genre*. The romantic appetite for exoticism, the lure of the strange, the faraway, the mysterious, the glamorous, of bizarre and recondite experience, had created a literary industry in the production of the travel book. From Irving and Cooper through Longfellow, Emerson, Hawthorne, Thoreau, and Melville, almost every major writer had tried his own variation on the pattern. To take ship for distant lands and do a book on one's sensations became a recognized method of initiating a literary career. Minor writers like N. P. Willis, George William Curtis, and Bayard Taylor had scored big popular successes in the mode. Whittier, relaxing in the midst of his long, fervent battle for the slave, knew he spoke for an army of readers when he praised the *genre* in reviewing Taylor's California volume, *Eldorado:*

'Blessings on the man who invented books of travel for the benefit of home idlers ! . . . When the cark and care of daily life and homely duties, and the weary routine of sight and sound, oppress us, what a comfort and refreshing it is to open the charmed pages of the traveller ! Our narrow, monotonous horizon breaks away all about us; five minutes suffice to take us quite out of the commonplace and familiar regions of our experience. . . . We look into the happiness of travelling through the eyes of others, and, for the miseries of it, we enjoy *them* exceedingly.'

With this in mind Howells began to keep a journal "registering" his "sensations" from his first arrival. His delight in the back-alley life of the Venetians was partly motivated by the ease with which he could turn it to account in the journal. Emboldened by the success of his various "Letters" to newspapers, he sent off some of this in "sketches" to Fields. And, like all the rest of his manuscripts for the *Atlantic* in this period, they were rejected. But where nothing had seemed to work for the poet, the reporter fell into luck. In the late spring of 1862 a youngish but important Bostonian came to Venice on a trip for his health, and Howells made a friend of Charles Hale, brother of Edward Everett Hale and publisher of the *Boston Daily Advertiser*. By the time Hale was ready to leave for Egypt and then home, he had contracted to print regular "Letters from Venice" in the *Advertiser*.

Although the pay turned out to be only five dollars per crowded column of nonpareil type, Howells was delighted. It was literary income, a footing, and he was to be read by the audience he wished more than any other to impress, literary Boston. He worked earnestly at the job, planning his sightseeing and outside trips carefully for their yield in material, and thinking the problems of the form out as he worked. His aim to impress Boston succeeded early, the letters winning a steady following among the Italophile Bostonian literati. More important, Howells learned a great deal on the job.

Probably helped by the necessity of reading his stuff aloud to the incisive Elinor, he began to rebel against the tendencies toward posturing romantic sensationalism which had often appeared in earlier series of "letters." Without losing the ideal of readability, he began to deepen and tone down his style, depending more on irony for his humor and deleting the slick stunting of the "paragrapher." He saw that an effective improvement in the travel book could be made by the man who would take his eye off his own "sensations" and give his pages over to revealing what Venice and the daily life of its people really looked like. With thought and practice together, his objectivity and his penetration increased. Invaluable perceptions of cultural relativity, of the textures and patterns of human life which may be observed by the mind which can stand a little aside from itself, began to come to him. And so his impatience with the old romanticisms, even romantic irony, increased. He tended more and more to define his purposes in opposition to them and to handle them derisively. Unconsciously, he had moved a little more toward realism. As he said in futilely proposing a book on Florence to the Harpers in 1864, he could promise charm, liveliness, and information, but above all "the flavor of an honest, unsentimental liking for the Italian civilization."

Something of the same effect came out of the education his wife provided for him in Venetian art. The painters he liked best were Bellini, Carpaccio, and their school, specialists in human life and character. But he seems never to have achieved much grasp of the "painterly" qualities of pictures. With architecture he was more successful, learning to analyze the reasons for his taste convincingly. Reflection and perhaps experiment, however, persuaded him that the effort to elucidate works of art is useless except in the presence of the works themselves. His own discussions of the treasures of Venice have much more to say about the Venetian crones, *ragazzini*, priests, or even cats present before and around them than about esthetics. Much of the art criticism he read moved him to satire. After reading Ruskin's description of San Marco, he said, "I, who had seen it every day for three years, began to have dreadful doubts of its existence." The "theories and egotisms" of Ruskin, especially the naivete of his morals-beauty equation, annoyed Howells, and yet he read Ruskin with care, confessed him the best guide of all to Venice, and used him as historical source for his own writings.

Reading in *The Seven Lamps of Architecture* and *Stones of Venice,* Howells could find much support for his own development as a writer and critic, along with much he felt forced to reject. One of the greatest lights on the path of the artist, Ruskin insisted, was the Lamp of Truth: there must be no deceit, no trickery, no pretense in art. Therefore beauty must be based on nature, and nature means what is "commonest in the external creation." One looks "from Frequency to Beauty" and argues "that on the shapes which in the everyday world are familiar to the eyes of man, God has stamped those characters of beauty which He has made it man's nature to love." Here was confirmation on high authority for the practice into which Howells had drifted in his own report on Venice. In *Stones of Venice* he found more. In the famous chapter on "The Nature of Gothic" were objections to the human cost of industrialism which the young man from Jefferson and Columbus could not appreciate yet. But the discussion of "Naturalism" might almost have been written for him. It called for a synthesis in art of abstract design with command of fact—taken to mean nature, the familiar, common, and everyday. Then it made another division of artists into dangerous Sensualists who pursue the fact morbidly

and see only evil, and Purists who pursue the good only, ignoring
evil, and are acceptable but lesser than the Naturalists, who pursue
good and evil together, "the whole thing as it verily is." Howells'
own condition was extenuated and his best ideal held before him
at the same time when he read in Ruskin, "We easily understand
the timidity or the tenderness of the spirit which would withdraw
itself from the presence of destruction, and create in its imagination
a world of which the peace should be unbroken. . . . That man is
greater, however, who contemplates with an equal mind the alterna-
tions of terror and beauty."

IV

The simplicity of Bohemian living and easy comradeship with his
wife out of which all this came was complicated on December 17,
1863, when Elinor gave birth to the first of their three children, a
daughter, Winifred. Elinor's sister Mary had come on to help out
with the house and baby, and Will began, happily enough, to feel
the pressures of new expenses and responsibilities. They marked
the beginning of the end of the Venetian idyll. He had to begin to
think more concretely of the future: of return to the States and of
actually achieving the career for which everything to this point
had been promise and education. Subjectively he began to make
ready to leave Italy. More practically, he had to supplement the
good preparation for a return to American literary life which the
Advertiser sketches were making. Now he found his scholarly
pursuits into Italian letters ripe for the harvest. Since the *Atlantic*
seemed closed and Fields out of sympathy, he turned to the ancient
organ of the Brahmins, at a new peak of vitality and importance
under the joint editorship of Lowell and Charles Eliot Norton, the
North American Review.

For Howells' purpose the situation on the *Review* was ideal. The
editors were both Italophiles who brought a high standard of
intellectual seriousness to the magazine, and Lowell was his own
most dependable literary patron. Under the guise of reviews, often
of a group of books together, they encouraged authoritative, original
articles. Therefore, Howells sat himself down to exploit at the very
top of his capacity the most original materials he commanded, the
Comedy which was the best of contemporary Italian writing. With
a baby in the house the center of attention for two suddenly very

domestic women, life that winter of 1864 was very different, and not very Venetian or exotic except for the coffee and card parties Elinor held for cosmopolitan little groups on Saturday nights. It was no doubt lucky that Howells could not know that her health would always thereafter be insecure. He enjoyed the new tone and his status as pater familias and was able to stretch himself and give his scholarly project all his strength.

The result, which appeared in the *North American Review* for October, 1864, as "Recent Italian Comedy," was an effective blend of history, cultural analysis, human interest, and literary criticism. He got into his subject by pointing out that where a foreigner in England or America can penetrate the "themes and people of the present civilization" through fiction, especially "the romance of society," he will be baffled in Italy by the almost total lack of anything but historical romance. Most foreigners have therefore overlooked the best index to "the manners, thoughts, feelings and lives of the modern Italian population" because that source, the comedy, has almost dried up in English. He theorized on the reasons in Italian history, social, political, and religious conditions, and the Italian temperament for the special dominance of the drama. Censorship had helped the play and hurt fiction, he thought, because "narrative fiction must bare the causes which produce character, and reveal all the feelings and explain the circumstances which influence men to action." Fiction is inescapably critical and overt; but the comedy may laugh unanalytically or make its point in a fleeting tone or gesture which the censor can hardly catch. Then he surveyed the history of Italian drama in the "commedia d'arte" and Goldoni, with high praise for the latter, his methods, characters, and morality, frequently coupling his beloved Spanish picaresque novelists with the Venetian genius. Chasteness, the "purity" of Italian comedy which could be read unblushingly by girls and never exalts gilded vice, he praised. And then he gave twenty pages to a careful survey of the dozen playwrights reprinted in the four volumes of plays and the one of dramatic criticism he had set himself to review. These were carefully analyzed, quoted, evaluated, and allowed to parade their wares before the article ended with a quotation from Dall'Ongaro on the duties of the Italian dramatist to the people: uplift and "Liberty!"

The experience in reading and theater-going from which so fine a bit of criticism came could not, of course, have left Howells without a new literary passion, and he disclosed it in his article. Carlo Goldoni, whose humanity recalled Goldsmith and whose characters the picaresque authors, Howells loved most for his "fidelity and truth." Twelve years later he recalled that Goldoni, an eighteenth-century dramatist, had "painted the Venice of his day so gracefully, so vividly, so truly, with so much more of the local human nature than of the mere manners of the age, that his plays mirror in wonderful degree the Venice of our own day." And somehow, as an antidote to Heine and romanticism, Goldoni had learned "the lesson that humanity is above literature" and helped to renew in Howells this bit of his own father's wisdom, just as a reading of George Eliot's *Romola* in the same period revived in him the Swedenborgian conviction that egotism is the root of all true evil. In later years the doctrinaire realist felt that knowledge of Goldoni had been the beginning of his revolt from the ideal of "romantic glamor" and hinted that the fountainhead of his realism might be the Venetian comedian. But this was at least partly the result of the foreshortening distortion of the afterview and must not be taken too simply. Goldoni was, as a literary passion, one impulse down the path which led to *A Modern Instance* or *Criticism and Fiction,* but hardly more.

V

The unstinted labor which went into the *North American Review* article produced a strain on Howells which revealed the limits to the firmness of his hard-won psychological adjustment. The results proved that he could do first-class work, even in an unfamiliar field, if he went all out. But the reaction showed, as it was always to show for the rest of his life, that supreme effort took its price in undermining his psychic security.

Early in May, when he had finished the job, he had a minor breakdown. He suffered a spell of sickness, and he was so jittery for a time that he could scarcely bear to write letters. Just when he was beginning to recover from that the fates dealt him a body blow. His brother John suddenly died at school in Cleveland of "spotted fever" (diphtheria) at the age of eighteen. Of his four brothers, John, the youngest child except Henry, was apparently the most sympathetic to Will. It was in saying goodbye to John in Jefferson that he had shed his tears, and he had used the leverage of his own deprivation to push Joe into sending John to school. He may have felt obliquely guilty because John died at school. Since this was the first rift in the family circle, it may have revived other guilt feelings for him. Whatever the causes, it sent him into a paroxysm of grief which took the bloom off any imaginable continuance of his European experience. It also moved him to seek an embarrassingly emotional reconciliation with his mother. In not too long a time he had recovered his poise; but the experience left its mark, and the lesson was clear. The adjustments he had shored up against his psychic dangers would stand the strains of careful living and hard but well-distributed work. They might give way before unusual shocks or the peak stress of supreme effort.

He was rescued from this crisis in August by a note from Lowell so heart-lifting that he was later to call its reception "The Turning-Point in My Life" when paid by a magazine to describe that momentous event. Undoubtedly conscious of how much it meant to Howells, Lowell was generous in praise of the *North American Review* article and told him that Norton and Longfellow approved too. In the name of "my interest in your genius" he undertook to read Howells a lesson: "You have enough in you to do honor to our literature. Keep on cultivating yourself. . . . You must sweat the Heine out of you as men do mercury. You are as good as Heine— remember that." Then he sweetened the homily with a last bit of praise. "I have been *charmed* with your Venetian letters in the *Advertiser*. They are admirable and fill a gap. They make the most careful and picturesque *study* I have seen on any part of Italy. *They are the thing itself.*" This praise and, much better, this understanding from the greatest living American critic of what he had slaved to achieve electrified Howells. Lowell called for more, and the pages of the *North American* were open to him. He blocked out a dozen things he could prepare. Lamenting that the stimulus came so late in his Venetian period, he could still apply the corrective of Western humor to his exaltation as he laughed to his father that he was really like the man who shot one coon and promptly cut 365 sticks to stretch coonskins on in the year to come. He went to work to convert the *Advertiser* sketches into a Venetian book with new fire.

Added to this stimulation was a sense of urgency which came from a half-admitted decision to resign his post, the four-year term of which was expiring with the end of Lincoln's first term. He must store away the best of the remaining opportunity in Venice for exploitation at home. When his brother Joe was threatened with being drafted into the Union army and his father proposed that Will should come home, if that happened, in the fall of 1864 to take over Joe's part of the newly thriving *Sentinel* enterprise, he fought for the chance to stay a few months more. And he tried to outline the possibilities for the future as he saw them. Of course, he conceded, if there were real family need for his services he would come dutifully. But living in Jefferson on permanent terms was psychologically impossible; the place had too many associations of terror for him. A business career was out of the question, and if he were to succeed in the world of letters he must establish himself immediately in the East before the glamor of his European residence had worn off—as he thought it would in three or four months. In short, he had no intention of returning to Ohio journalism if he could avoid it.

In November he was given a two-month leave from his post and turned the light responsibilities of the consulate over to Larkin Mead while he took his family on a tour of the rest of Italy to see the sights and gather material, especially in Naples and Rome. He and Elinor enjoyed themselves and fell in love with Rome; but the enchantment was gone (which accounts for the difference in tone between *Venetian Life* and *Italian Journeys*), and his reactions were often colored by sardonic self-defence against the tawdriness of tourism. The Howellses were ready to go home.

On returning to Venice at Christmas time he applied for leave to go to the States and finally got it after his father's protege, Congressman James A. Garfield, had interceded with Secretary of State Seward. By this command of practical politics he was able to hedge on the risk of not finding a job when he went home. Seward, reported Garfield, "spoke in very high terms of Will" and affirmed that Venice was safe for him, even if he came home on leave; except that he must not leave until after the Inauguration. "I am very anxious that the Tennysonian mind of your son shall have full range over the fine materials open before him in the old world and I hope he will stay there until danger of change is past," Garfield wrote.

On June 21 Howells received confirmation of his four-month leave of absence, and on July 3 the family left for London. There, although nothing came of Trollope's invitation to dinner, the influence of Conway got Trübner and Co. to promise to publish his Venetian book if he could find an American firm to take over the sheets of half the printing of one thousand copies. Then he took the steamship *Asia,* which arrived in Boston on August 3, 1865.

His three years and nine months abroad had done a great deal for Howells. His American reputation as a poet and journalist of promise, if dimmed by the passage of eventful years, was still intact, and he had added a sparkling new reputation as traveler, commentator, and scholarly critic to it. With luck, excellent career possibilities stood open to him. A good marriage had given him the means to subdue the inward demons which once threatened to devour all his promise. Finally, Venice had enabled him to complete, by his own definition, "the education of a gentleman (by which I do not mean a person born to wealth or high station, but any man who has trained himself in morals or religion, in letters, and in the world)." He felt ready to compete for his place in the sun anywhere in America, preferably Boston. As felicitous Lowell put it, "Venice has been the University in which he has fairly earned the degree of Master."

Chapter Six

A NEW YORK FREE LANCE

ALTHOUGH HOWELLS CAME HOME ON LEAVE, KEEPING THE DOOR open in case he found nothing with which to support his wife and baby in the United States, that arrangement was really only disaster insurance. He had no intention of going back to Venice if he could help it. As he wrote that fall for *The Nation*, American diplomatic service, especially at the consular level, "is not a career for any man ambitious of distinction and usefulness, and it is not a support for those willing to go into exile for a living." Low pay, no prospects for career advancement, and the fast turnover of the political spoils system made consular service attractive only to political hacks, glorified tourists, or failures. Or to writers and artists in need of a subsidized term of foreign residence. Having made good use of his term, William Dean Howells, now in the full powers of young manhood, was determined to try his luck at carving out a literary career, if possible a distinguished career, for himself in post-Civil War America.

Though he feared that at the worst he would have to go back to typesetting in Jefferson, still haunted by associations of psychic horror, Howells hoped that a degree of kudos attendant on his return from foreign parts would help him land a literary job in the East—where, and only where in his generation, literary careers were to be made. What he found, naturally, was a situation not nearly so bad as his worst fears and not quite so good as his best hopes. Landing in Boston, he went at once to see Lowell and was overwhelmed with friendship. In just the right mood, Lowell kept him talking Italian, drinking Elmwood's choicest wines, joking and laughing, and best of all canvassing Howells' future, until the dawn birds were singing in the shrubbery outside when they said goodnight. It was an experience such as Howells could scarcely have dared to dream of. Next came family visits to show off the baby in Brattleboro and in Jefferson, and then he was up against it. Could he get his foot on the ladder? And on what ladder— going where? He would never again have to face so critical a question of his future.

Somewhat unexpectedly, he found hands ready to give him a boost up one kind of ladder, to help him get a new footing in the career at which he had thus far done best: Western journalism. Things were looking up in post-war Ohio. The family in Jefferson was financially secure. Not only was the *Sentinel* doing well and William Cooper Howells in the Legislature, brother Joe had made a small killing by flooding the Union armies with a fast-selling soldier's song-envelope. He was solvent enough not only to dispense with Will's assistance but to offer help to him outside the family circle. Old Columbus friends were eager to have Howells back. Dr. Smith and William Cooper discussed getting control of *The Ohio State Journal* for Howells and young brigadier general Comly. There was other talk of starting a new Columbus paper, with backing from Squire Mead, among others. But Howells, in all friendliness and gratitude, turned his back on that opportunity, wrote out his consular resignation, sent wife and baby home to Brattleboro, picked up his free lance and, like so many hundreds of literary aspirants from the West since, went, on September 11, 1865, to New York. He was far from ashamed of journalism. All his life he claimed with pride to be a newspaperman. And he knew he could succeed in Columbus. What that success pointed toward, in the dawning Ohio Period, was political power, perhaps high public office. But what Howells wanted was to be a man of letters.

I

With the sharp eye of the returned traveler, in his case doubly sensitized by professional practice in Venice, Howells saw around him a changed America. To be sure, he had changed. He always, somewhat erroneously, charged his "sense of superfluity," his not quite being in the American mainstream at first, solely up to his having been away so long. Yet it was also true, as it would take Howells some years to realize clearly, that the American rate of change had been speeded up by the war. Life in the States would continue to change, at constant acceleration, all the rest of his life, and he would become a notable recorder of the changes. But now he wondered at his feeling of strangeness.

Not that he had not been warned. His publisher friend Frank Foster had written him from the depths of the war years an unusually perceptive document on the moral and social phenomena which were shaping the "Gilded Age." Having moved from Columbus to New York, Foster's eye was sharpened to see in 1863 that "the Country is in a curious condition." On the one side there was the heroic "self-sacrifice and devotion to country" of soldiers and their civilian supporters, especially women. On the other side events shocking and puzzling to a people who had lost all real memory of large-scale war. Foster hardly knew what to make of it: "Material prosperity unparalleled, money very abundant, the necessaries of life advanced to twice or three times the usual price. Extravagance is the rule, and the small vices accumulate rapidly. Thousands are dying in the field or in hospitals, but we have got used to it, and with all this *Wo*, the gaiety of our people seems to be higher than ever. You would be shocked to revisit us and see the abandon of our people." That was, of course, just one of the many swift-flowing social changes which would become obvious only in the perspective of years. And its evil aspects were, like those of other changes, easily veiled for the present if not obscured by optimism.

During most of the war Howells' view of American prospects had been dark. His radical abolitionist leanings had made it hard for him to give full sympathy to Lincoln's Unionist position. Doubts about the righteousness or even the entire desirability of a mere Federalist Constitutional victory had come naturally to him. But the finally prevailing view of the war and its aims, propagated especially from New England by such revered men as Emerson, Lowell, and Charles Eliot Norton, had been quite different. Appalled by the ethical torpor and confusion, the futile compromise and the overriding materialism of the pre-war decade, they hailed the war as a thunderclap which cleared the atmosphere and recalled the nation to idealism and to duty. Increasingly as the price of war mounted, they justified the loss of lives and treasure as a sacrifice to righteousness. Emerson was exhilarated that

> When duty whispers low, *Thou must*.
> The youth replies, *I can*.

While Lowell and Norton, as joint editors of the *North American Review* which meant so much to Howells, were prophesying that such a national experience would produce an America cleansed of sordid pettiness, redeemed by the blood of heroes to a future of spiritual greatness. Disillusion came slowly, and in some ways not at all for many years. Even Henry James, no ordinary optimist, was to account at the end of his life for the shock of World War I by the persistence throughout "well-nigh my whole lifetime" of that post-Civil War mood of "innocent confidence." "Just after the Civil War," he recalled, Americans felt "publicly purged of the dreadful disease which had come within an inch of being fatal to us, and . . . by that token warranted sound forever, superlatively safe."

Fortunately for Howells, however, the dominance of that mood did not preclude earnest criticism of the persisting wrongs and absurdities in American life. For he was to get his first toe hold with a robust new magazine, destined to greatness, which was dedicated to that sort of criticism and prepared to welcome his talents. The practical logic of free lancing then as now was to get "a basis," a sure part-time connection with some publication which would guarantee a minimal income but which also left time and talent free to play the literary market. During the first weeks in New York Howells found that his services were acceptable. He could sell special prose as well as items out of his poetry portfolio to magazines and newspapers. But he could not catch on anywhere. He had interviews, including one with Raymond, the great editor of the *New York Times.* He had good leads, sometimes even unkept promises as he worked his way from office to office; but nobody really offered him a basis. And then his break came. Godkin, editor of *The Nation,* the newest and for Howells the most desirable publication in New York, offered him a place on December 17.

Though at the periphery, he was now forever placed in his field. All the rest of his career was possible. As such things go, it had not really taken him long to get his basis, and he had in the meantime proved his power to get along as a real free lance. Yet the time had been long enough, and the pressure of anxiety on him strong enough. It was not the New York experience alone, of course. The tension of all the years of fighting to break through the barriers of self-education and small-town poverty also mattered. But Howells was henceforth to become famous for the imaginatively

sympathetic warmth with which he helped out the young man
trying to climb up from below.

II

His forty-dollar-a-week *Nation* job made Howells practically no free
lance at all, though he managed to add another fifteen per week from
outside sales. By working Sundays he could keep up a weekly
"Letter from New York" for the *Cincinnati Gazette,* but he had to
beg off regretfully when the *Ohio State Journal* asked for another
column from him. Work at the *Nation* was too absorbing, too exciting. Edwin Lawrence Godkin, his often irascible, morally arrogant
chief, took a strong liking to Howells. They worked back-to-back
at desks in the same office, and Howells, to his surprise, found himself drifting into much the same relationship with Godkin as that
he had shared with Reed or Price in the Columbus days. Godkin
loved to laugh with him over the absurdities of the morning news
as they searched together for the editorial grist of the day. At
night they often walked together up through the tidal roar of
horse-drawn Broadway traffic, still talking, inspiring each other's
thoughts as Howells headed home to his wife and child in the Ninth
Avenue boardinghouse he and Elinor called "Barickety-Barackety."
It was there, by the way, quite calmly in spite of all the years of
youthful terror, that Howells saw what his landlady insisted was
the house's familiar ghost walking.

There were a number of reasons, other than merely temperamental ones, for Howells' easy friendship with the formidable man
who was well on his way to becoming the most distinguished
American journalist of the second half of the nineteenth century.
Godkin was a North of Ireland idealist with a good university
education, who had become an American out of strong liberal
convictions. All his convictions were strong, if not impatient; but
he was also a born journalist of wide experience who was determined
to make the *Nation* go, to make it a morally powerful, widely
influential organ of public opinion. Therefore he valued Howells'
humor, his satiric touch, for more than its making him a pleasant
office mate. When Howells was still in Europe, Godkin had been
complaining about how very difficult it was "to get men of education
in America to handle any subject with a light touch," or "to find a

man to do the work of gossiping agreeably on manners, lager bier, &c., who will bind himself to do it whether he feels like it or not." What Godkin was asking for was a writer who could do the sort of thing done effectively in our time in *The New Yorker*'s "Talk of the Town." And of course that was exactly what the Ohio student of Heine, the erstwhile Columbus columnist of "News and Humors of the Mail," the experimental innovator in travel writing had long been training himself to do.

Godkin believed in criticism, serious criticism in something very like the sense given the word by Paul Elmer More or Robert Shafer, a searching evaluation of human (and in this case especially American) life measured by the highest standards. He proposed to fight for democracy, particularly for the negro freedman, but he also proposed to raise up an adequate standard for public morality, education, intellectual life, literature, and the arts in a post-war America whose popular standards really were just about as sloppy as Godkin thought they were. That suited Howells, who had felt "a distinct call to the larger criticism" since his success in the *North American Review* the previous year.

It was also true that Howells and Godkin suited each other politically. The *Nation* had been founded and was financially continued by a group of well-to-do Northern idealists, ultimately a group of New Englanders dominated by Charles Eliot Norton, who wished to propagate the Republican idealism which they believed had won the war and freed the slave. They were rich Eastern counterparts of Howells' father, who had been pushing a bill through the Ohio legislature to enfranchise the negro voter. Their conviction that racial reactionism must not be permitted to overwhelm the freedman in the South made them (and the *Nation*) Radical Republicans. But their long-run hope was to stiffen the fibre of American life with a newly vital morality. In this they were the heirs of generations of New England idealism culminating in Emersonianism. Howells was the heir of his father, and he and the *Nation,* he and Godkin, agreed wholeheartedly.

Quickly recognizing Howells' forte, Godkin set him to writing a weekly column headed "Minor Topics," in which he had much the same scope as the present-day "Talk of the Town" writers and in which, at his best, he achieved the same subtle blend of laughter, familiarity, and force. With perhaps something borrowed from Holmes's "Autocrat of the Breakfast Table" papers in the *Atlantic,*

Howells brought all his self-training and skill to bear in pieces that were just what Godkin wanted them to be—light, and enlightening. He was up-to-the-minute with the new intellectual gossip. Of fashions he said, "La Marck and Darwin assert that mankind sprang from some gorilla in advance of his age. If so, it must be this monkey element, not yet worn out of our nature, that drives us into these absurd imitations." In 1866 that was probably an original joke. He could even use craniometrical evidence to refute the "learned" assertion that Negroes are intellectually inferior.

And his own intellect was functioning lucidly. He knew how to flay the robber baron callousness and corruption of Gilded Age business practices. Describing, with no squeamishness at all, the latest in a series of horrible railroad accidents in New Jersey, he wrote:

'Let New Jersey reflect what renown she might win by convicting the officers of the Bloomfield and Newark Railroad, for example, of manslaughter; by shaving their highly respectable heads, and by teaching their universally esteemed legs the lock-step! But we dare say New Jersey will not do anything of the kind. At least we cannot . . . hope for such greatness from New Jersey, in view of the fact that her Governor has just declined to renominate one of her judges, because he decided that New Jersey had no right to sell a monopoly of the public carriage of passengers over her territory, to any one railroad company.'

Then as now, a critic of sensitive conscience working in New York had to be concerned with its social horrors. Spectacular personal crime and the often absurd disorganization of city government occupied columns both in the *Nation* and in the letter to Cincinnati. There was nothing small about the ills of New York: "while it rivals Naples in the filth of its streets, [it] may well challenge the most favored regions of California [then the Wild West] to equal the daring and impunity of its brigands." And the social criminality of the existence of New York slums was intolerable. Better housing, publicly financed, was the answer, Howells thought. He cited a distinguished traveler as saying that there were people in New York living in "the vilest condition . . . in no barbarian tribe is anything to be seen so filthy, shameless, and utterly and hopelessly degraded."

In the light of future developments, it is important to notice two aspects of his thought in this period. In 1866, as always, Howells was a convinced, theoretical democrat. In spite of all that "history, art and the poetry of association" could offer in European life, he had felt in Europe the necessity of reverting to America and the "opposite faith," to "that social and civil life which permits every life to be at once grand and simple, that makes man superior to classes and only subject to freedom." Along with this went his theory of labor and of competition, in 1866 according with the dominant "political economy" and Herbert Spencer Social Darwinism of the age, which Howells was gradually to grow away from— against which he would become, in fact, the leading literary rebel of his time.

"In democratic theory," he said in 1866, "and in democratic practice all labor should be equally honorable. . . . Every man should have a fair start in life . . ." —and natural inequalities and money will sort men out in the course of a free competition. Therefore, having been poor should be "no barrier against any man's advancement," and "no honest work . . . dishonoring to the worker." That theory was not only eminently respectable at the time, it fitted Howells' own case very well: he was in the midst of being thoroughly successful in his kind of competition. It did not fit his training in his father's thought, however; and during the next twenty years Howells was to find that it did not fit into his own mature view of man's life in this world, either.

III

As always with Howells, the main job of the moment was only the main job. He had other literary fish to fry. There were poems to sell to magazines; there were two books to try to place; and there was the New York world of letters to explore. Journalism and printing poems in magazines were all very well, but only through book publication could he move on toward the literary pinnacles above him. The road of Tennyson and Longfellow remained barred. His too-aptly named manuscript volume, *Disillusion*, was unplaceable. And when he remembered, strolling down Broadway one day, that a box of *Poems of Two Friends* had been sent before the war to a publisher whose offices he was passing, he turned in on the scent of a windfall. After a dusty search, the publisher's boy found the box from Columbus—never opened. But his Venetian book went much better. His London publisher had agreed to print a thousand copies if an American firm would take half of them. Prosperous brother Joe had offered to act as the American firm if no one else would, but good luck brought Howells a better chance. On board ship coming back he had played shuffleboard and euchre with an American publisher, Melanchthon M. Hurd, of Hurd and Houghton. The first week Howells was in New York he bumped into Hurd on the street, went to lunch with him, and left with Hurd's agreement to take over the American edition of the book as a matter of friendship, sight unseen.

If Hurd thought he was probably throwing a small investment away as a bet on the future of a promising author, Howells knew better; and for once the author's optimism was more correct than the publisher's caution. At any rate, the transaction gave Howells confidence in renewing his contacts with the literati of Manhattan. With Whitman gone to Washington, the flock of Pfaff's lesser Bohemians had split up during the war, and new groups were forming. Howells made his peace with Clapp, but the men with whom he was closest were those who had become his friends, in spite of his clash with Clapp, before he went to Venice. Thomas Bailey Aldrich, with his sprightly wit; Edmund Clarence Stedman, who supported the literary life with a successful brokerage in Wall Street; Richard Henry Stoddard and his poet-wife who were beginning the tradition of one of Manhattan's most flourishing *salons;* Bayard Taylor, the furthest-ranging and most glamorous travel writer of Howells' youth, who was now settling down to more solid literary work at home—these were New York writers of the day with whom Howells became intimate.

All through the Venetian years he had kept up some sort of contact with Aldrich, Stedman, and Stoddard. Aldrich was soon to become a colleague in Boston and one of Howells' favorite playmates. With the others his personal contact was to be less frequent over the years, but his gift of creating and holding friendship, a gift which seldom failed him, was nonetheless to bind them fast and keep his own place in the New York literary circle open for many years before he went back to reoccupy it.

Stedman, four years older, had been from the start strongly impressed by Howells. On seeing Howells again in 1865, Stedman underscored in his diary his conviction that Howells had matured abroad and on returning jumped "into a most deserved foremost

position at a bound. *Our most rising young poet and essayist—"*
Expelled from Yale in 1851, Stedman had belonged briefly to the
Fourieristic "Unitary Home" in New York in 1856. He had been
a strong abolitionist but was now, after the war, developing more
exclusively poetic and esthetic interests. Never more than a minor
poet, he became, partially through Howells' prodding, the widest-
ranging American critic of poetry in his time and an important
anthologist. He was one of the few who insisted on believing that
Howells was at heart a poet and who continually urged him not to
forget or neglect his poet's practice.

These men were not only his friends; they tended, especially
those of his own generation like Aldrich and Stedman, to be his
allies. While neither Aldrich nor Stedman would prove to be able
to go all the way with Howells in his mature advocacy of realism,
they went as far as they could, and even in opposition they remained
personally friendly. But just now they were altogether willing to
join Howells in that revolt against the stereotypes of popular
literary sentimentality which he signalized by declaring war in the
Nation against the immensely popular lecturer and author of sentimental monstrosities, the monumentally respectable Dr. Josiah
Gilbert Holland.

Perhaps the easiest way to understand Holland is to say that he
was the sort of man whose worst crimes are blissfully veiled from
his consciousness. It is a kind of tragedy as well as an indictment
of his type in American society that he was the "man of letters"
whom Emily Dickinson knew best. The fact must have had something to do with her determination to keep out of the world and
not be like a man of letters at all. Holland was the type of unconsciously pompous, arrogantly humble, tyrannically respectable, and
irresponsibly emotional man who made Mark Twain hate the Sunday
School with fervor all his life and who provided such a fine target
for the first half of the twentieth century's more or less deliberate
misrepresentation of Victorianism. He wrote like the kind of man
he was, and, being no artist, he wrote badly. What infuriated
Howells was that, writing so badly, he was so popular. His popularity had a negative factor: being respectable, and ostentatiously
evangelical, he was "safe," noncontroversial. Howells and his group
were morally and socially respectable, but as, on the whole, agnostics
they could not shelter beneath the shield of evangelicism. And

they thought Holland's doing so dishonest as well as irrelevant. Even worse, there was a positive side to Holland's appeal: he was a sentimentalist, and then as now the popular appetite for sentimentality was as insatiable as it was profoundly corrupting to its addicts. A most fundamental part of Howells' revolt against his time was his revolt against sentimentality. His personal and social morality, much of his literary practice, and much of his battle for realism stemmed from that revolt, and it is worth understanding what he was about.

The most concise way to define "sentimentality" is to say that it is irresponsible emotionality. It had been common, it was so among Howells' critics, to say that anti-sentimentalists are monsters of rationalism or sheer coldness, devoid of feeling. Nothing could, of course, be more absurd. No human act or reflection is ever divorced entirely from emotion. On the contrary, normally thought and deed are inseparably fused with emotion. They move together, one supporting, even defining the other. And it is precisely for that reason that sentimentality, the effort to indulge oneself in the pleasures of strong feeling while escaping from responsibility to think, to decide, or to act in accordance with it, is a form of human perversion. It is a dangerous perversion because the practice of it distorts one's fantasy-life, destroys or weakens the power to respond properly to true emotional stimulus—or even sometimes the power to experience proper emotion at all in the low-charged but complex situations of common, everyday life—and leaves the mind available only to over-intense, lurid approaches, often entirely too available to them.

In Howells' time the principal mass entertainment media were oratory and the theater, newspapers, the rising magazine industry, and the novel. Sentimental writers of fiction for the last three media seemed morally vicious for the reasons cited; and Howells was to devote broad spaces of his creative as well as critical output to dramatizing the case against them. But the sentimentalists were almost always bad artists, too, because they inevitably went in for what Howells was eventually to call "effectism." That is, they became interested mainly in producing unlimited, intense, and irresponsible emotional effects. Their literary means were therefore apt to be broad and crude, if not wooden. Style and dialog were high-flown. Characterizations, symbolism, and the cruxes of action tended simply to conform to well-worn conventional patterns which served to trigger-off the desired sentimental reactions in readers and nothing more.

Holland was only one of thousands of such writers, and by no means the worst. But he was the highly successful "Apostle to the Naive," as his biographer calls him, and he had set himself up as a target which the bright young critic of the *Nation* could not resist knocking down. It was high time, he said, in "Concerning Timothy Titcomb" (one of Holland's *noms de plume*) on November 25, 1865, for American criticism to wield a more vigorous cudgel. "Titcomb's" success, he said, proves that because of a "slovenly and timorous criticism . . . an order of mind has been allowed to flourish up into a thistly rank in our literature fit only to browse donkeys." The following year, as reviewer for the *Atlantic*, he sneered openly at Holland's narrative poem *Kathrina*. The only reason the heroine did not laugh in the face of the hero when he spouted his atrocious verse to her, Howells surmised, was that Kathrina was "herself scarcely other than a name for a series of arguments, with little of the flesh and blood of a womanly personality." The whole poem, he concluded, was "puerile in conception, destitute of due motive, and inartistic in treatment."

When Howells became editor of the *Atlantic*, none of Holland's still popular novels was reviewed. None of his reviewers could promise not to scarify their author. Naturally, Holland was bitterly hurt and resentful. Even when he once tried to turn the other cheek and dropped in on a group of the Young Turks during one of Howells' later visits back to New York, he found them mad about Turgenev and other incomprehensible people. And he satisfied their Young Turk malice by making himself ridiculous with a pompously impersonal speech when he rose to go: "I have been listening to the conversation of these young men for over an hour," he said. "They have been talking about books. And I have never before heard the names of any of the authors they have mentioned." Gleeful balm though that may have been to the heart of a young literary radical, Howells had made an influential enemy. As editor of *Scribner's*, Holland belittled Howells' writings, threatened to resign if anything of Howells' were accepted for the magazine by its publisher, and refused to have Howells reviewed in his magazine. That inspired Stedman to a happy epigram (in which Howells is, of course, "H. number I"):

H. number I will not review
The poems of H. number II,
   Because he can't defend 'em;
II. number II has nothing done
With novels of H. number I
   For fear he must commend 'em!

Nevertheless, Howells had his first good lesson in the enmity of the old conservative for the Young Turk, and it was only by humbly paying a personal call to Holland on his deathbed that he was able to achieve a personal (since he could not, indeed, wish for an ideological) reconciliation.

But the New York crowd were most important to Howells simply because they admitted him on equal terms to the society of creative and cultivated people he had longed to live among. Stedman introduced him around. Stoddard, old enough to be his father, took him in with special warmth because Howells had been a poor boy, and Stoddard, the impoverished son of a ship's captain lost at sea, had come up out of the slums as an iron molder before he could break into the literary game. At one of the parties there came an incident which left Howells' sensibility reverberating with its tragic implications all the rest of his life. Edwin Booth, the actor, was among the guests, and moodily looking over the *objets d'art* he came across plaster casts of two interesting hands and picked up the huge one clenched into a fist. "Whose hand is this?" he asked the host.

"Tennyson's."

"No, I mean this one," Booth insisted, until the host had to answer, "Lincoln's."

IV

It was at Bayard Taylor's New Year's party (Sunday, January 7, 1866), that Howells' most fateful New York social experience took place. James T. Fields, the Boston publisher and editor of the *Atlantic* who had been virtually barring Howells from the magazine, was there. And he was lavishing on Howells the robust charm which had captivated the skeptical Hawthorne and the touchy Dickens, among hordes of other authors. As they shook hands at the end, Fields put out a subtle feeler to sound out the newly successful New Yorker, "Don't despise Boston!"

And he got an equally subtle but reassuring response, "Few are worthy to live in Boston."

The next two days Howells was snowed in. But when he came down to the *Nation* office on Wednesday, he found concrete evidence that he and Fields had not been simply joking. There was a note on his desk from Fields, inviting him to dinner and hinting at a fine proposal. Having missed the date, Howells wrote explaining and indicating his interest in the proposal. In reply Fields offered him the assistant editorship of the *Atlantic Monthly,* for Howells the most attractive job he could then imagine filling. Always a good businessman, Howells did not jump at the chance. He negotiated. Godkin was willing to release him. He bargained for fifty dollars a week from the *Atlantic,* with his literary contributions to pay extra, and got it. He was invited up to Boston and suitably entertained by the Fieldses, came back home, and on February 6 wrote to accept the job effective March 1, which would be his twenty-ninth birthday.

Chapter Seven

CAMBRIDGE AND THE
ATLANTIC MONTHLY, 1866–1871

A LERT AND SENSITIVE AMERICANS FELT A SHOCK OF RECOGNITION at the news that young William Dean Howells was assistant editor of the *Atlantic Monthly*. A Western writer first in the line of succession to the birthright of the Brahmins ! Just at the peak of New England's triumph in the competition for provincial supremacy in American cultural life, the great symbol of its supremacy bade fair to pass into the hands of an Ohioan, whose only objective link to New England was through marriage. By that token, American letters began to become national, no longer provincial.

There was no lack of witnesses to that recognition. Howells had it confirmed to his face during an accidental meeting with Samuel Bowles, the brilliant editor of the *Springfield Republican,* on the train trip up to Boston to begin the *Atlantic* job. Bowles took pleasure in musing aloud on the dramatic meaning of Howells' pilgrimage. The following October, Lowell subtly underscored the same theme in reviewing *Venetian Life.* The *Saturday Press* was so bowled over that it prematurely (by five years) made Howells editor of the *Atlantic* and set the Western newspapers ringing with hosannas of inaccurate praise which made Howells feel as if his obituaries were appearing. Artemus Ward, knowing he would be heard as the spokesman of the Western authors, wrote his hearty congratulations.

I

In later years, looking back on his Boston and most especially his Cambridge years, Howells developed a mood of acute nostalgia.

Boston was fascinating and instructive. Cambridge was the perfect home for his spirit. Yet in the long run the most important feature of the Cambridge-Boston period in his life was the education it gave him. Perhaps the most astonishing thing about Howells was his mental ductility. His mind did not crystallize, he did not lose his power to learn and adapt, even at deep psychic levels, until after his fiftieth birthday. This prolonged power to change creatively, to grow, is one of the secrets of his greatness; and he displayed it to the full in his *Atlantic* period. His relationship with Cambridge and Boston, for all they were emotionally profound, were *désengagé*. He was like a good cultural anthropologist at work—sympathetic but detached, critical, intelligent, professional—in the last analysis an outsider with too much integrity to pretend to be inside. It was Aldrich, born in Maine, who wittily summed up his own career by saying, "Though I am not genuine Boston, I am Boston-plated." That was never true of Howells. And if his ultimate detachment accounted for some of the coldness critics felt in his handling of Bostonians, it also accounts for the penetration they recognized in his Bostonian portraits.

Yet as an American writer, Howells could be, and was, happier to be in Boston than anywhere else. This was the "Flash Age" of New York, the era of Boss Tweed and Jim Fisk, when the arts counted for little in Manhattan. In Boston, quite the contrary, they counted for a great deal. Literature was queen in a city ruled by college men bred in that time, just before the cultural explosion caused by the new sciences, when American higher education had been dominated by *belles lettres*. "In Boston," said Howells, the standard authority on the epoch, "literature was of good family and good society in a measure it has never been elsewhere." To provide a thumbnail characterization of Bromfield Corey, his most famous Bostonian creation, Howells once wrote of him simply that he was "a society veteran of that period when even the swell in Boston must be an intellectual man." On March 26, 1866, Aldrich wrote Bayard Taylor that the luckiest day of his professional life was the day he moved to Boston. "The people of Boston are full-blooded readers, appreciative, trained," he said. "A knight of the quill here is supposed necessarily to be a gentleman. In N.Y.—he's a Bohemian ! outside of his personal friends he has no standing."

What Howells and Aldrich both remarked was the effect of a unique pattern of events, which has not yet been thoroughly studied.

How can one account for the special position of the writer in Boston? Part of the answer lies in the Puritan tradition of the prestige of the minister-scholar. With the demise of Calvinism and the rise of Unitarianism, transcendentalism, and other varieties of free thought, that prestige had been transferred to the secular scholar and, increasingly, to the artist-scholar, even the pure artist. And since the intellectual and esthetic experience of New England had been intensely sophisticated in letters and ideas for generations but was on the whole shallow and naive in the other arts, literature was enthroned.

All that has long been known, but it leaves unaccounted for the fact that literature was "good society" in Boston—Society-Page Society, that is. And the best way, though it must be a theoretical way for lack of historical study, to account for it is to say that, before and during Howells' time, there had been a unique fusion of Proper Bostonians and New England Brahmins. That this fusion created some "Boston Brahmins" is undeniable. It ought, however, to be denied that the popular tradition is correct which would make "Boston Brahmin" one term in the usage of American cultural history. It ought to be denied because the Brahmins were very often not Bostonians, because making them so confuses and distorts one's view of their nature and their significance in the history of New England and American culture. Furthermore, that history— and William Dean Howells' place in it, understanding of it, and fictional treatment of it—is much more readily comprehensible when one maintains the distinction between "Brahmin" and the term so happily given us by Mr. Cleveland Amory—"Proper Bostonian."

Proper Bostonian Society, says Mr. Amory, is nineteenth-century commercial Society, resting on the wealth garnered by nineteenth-century merchants. He feels that one can take 1878 as the latest date by which the fortune must have been made, the social entree secured. The Brahmins, however, were labeled by Dr. Oliver Wendell Holmes in 1861. A medical professor much interested in genetics, Holmes distinguished between "pitch-pine Yankees and white-pine Yankees," the latter "a native aristocracy, a superior race." He admitted the possibility of mutations, genetic "sports," who might turn out to be natural *aristoi,* as Thomas Jefferson and John Adams had called them, nature's gentlemen. There was always the "large uncombed youth who goes to college and startles the hereditary class-leaders by striding past them all." But the true, enduring aristocracy of New England, its Brahmin caste, were the "Academic Races," a "harmless, inoffensive, untitled aristocracy" among whom "aptitude for learning" was "congenital and hereditary." They had filled the college catalogs and learned professions, especially the pulpits, of New England for generations. Around them the extraordinarily tenacious and successful culture of the New England villages had grown.

Blended, as in Holmes himself, with Proper Bostonians and their wealth, the Brahmins, thus become Boston Brahmins, produced a society and an intellectual life dominated by such names of "first citizens" as (to use Howells' own list) "Prescott, Motley, Parkman, Lowell, Norton, Higginson, Dana, Emerson, Channing." For just so far as it was Brahmin, that society could command Howells' admiration, even affection. But the Proper Bostonian, said one contemporary observer, "is furnished with an icicle in place of a spine, and he is in terror if he thinks a new person is really going to know him. . . . A morbid reserve, a contented selfishness, and distinctions set up with an arbitrariness that is ludicrous, hamper intercourse at all points." Insofar as it was like that, Boston society stimulated Howells to sharpen his satirical knife for its scalp. By native endowment and rigorous training he had come to the point where he might hope to be accepted, outsider though he remained, as a "natural" Brahmin. But against Proper Bostonism he could have no defenses save his wit.

When the Howellses moved into a tiny apartment at 22 Bulfinch Street, Boston, in March, however, they were certainly not without friends. Holmes, who had continued to be fond of young Howells, made a point of calling on them soon. And the Fieldses, the genial, glamorous, wealthy Fieldses with their marvelous collection of literary souvenirs, their boundless prestige and *savoir faire*, their famous breakfasts and celebrity-packed "evenings," could introduce the Howellses into every compartment, however normally airtight, of Boston's literary-social life. Not only was Fields the "chief" on the *Atlantic*, Mrs. Fields had a certain stake in Howells' success. It was she who had persuaded her husband to pick him for the job. Together they saw that everybody met him and his wife. And, on the whole, they caught on well. Everybody was charmed with Mrs. Howells, and Howells had by no means lost his ability to win friends, especially ladies. Even the redoubtable Julia Ward Howe, meeting them on April 4, found that "Howells is odd-looking, but sympathetic and intelligent."

Like most of the Howellses' actual residences in Boston, this first one was destined to be brief. On the *Atlantic*, Fields most wanted help at the editorial-production end. Howells would be more convenient to the printer living in Cambridge. Only the desperate postwar housing shortage had made it necessary for him to alight in Boston at all. And powerful assistance was at work for him in Cambridge. When nothing could be found to rent, a little place for sale was finally uncovered. Squire Mead put up Howells' payment for an equity. Charles Eliot Norton found a rich friend to take the first mortgage and took the second himself, and so Howells became on May 1, 1866, the "owner" of a "little wooden pill-box on Sacramento Street" in a bucolic and unfashionable outskirt of Cambridge. Yet if Sacramento Street was a small beginning, it was anything but unpleasant. The house was snug, and Elinor got a good Irish cook. There were pear trees, grapes, and currants in the yard, and room for the vegetable garden Howells planted every spring of his life, circumstances permitting. Most important, it was in the town in which Howells delighted above all others. "After we went to live in Cambridge," he said, "my life and the delight in it were so wholly there that in ten years I had hardly been in as many Boston homes."

II

Settled in "Cottage Quiet" to begin, as Howells wrote Norton, the task of growing old, the young writer and his wife also had ahead of them the task of coping with a new life. It was good to be a publishing author as well as an *Atlantic* editor. Household expenses could be covered by selling verse to outlets like *Galaxy* and the *Nation*. Squire Mead happened to be visiting when the winter's coal was delivered the same morning as a check in payment for a poem. And he roared with laughter when Howells admitted that the check just covered the price of the coal—the hard plebeian stuff crashing into the cellar was the wage of the delicate Muse. But the real job on hand was, after all, the subeditorship of America's most distinguished magazine.

He was working for the best known publishing house in America

—Ticknor and Fields, due to become Fields, Osgood and Company in 1868 and James R. Osgood and Company in 1871 without disturbing him in his job. Not only were Ticknor and Fields publishers of the galaxy of New England authors who had dominated American intellectual life since before Howells' birth, they were also in control of a whole stable of influential magazines. To the *Atlantic,* which Fields had taken away from the editorship of Lowell, they had added the *North American Review,* Boston's ancient and powerful quarterly, still edited by Lowell and Norton, in 1864. They also put out *Every Saturday,* an effort to compete with *Harper's* for the English reprint market, which Aldrich had been imported to run, and *Our Young Folks* under Lucy Larcom and J. T. Trowbridge. Boston or no, Fields's enterprise was worth joining, and the more because Fields knew how to run a happy ship. In the spacious converted mansion at 124 Tremont Street where Fields had his office, humor and good-fellowship were encouraged. Lunch was brought in from the Parker House every day, and visiting authors were cordially welcome to sit down with Fields, Aldrich, Trowbridge, Howells when he had come to town on the horsecar from Cambridge, and other staff members and join in the fun.

Howells contacted the office mostly by mail and messenger, however, because his job was easiest to do in Cambridge. With many other responsibilities and a waning enthusiasm for personally editing magazines, Fields needed a man to take off his shoulders two troublesome technical jobs. Part of the distinction of the *Atlantic* rested on the nearly impeccable results in stylistic competence, accuracy, and good printing which had been achieved under Lowell by a rigorous system of proofreading. In what would nowadays be an impossibly expensive process, typographically perfect proofs came from two corrections in the print shop to Howells, with margins already filled with stylistic queries from the head reader. Howells then altered style to suit his idea of the *Atlantic* standard, verified every proper name, date, quotation, accent, technical term or other reference, consulted the author or another authority if he pleased, and returned the proofs for resetting at the press. When that was all done, there came the final, often frantic, job of actually seeing the monthly issue into and through the press, of begging the main office to let him have a few more pages and hang the expense, or, denied, slicing and hacking at the table of contents or even the text until the budget had been met and he could tell the printer to let 'em roll.

The job demanded competence in areas ranging from typography through esoteric fields of scholarship to literary esthetics. It demanded diplomacy, stamina, and dedication. Sometimes it took courage, as when he had to point out unconscious plagiarisms to Holmes and Lowell, or when he had to go, hat in hand, to point out lapses in the Latinity of the egomaniac Senator Sumner. Howells' hours were often long, his responsibilities complex and hard to define. His opportunities to infuriate people were numerous. Yet he succeeded excellently in his job and had energy to work beyond it at the hopeful tasks which were some day to free him from bondage to editorial technicalities.

Howells had raised Fields's original salary offer partly by engaging to write reviews for the *Atlantic,* and he did them enthusiastically. He reviewed eighteen books in his first calendar year on the job and soon advanced to the place where he could say to Thomas Wentworth Higginson that he "almost wholly" controlled *Atlantic* reviewing. He had a high sense of responsibility about it, trying to cover all important American books but beyond that "choosing books that I can write intelligently about" because "I do nearly all the writing myself." He kept up the faith in the importance of serious criticism to which he had subscribed while with the *Nation,* yet tried to be *"entertaining* and . . . worth the reader's while," as he explained in laying down the rules of good reviewing for his neophyte sister Annie in 1873. The art of fair quotation is most important, he pointed out: "Set the author honestly before the reader. If you don't like an author, say *why* and let him *show* why. Never try to be funny at his expense; that's poor, cheap, cruel business. Read a book, or else don't write of it." And twice in the period he anonymously won almost the highest praise the *Nation* could give. It said in 1868 and again in 1870 that the *Atlantic*'s reviews were usually the best written and "the most profitable part of the magazine."

Surprisingly, and the powers liberated in Howells by his *Atlantic* and Cambridge opportunities were surprising, he still had time and strength left to take advantage of his magazine's unusually high pay rates as a contributor over and above his contract. Occasionally he published in the *North American Review* or other magazines. Some of these pieces came out of his portfolio, like the popular bits which were chapters from his second travel book, *Italian Journeys,* 1867. Some were outright sketches, and some the experiments, half sketch and half fiction, which became *Suburban Sketches,* 1871. In 1868 Howells flashed back to his Ohio days and wrote a strong political endorsement for Radical Republicanism and Grant. The *Atlantic* had been bitterly anti-Johnson, as of course the *Ashtabula Sentinel* had, but now it was time to make General U. S. Grant "The Next President." Politically passive but a great leader with a "thorough knowledge of men" (!) Grant should be the perfect Radical Republican man, Howells argued. He would free the Congress to lead the nation toward an ideal democratic future under "a President without a policy and a people without a master."

Health failing and many affairs pressing, Fields was increasingly glad to let his young dynamo take over. For Christmas 1868 Elinor Howells got a complimentary check for one hundred dollars from Fields and Osgood, though the previous March her husband's salary had been raised to $3500 a year. More and more all but the most ultimate decisions about the *Atlantic* fell into Howells' hands. That meant Fields's gradually resigning to him the most delicate and decisive of editorial jobs: accepting, rejecting, and requesting revision of manuscripts; paying and otherwise dealing with contributors; recruiting new talent. Handling new talent, especially from among the writers of his own generation, had been left to Howells from the start. It was probably one of the functions for which he was hired. Hence he dealt with Stedman, Aldrich, Harte, Clemens. When Sarah Orne Jewett first began to submit poetry and tales under the name of "Alice Eliot," it was Howells who rejected her early things with letters so kindly encouraging that she kept writing and growing toward her future excellence. He was early given the job of negotiating with an old but distressingly uneven contributor, his New York friend Bayard Taylor. Most important, perhaps, Howells coached, and wheedled *Atlantic* space for a young man not yet quite sure of his literary vocation. He did much to assure a career in letters for a desultory law student who then perforce signed himself Henry James, Jr.

Fields had less and less hesitation about giving Howells extra work, and as a young man in love with his job and confessedly on the make, Howells was glad to take it on and do it well. It meant increased responsibility and opportunity. He came to read virtually all manuscripts and have the right of choice. Only occasionally did

Fields overrule by accepting things not seen by Howells or by soliciting items without consulting him. And the more he let Howells' power grow, the more friendly and considerate Fields became. The one ultimate control he retained was final decision on what should or should not actually appear in each month's issue. Finally in 1869 Fields felt secure enough to go to Europe from April to November, leaving the magazine in Howells' hands, with Osgood, Lowell, and Holmes to consult if he needed help. After that, the *Atlantic* was almost wholly Howells' until he finally became editor-in-chief in 1871.

After his childhood in a newspaper shop and his experiences with the *Ohio State Journal,* Howells did not have to learn on the *Atlantic* how important the business office is in journalism. Even the prosperous Fields kept his eye on the circulation list, which he had built up impressively. And three episodes during Howells' assistantship taught him dramatic lessons about what the constituency would not stand. He learned that even the *Atlantic* was vulnerable to the religious prejudices of the great church-going audience to which Dr. Holland played so successfully. And he learned that, whatever globs of sentimentally-flavored sexual nasty-nicety the American Victorian audience would swallow eagerly as long as it conformed to the conventions long ago established by the novelist Samuel Richardson and his imitators, frank talk or non-sentimental speculations about sex met with instant, indignant rejection.

The great drawing card of the *Atlantic,* the writer who more than anybody else had built up its circulation with his gay poems and effervescent essays, was of course Dr. Holmes. Fields was always eager to get contributions from him, and in Howells' first year accepted and published with joy the second of Holmes's "medicated" novels, *The Guardian Angel.* And it cost the magazine very heavily in cancelled subscriptions. Among evangelical Americans Holmes had long been theologically suspect. He was an aggressive anti-Calvinist, freely castigating "The Moral Bully" of an evangelical preacher who tried to scare poor parishioners into meek faith under the threat of hell-fire, and often lightly satiric in his treatment of the cloth in general. In *The Guardian Angel* he sketched a beautiful heroine suffering dramatically from what would nowadays be called serious neurotic disturbances. Eventually she is saved by true love and the wise machinations of her kindly, old guardian—a rational, humane "guardian angel." But one of the dangers from which he must rescue her is the ministration of a smooth and lecherous clergyman, already married, who has salvation on his lips but seduction in his heart. The public reaction was devastating. Holmes and the magazine were pilloried in the evangelical press. Even the *Nation* objected to what it called Holmes's materialistic way of treating "the physical influence of sex" so that the novel gave off an "atmosphere of carnality." The impact of this on a young editor must have been heavy. If such a thing could happen to the *Atlantic Monthly* when it published what Fields said was the best thing Dr. Holmes had ever written !

The same year popular British novelist Charles Reade's *Griffith Gaunt* stirred up another hornet's nest. Paying then unheard-of fees for exclusive rights to the novel, Fields had hoped to create a sensation and did—but it was a disastrous one. Heading its review "An Indecent Publication," the New York *Round Table* called Reade's book "an unpardonable insult to morality" and charged that the *Atlantic* had printed something "declined by some of the lowest sensational weekly papers in New York." There was more publicity when Reade replied in wrath and sued for libel; but it only hurt Fields's subscription list the more.

If Howells could stand by wide-eyed at these first disasters, he had to share responsibility for a real catastrophe which happened while he was in charge of the magazine during Fields's European vacation in 1869. In the September *Atlantic* he published Harriet Beecher Stowe's "The True Story of Lady Byron's Life," which made public Lady Byron's charge that her husband had committed incest with his half sister Aurora Leigh. The article attracted public attention; in fact it created a volcanic international sensation. But it cost the *Atlantic* fifteen thousand subscribers and seriously damaged the public attractiveness of the most famous name among its contributors. Appalled though Fields must have been by the result of a venture over which he had no control, he neither blamed nor penalized Howells for it. Nor should he have done so. The affair had been almost entirely out of his hands because Mrs. Stowe had determinedly ignored him (and almost everyone else) while bulldozing her way toward destruction. Perhaps the only real blame Howells deserved was for his believing at the time (as he did not later) in the rightness of the project, however much he deplored her way of doing it.

Burning with personal vanity, moral indignation, and Victorian female outrage at masculine depravity, Stowe wrote her article and in May, 1869, sent proofs of it to Dr. Holmes, announcing her determination to print it in the *Atlantic* no matter who said what but begging him to help her improve her presentation. Had Holmes objected, the article would probably not have appeared—at least not in the *Atlantic*. And there was the rub. Mrs. Stowe, as author of *Uncle Tom's Cabin,* was the most prestigious woman in America, the confidante of Lincoln, the Boadicea of reform, an unquestionable authority on household affairs and the life of women—like a modern-day equivalent of Mrs. Roosevelt, Helen Keller, Mary Roberts Rinehart, and Simone de Beauvoir rolled into one. Fields subsidized her freely with advances just to keep her contributing, though what she wrote was often so careless and hurried that she gladly depended on *Atlantic* editors to rewrite her into respectability. How could Holmes and Osgood, much less Howells, risk her wrath when she was so determined? They gave way, as did Lowell —though much more reluctantly because he thought her wrong both in believing Lady Byron and in publishing her charges.

Except Lowell, everyone concerned, including Howells, was also giving way to prejudice against Byron, the god of one kind of romanticism. There was an ancient Bostonian grudge against Byron's wickedness and Byronism's emotional incontinence. Holmes put it perfectly in trying to console Mrs. Stowe for the storm which howled against her in the press of two continents. Only "scum" would so resent her, he said, "the model-artists and the cancan dancers." Really it was high time "that the true character of a man, who has diabolized the literature of his century . . . be known in his true character to posterity." Howells shared that grudge, and had a new proto-realistic one of his own. He was not allowed to see the Byron article until it was in type. When he corrected the proofs and sent them back to Mrs. Stowe, she ignored him and dealt only through Holmes. Thus his skirts were almost clear and no personal retribution followed; but the lesson must have been really painful.

III

Personal life, more and more successfully blended in marriage, went on for the Howellses in the meanwhile. Will might slave late into the night on proofs or might have to wade knee-deep through drifts to get materials to the printer's on time when a blizzard stopped the horsecars, but he worked at home. His professional and domestic lives were permanently intertwined. In a household un-ashamedly child-infatuated there was exultation when a second baby was born, a son named John Mead (both parents had lost beloved brothers John), on August 14, 1868. That complicated life, be-cause of course children fall sick, and Elinor Howells was weak and recurrently ill for a long time after John's birth. Yet in sum it made for great happiness and content, especially as the children grew more companionable. Trying to cheer his recently bereaved father on Halloween of 1868, Howells wrote of how little Winnie was enjoying Christmas in prospect through Clement Moore's "A Visit from St. Nicholas":

'Every night after dinner I have to come down the parlor chimney 'with a bound'—the idea being represented by hiding in the screen and then jumping out into the middle of the floor. Then I am Winifred Howells, and lie asleep on the sofa while she brings me a Christmas Tree.'

With his increased income Howells was eventually able to leave the deteriorating Sacramento Street neighborhood and buy a house at 3 Berkley Street, near Harvard Square and Longfellow's house, in 1870.

There a handsome young Norwegian immigrant, a Swedenborgian professor and aspiring author, Hjalmar Hjorth Boyesen, recorded an idyllic picture of the Howellses at home in 1871. Lonesome in his adopted homeland, Boyesen had concluded that family affection was unknown in democratic America. But in coming to Cambridge he had better luck. Professor Child picked him up in the Harvard library and, learning that he had written a novel, invited Howells to lunch with Boyesen, who read a chapter of his *Gunnar* after lunch. He and Howells liked each other at once, and Howells took him home for a two weeks' visit "in a rose-embowered cottage in a secluded nook of Berkley Street, Cambridge. He had a study . . . fronting upon a small garden, and lined with books up to the very ceiling," Boyesen found.

As young writers they had a glorious time together, sitting up to all hours in "splendid conversational rages" and reading chapters of work in progress to each other. Then they would raid the cellar in the middle of the night and improvise suppers of "cheese and crackers and . . . a watermelon and a bottle of champagne." But what meant most to Boyesen's charmed eyes was the atmosphere of Howells' family life. He was smitten by seven-year-old Winnie, a "dear, confiding, affectionate little girl . . . with large, thoughtful eyes." His hasty conclusion about the chilliness of the American home vanished when he saw that in Howells' house "the tender and considerate conduct of each toward all made domestic life beautiful, and love found expression in caresses . . . naturally." Years later Boyesen said, "I have never seen a more beautiful instance of the spontaneity, the inevitability with which a rich and loveable personality radiates its own genial warmth and light through all relations." He joined the growing ranks of those who were to be Howells' friends for life.

But of course it was not all just fun and felicity. There were personal sorrows. Mary Dean Howells, worn out with her hard-won victory for her family in Jefferson had been "ailing" all summer but insisting that "Willie" not be made anxious about it. In the fall she collapsed suddenly, and though Howells raced home he arrived four hours late, tiptoeing in at night so as not to disturb her and then having to be told. Forever after he could remember walking with his father and brothers out in the dim-gold October sunshine under the grape trellises in Jefferson trying to reason out his agony. The next year he was involved in a very different scene in Brattleboro, when Squire Mead died and Howells saw the concealment of sorrow among mourners whose heritage of Puritan discipline had brought them to the conviction that grief is a private affair. Upon acquaintance, the awful thing, death, which he had feared with such hysteria in adolescence, turned out to be less fearful—and more inevitable. He found that there had been an error in his theory of life, he told Henry James. Henceforward he was not to try to "forget death."

IV

At the same time, he was gradually mastering a unique and tricky feat of social balance—the art of living in Cambridge, Massachusetts. Though on the point of changing completely and for that reason perhaps more acceptably cosmopolitan than it had ever been before, the Cambridge to which the Howellses came was a distinctive town. In brief, it was typical of the New England village at its best, but made unique by having since 1636 been the seat of the oldest college in the nation. The people of the town and their lives had all the character of the Yankee village—with a most important added leaven. Almost everyone was Yankee, and "everybody knew not only everybody else in person, but much of everybody's tradition, connections, and mode of life," as Charles Eliot Norton remembered. They were democratic, yet kept the New England tradition of respect for "the natural distinctions of good breeding and superior culture." But if village intimacy, rigorous Yankee morality, and social distinctions threatened to establish the tyranny of the community, they were firmly restrained by another New England tradition—that of Yankee individualism—as another native son recalled. In the Cambridge of his boyhood, said James Russell Lowell, men felt that "their personalities were their castles in which they could intrench themselves against the world." Altogether, as Norton summed it up, "there was simplicity in its best sense. The households were homes of thrift without parsimony, of hospitality without extravagance, of culture without pretence."

In small-town Cambridge, nature was close at hand and very lovely—as indeed it was almost everywhere in preindustrial America. But after all, what made the town famous was, first, the college and, second, the Brahmin literati who sprang up in the generations between the decline of theology and the rise of science. Their special tradition, whether they were native sons or adoptive ones like Longfellow, had become that of Andrews Norton, Charles Eliot's father, as Thomas Wentworth Higginson remembered him: "His refined and exquisite taste cast an air of purity and elegance around the spirit of the place. His habits were as severe as those of a medieval monk. His love of literature was a passion." If they suffered from parochial restrictions and village respectability, they were able to turn their liabilities into certain kinds of advantage. Devoutly worshiping the best as they knew it, they achieved the quality of life which most impressed Howells when he recalled it —the phrase for it was *"intense and simple."*

Of course that is a portrait taken, for the most part, from the nostalgic praise of backward-gazing local boys, and no doubt there were things to be said on the other side. Nonetheless, their vision should stand here as recorded because Howells saw the Cambridge he loved very much the way Lowell, Norton, and Higginson saw it. He arrived barely in time to see it at all, for as soon as the immediate postwar paralysis was overcome the town began to change swiftly from an academic village into the university city, Boston suburb, and manufacturing center it has since become. Even by 1871 John Holmes, the Doctor's home-loving brother, saw with "the calmness of despair" that "Old Cambridge is almost gone and the New has taken its place" and found that old-timers could find refuge from "the uproar" only in memories. As the place changed, its society began to change also, of course, and that was one of the reasons why Howells eventually left Cambridge. But for about a decade to come, he found the society of Cambridge the most nearly perfect he could imagine for himself.

Cambridge people, especially the most distinguished, were well-impressed by Howells and kind to him. They had liked him on his pilgrimage in 1860, had followed his Venetian letters in the Boston *Advertiser* with pleasure, and read and esteemed the *Nation* second only to the *Atlantic*. The *Atlantic* they regarded with justification as peculiarly their own creation, and their pride in it was indubitably sinful. They took it for granted that *Atlantic* editors should live in Cambridge as every one (except Fields) prior to 1900 at some time did, and they were prepared to make the editor glad he was there. But their unbounded devotion to Italy, its language, culture, and art, was what won the newest American Italianist favor and acceptance in Cambridge.

The American intellectual's delight in Italy has long been known but never well studied. There may be good Americans who go to Paris when they die, but there are probably a lot more who go to Venice, Rome, or, even better, somewhere in Tuscany or Umbria. And the hard-working college professors, writers, and magazine editors who made up the core of Cambridge society in 1866 loved to play at the game of pretending to be rich and leisurely *dilettanti* basking in a world of warm, colorful, ancient Italian culture. The center of the game was the Dante Club, meeting weekly at Longfellow's home to hear him read a canto a week from the proof sheets of his translation of Dante's *Divina Commedia*, which he had begun as a shield for his mind from the shock of his wife's tragic death by fire. When Howells arrived, Longfellow was working through the *Paradiso*.

Dante Club meetings were delightful free-and-easy social affairs as well as times of high scholarly-poetic converse where Longfellow's renderings were subject to the debate of the membership. When the group had gathered, Longfellow would say "School-time !"

and pass out copies of Dante in the original. Then he would an-
nounce and perhaps defend decisions he had made after the past
week's discussion and proceed to read, in his soft, foghorn voice,
the canto of the night, pausing for query or objection whenever
anything was offered. To hear Lowell and Norton and sometimes
E. P. Whipple, Fields, or other luminaries so engaged with the man
he thought perhaps second only to Tennyson as the greatest living
poet was a profoundly moving experience for Howells. He dared
open his mouth only once to make a suggestion. And then, the
work done, came supper: oysters, and turkey, or venison, grouse,
or quail with salad and Longfellow's famous wines—"very plain" by
the standards of the Gilded Age. Even more delectable to a young
participant, however, was the play of humor and fancy around the
table. Howells discovered that his wit could score even in the big
league—with Lowell, and Holmes, and Tom Appleton, Boston's
premier *bon vivant*. He used to walk home to Sacramento Street,
in the wee hours, with feet which seemed to float above the frozen
paths.

Howells proved acceptable for his wit, and because Lowell had
long liked him and Longfellow's liking of his poems quickly turned
into personal affection. But there was another excellent reason why
he was one of those privileged to walk freely into Longfellow's
study on Dante Club nights when tradition said that no one who
rang the doorbell could be admitted. The Cambridge Italianists,
including pioneer professors of modern languages Longfellow and
Lowell, were philologically and literarily learned far beyond Howells'
ken. But their oral facility with their multiple languages was not
equal to their ocular command. Newly returned from Italy and
with intensive oral experience only in Italian, Howells could speak
the language with a swing and a style decidedly impressive in
Cambridge. Buoyant with high feelings one day, he marched into
Lowell's study chanting from Dante some, perhaps unconsciously,
all too appropriate lines:

> Io son, cantava, io son dolce Sirena,
> Che i marinai in mezzo al mar dismago.*

And Lowell could only listen in admiration and say, *"Damn!* Let's
go out for a walk."

* "I am, I, she sang, am a sweet Siren, who bewilders the sailors in the
midst of the sea."

When *Venetian Life* appeared, most opportunely, in June, 1866, and when it achieved a fine international success, Howells took full rank as an Italianist in Cambridge. In later years annotating for a friend the flyleaves of a "set" of his works published by Douglas of Edinburgh, Howells wrote in *Venetian Life:* "The book that made friends with fortune for me." Few of his many, many other books were so unqualifiedly successful. First publication in England was lucky, for the English journals reviewed it, all happily, and English approval still exerted strong pressure on American critical opinion. Then in America his powerful new friends drove home and clinched his friendship with fortune. Lowell in the *North American Review* praised the charm of his blend of honesty and "airy elegance" and marveled that "this delicacy" should be the fruit of "our shaggy democracy." George W. Curtis from *Harper's* "Easy Chair," himself the reigning dean of travel commentators, found it "the most vivid, accurate, and poetic description of Venice that we recall." He lauded its fresh originality, its "delicate and airy humor," thought it politically sensible and morally sound as well as "gay and graceful." To complete the cycle, Norton in the *Nation* pronounced this "a delightful and excellent book." He too enjoyed the humor, the "graceful and original" fancy, guided by "sympathetic imagination and cultural intelligence . . . together with good common sense and moral feeling." Norton applauded Howells' unobtrusive scholarship, and the "individuality . . . beauty and finish" of his style.

The pecuniary fortune Howells got from the first editions of *Venetian Life* was not exciting. With all charges subtracted, he made ten shillings on the English and $29.95 on the American first issues. But from that meager beginning the book went forward to a long and very popular life, re-edited and reprinted again and again up to 1907–08, when there were three more editions. Not only did *Venetian Life* make Howells his first great reputation and, in the end, a good deal of money, its success also deeply affected his literary future. His development of the skeptical eye, the detached, antiromantic traveler's view, had been natural to him, given his experience. But he had also shown how to fall in love with a fascinating place without sloshing around in a lot of bosh and fake sublimity. He debunked romantic Venice, or more especially the conventions of the romantic visitor to Venice. Yet he became the standard author on it, his book the traveler's guide, the honeymooner's *vade mecum*. If *Venetian Life* is not Howellsian realism (and it is not any kind of realism), the loud critical approval its method won set him more firmly on the track toward his eventual realism. The English *Contemporary Review* even used "realistic" to describe his Italian characterizations. And Lowell rang the bell by praising his "pictures having all the charm of tone and of the minute fidelity to nature . . . of the Dutch school of painters." It was certainly not altogether true, as Henry James said looking back from 1886, that *Venetian Life* began Howells' "existence as a man of letters" and "he has produced nothing since of a literary quality more pure." But it was true that Howells was confirmed in the experimentalism of his second period of literary growth by his book's amazing success and that with it he won an audience which expected him to go on doing the same sort of thing for its delight forever.

Such new celebrity must have helped in the blossoming of Howells' friendship with Lowell into affection and comradeship. For a period of years their relationship was almost as close as father and son. Howells dined at Lowell's every week. There were frequent exchanges of calls. They agreed in craving long walks and often took them together. Lowell therefore not only continued to praise him in print at every good opportunity but saw to it that distinguished visitors were introduced to him as Lowell's protege, a young man with a great future. With Lowell and such allies as Longfellow, Norton, and Professor Child behind him, Howells became "to all intents and purposes an alumnus with right of voting at elections of Overseers, eating Commencement dinners and the like," when Harvard awarded him an honorary M.A. in 1867.

All this, with continued study and writing on modern Italian literature, brought him close to the academic career he had considered as a possibility from Venice. In 1868 he refused the offer of a professorship in rhetoric from Union College. The next year he was personally urged by President Eliot of Harvard until he consented to become a University Lecturer in modern literature for one of the two series of courses which Eliot initiated with the hope that they would become the germ of the graduate school. Although the lectures were so sparsely attended as a group in 1869–70 and again the next year that Eliot gave them up in despair, Howells must have been fairly successful. Child got him a chance to give the famous Lowell Lectures in Boston in 1870. Always thrifty with material, Howells eventually made a book, *Modern Italian Poets,* 1887, out of his lectures. Perhaps his worst book, it shows clearly that he was wise to desert scholarship for the novel. Sometime in the seventies he declined a professorship at Washington University (in St. Louis?) and another at Johns Hopkins in 1882. In 1886 Harvard offered him the Smith Professorship which had been held by Longfellow and Lowell, but, still wisely, he preferred to keep his freedom for the work only he could do.

These gratifying academic temptations, as well as a great many important intangibles, Howells owed to his friendship with the famous older generation of Cambridge worthies. He has written so extensively and so movingly about them and his debts to them that it has often been mistakenly assumed that they filled his whole horizon. Nothing could be further from the truth. There was a great generation of men his own age in Cambridge. And he was closer to the men who made it up than he was to the older demigods. He did not write of his contemporaries as much as he did of his elders for two reasons: one does not write intimately of his friends while they are alive; his literary memoirs were originally magazine pieces, and the older names had more appeal for a magazine audience than the names of contemporaries who were as yet less famous.

V

In these Cambridge years Howells' many friends among his contemporaries may be said to fall into three loosely overlapping and interlocking groups. There were the young journalists—whom he knew for the most part outside Cambridge—men like Aldrich, Clemens, Gilder, Harte, Hay, Stedman, and Warner. There were the intellectuals, somehow connected with Harvard—Child (between Lowell and Howells in age), John Fiske, the younger Holmes, Charles Saunders Pierce, Chauncey Wright. With intellectual and journalistic ambitions as well as artistic and sometimes political hopes, but forming a group within all groups, were the *jeunesse dorée.* They had money, family standing, cultivation, and distinction in their backgrounds, and they had to fight, sometimes unsuccessfully, against a tendency toward snobbery—Brooks and Henry Adams, William and Henry James, Thomas Sergeant Perry (among others). Obviously these were not exclusive groups, and one might hesitate over which circle to place certain figures in; but the classifications are meaningful, and Howells got education as well as companionship out of each.

From the young intellectuals he received an education in ideas and ways of handling them. His self-education had been weakest on the philosophic side. He certainly never became a philosopher, hardly an intellectually respectable "thinker." But, then, very few creative artists are either, and what he did learn from his young Cambridge friends was invaluable. Not only was it stimulating, it was fresh, up-to-the-minute, and put him in touch with the issues and problems most troublesome and most relevant to his age. His was perhaps the last generation, at least the latest one in modern history, in which creative minds—artistic, intellectual, and scientific —formed a genuine international community. For there were at that moment in the American Cambridge, Charles Darwin is supposed to have said in a moment of generous hyperbole, enough fine young minds to staff all the universities of England.

Aside from ordinary social and neighborly contacts, Howells knew the possessors of these fine minds intimately in two of the three centers about which they gathered. Married, hard-working, and no philosopher, he was not a member of the informal Metaphysical Club which met on call to thrash out ideas, often over a bottle of whiskey in student quarters. But he knew all its members in the slightly more formal organization called simply The Club, which met for dinner on the second Tuesday of every month and had as charter members the James brothers, Holmes, Fiske, Adams, Perry, and Howells, among others. The other great nucleus was the home of the mystical, exuberant, cosmopolitan, intellectually brilliant, one-legged philosopher, Henry James, Sr.

Independently wealthy, James had devoted his lifelong leisure to the cultivation of his mind and his family. After wandering widely in the ultimately futile effort to find the perfect place to educate his children, James had settled down for good in Cambridge in 1866. His sons William and Henry, the most successful members of a distinguished family, belonged to the two groups among his contemporaries most interesting and useful to Howells. William, having renounced painting, was working his way from biology to psychology and at last philosophy. He was one of the guiding spirits of the Metaphysical Club. Henry, then with Howells' help in the process of discovering his literary vocation, was naturally drawn toward the young humanists of Cambridge. Both sons reinforced the magnetism which drew eager minds to the sparkling talk and ready affection awaiting them in the James household on Quincy Street. And since the elder James was a kind of Swedenborgian, there was a special dimension to the welcome the Howellses felt there. They spent many a gay Sunday afternoon with the Jameses at home.

Though the two greatest friendships of Howells' life were with Mark Twain and the almost totally dissimilar Henry James, his intimacy with William was certainly warm. William read his novels, sometimes belatedly, and acknowledged them with the loudly admiring letters Howells called "whoops of blessing." Intellectually William's friendship was significant, because Howells began by listening to his conversation and continued on to read his books, thus profiting by exposure to one of the most sensitive and energetic minds of the age. And though it was with a decidedly lesser figure, another of his Cambridge friendships had, especially for the immediate Cambridge years, much the same value. One of his Sacramento Street neighbors who became an across-the-street neighbor in Berkley Street was the ardent young Darwinian apologist John Fiske. Encouraged by Howells to expand conversations into *Atlantic* articles in 1870, Fiske produced his first significant book, and the dedication of his *Myths and Myth-Makers,* 1872, reads:

To My Dear Friend
William Dean Howells
In Remembrance of Pleasant Autumn
Evenings Spent Among Werewolves
and Trolls and Nixies
I Dedicate
This Record of Our Adventures

The years of this intimacy were those in which Fiske was developing the thought, soon to be published, which would make him the principal apostle of reconciliation with Darwinism to the American people.

And "Darwinism" was the magic word—benign or evil according to the user—of an age caught up in a grand but menacing intellectual drama. Not all Darwinism was properly chargeable to Charles Darwin, of course; but his was the name which labeled the New Thought, however much it owed to Comte, Spencer, Buckle, Lyell,

Huxley, or Taine. Robert Frost has summed up the situation in a typical stroke of neat wit, making a New Hampshire farmer say, on hearing a pack of hounds baying along a mountain: "The matter with the Mid-Victorians seems to have been a man named John L. Darwin."

The story of the impact of Darwinism on American thought has been told so well and so often it needs only the briefest coverage here. Whether truly scientific or merely wishfully related to science and so "scientistic," the New Thought forced thinking people into painful, profoundly unsettling intellectual explorations. Not only did there seem to be a warfare between science and theology which made traditional, orthodox religious faith impossible to many people, their fundamental assumptions, the unquestioned beliefs on which their formal ideas had rested, were also shaken if not shattered. Almost no matter what one's faith had been, it seemed threatened. People who had long ago, with the deists and Unitarians, given up belief in the absolute historic accuracy, authority and divine inspiration of the Bible, or with Emerson resigned the idea of a personal God and personal Providence, were still in trouble. Darwinism threatened to deprive them of faith in the morality or spirituality of Nature. It stressed the vulturism and parasitism of life, "Nature red in tooth and claw." It seemed to reduce the secret of life to chemistry, creation and growth to blind chance, progress to brute force, intelligence to camouflage and treachery. It threatened the final obliteration of the heritage of Christian culture. Perhaps it would leave behind it as the sole possibilities for human life those ultimate horrors which thinking men had feared since the Renaissance: practical atheism and Machiavellianism—the morality of power.

Obviously men would resist being pushed to that conclusion if they could. Some simply refused to accept Darwinism at all. "Perhaps Mr. Huxley's grandfather *was* an ape—mine wasn't," Gladstone is reported to have said, thus paving the way for the ultimate disgrace of the Scopes trial. Harvard's most influential scientist, Louis Agassiz, refused to countenance the Darwinian thesis and fought it publicly until his death. But his colleagues and his very students defected to the new ideas. Most intellectually responsible people felt compelled to come to some kind of terms with Darwin, to achieve some kind of reconciliation between whatever old ideas they could not bear to part with and the new. In an interesting

way these reconcilers tended to group themselves and their reactions by generations. Each in his own way, men whom Howells
knew like Lowell, Holmes, and Norton, came to uneasy and sometimes superficial compromises with Darwinism. Regardless of
theology, they had grown to maturity in a culture dominated by
Christianity and idealism. They suffered and sacrificed as they
had to, paid what forfeits in comfort and belief they had to, but
kept all they could of the structure, particularly the ethical and
emotional superstructure, of the idealism in which they had grown
up. Their generation was particularly hospitable to so-called "soft"
Darwinism, the rationale which reconstituted idealism by holding
that God or the cosmos had really designed the whole mighty effort
in order to achieve the ultimate evolution of the human mind and
spirit and thus, by slow creation, place man but a little lower than
the angels.

The second generation, Howells' age, were not so sure. That was,
in fact, for many years their badge. They were not so sure of anything. They learned to say their prayers from Thomas Huxley:
"I do not know." Agnosticism was their church. The members of
the Metaphysical Club and The Club averaged between thirty and
thirty-five years of age in 1870. Their boyhoods had been spent in
the world of idealism. But they were terribly conscious that the
world moved; change was constant and swift, perhaps swifter all
the time. As a group they devoted themselves to the resolution of
their philosophic, religious, and esthetic problems, and some of them,
notably Peirce, the James brothers, and Howells, achieved important
results. But they had to go slowly and along the road of agnosticism.
They tended, consciously or not, to use Occam's Razor and to insist
on pluralism and relativity, on the fallibility and individuality of
the human mind in an immensely complex world. In thought their
destination was pragmatism. In literature it was, and for closely
related reasons, realism.

It was not only through friendship and conversation that Howells
acquired a command of the New Thought, of course. Through the
North American Review and the *Atlantic* his firm was playing a
leading role in the dissemination of Darwinism. And everything in
the *Atlantic* he read and reread and checked until he must nearly
have memorized much of it. Then there were books to be reviewed,
inevitably some of them scientific or polemic, though Howells usually
avoided religious volumes. But the easy optimisms of Herbert

Spencer, the rationalizations which became "the gospel of wealth" and "the religion of humanity" were suspect among the members of the Metaphysical Club. They argued and withheld committing themselves. Howells hung back, too, even from the attractive enthusiasms of John Fiske.

That was partly because he strongly felt the pull of his father's and now the elder Henry James's Swedenborgianism. How deeply James affected him it is not easy to say. Howells was intimate enough to be in on the family jokes. It was he who said that Henry James had written *The Secret of Swedenborg* and kept it, though his review of the book was respectful enough. Surely the Swedenborgian metaphysical "dramatization of love" and the contempt, almost hatred, of selfhood and selfishness as preached by James continued to appeal intensely to Howells' ethical imagination. When Mary Howells died, he felt a sense of support from a source not inward and was given pause. But in the long run he felt compelled to revolt, even openly, against his father's religion. He could accept its ethical insights with humble gratitude. Its theological faith, and particularly its mystical assurance, he had to deny. He was left, much like Henry James, Jr.—and this is a fact of great importance to the understanding of the thought and work of both men—an agnostic Swedenborgian. Where Swedenborgianism had insisted on the duality of existence, on spiritual reality in direct correspondence with physical reality, this agnosticism cut off the top, denied the "spiritual" or supernatural, and was left with the physical, human, ethical part of the faith. Howells' agnosticism truncated his inherited Swedenborgian religion.

And there can be no doubt about his agnosticism, though it would be dangerous as well as unnecessary to label it the agnosticism of any one school. Not since he had read Strauss's *Life of Jesus* with his father over the type cases in Jefferson had ordinary supernatural religion been possible to Howells. In Cambridge not only were his contemporaries overwhelmingly agnostic, the elders by whose confidence he felt so honored were increasingly so. Holmes, Lowell, Norton, even Longfellow grew in doubt rather than affirmation in those years. This agnosticism wore no collar. It was pure, affirmative doubt. Thomas Huxley spoke for it when he defined agnosticism as "suspension of judgment," the refusal to pretend to solve the problem of knowledge when there was no clearly demonstrable solution. And Huxley was speaking for the best of

Cambridge, Massachusetts when he proceeded to denounce pseudo-scientific, or scientistic, transferences of terms and principles from scientific to non-scientific considerations. Positivism, he said, was an "incongruous mixture of bad science with eviscerated papistry." The agnostic might believe where he must and hope where he could, so long as he did not claim to know. After a lifetime of reflection, deep exploration, and much wavering, Howells returned, as he always did, to say, "There are many things that I doubt, but few that I deny; where I cannot believe, there I often trust. . . ." He never truly went beyond this conclusion:

'As a matter of fact, we see nothing whole, neither life nor art. We are so made, in soul and in sense, that we can deal only with parts, with points, with degrees; and the endeavor to compose any entirety must involve a discomfort and a danger very threatening to our intellectual integrity.'

VI

This skepticism, unpretentious but firm, naturally affected the development of Howells' writing, and pushed it further toward realism. He simply could not share the romanticist's sense of cosmic drama involved in the symbolic actions of his creations. The sublime pathos of spiritual infinities at work behind the veil of an author's fictional illusions could not exist for him or young Henry James as it had for Dickens or Hawthorne. An agnostic could not believe in such things. His dimensions must be human, not sublime. Howells' ironic distaste for romantic emotional inflation and hypocrisy acquired a deep-searching intellectual ally. Others early noted his detachment. When his realism was fully developed in the eighties, perceptive hostile critics would use his agnosticism as a weapon against him. And even this early, Whitman and his followers disliked him for it, and it was probably one of the reasons why he did not get along well with Emerson. But his contemporaries praised it. William James saw how deep it went in the work of Henry, who was experimenting in the closest intimacy with Howells in 1868, and commented significantly, "The skepticism and, as some people would say, impudence implied in your giving a story which is no story at all ["Extraordinary Case," *Atlantic*], is not only a rather *gentlemanly* thing, but has a deep justification in nature, for we know the beginning and end of nothing."

The last paragraphs Howells ever wrote, from his deathbed, were concerned with "The American James," whom he thought libeled by cultural patriots. He had flashed back in memory to the early acquaintance in Cambridge, the time of long talks, always somehow about fiction, which were so fateful for both. It is a rare, an almost uniquely fortunate event when an artist can find the kind of friendship Howells and Henry James could give each other at that moment. In the summer of 1866, when they met, James had published a number of book reviews and three stories. James was younger, his experience of the world of men and the practical world in which one sold and published writing much less than Howells'. On the other hand, James's peculiar education had given him opportunity and encouragement to find his way toward his eventual greatness by reading rather broadly in the French novel, which with Balzac, Stendhal, and Flaubert had taken over from the British the mastery of the form, and he was experimentally advancing it toward new heights of achievement and a far greater range of technical capability.

Though James had been printed, apparently somewhat tentatively, in the *Atlantic* before Howells came, Howells at once claimed him as a permanent *new* contributor of the type he was supposed to handle and interceded with a slightly reluctant and sometimes amused Fields to confirm James's permanency. That charmed James, naturally, for it gave him his first status as an author and opened the door toward a career for a life which had previously been painfully lacking in direction. But even more important were the talks. Returning to Columbus for a visit in this period, Howells was asked with whom he took his well-known long walks now. He might easily have said "Lowell" and basked in reflected glory; but he gave the name which most intrigued him: "With James." Walking the streets, often at night, strolling out to Fresh Pond, a favorite spot, or sitting late in Howells' study, they talked on and on. They had information and advice to exchange. Entire new vistas opened for Howells, a journalist and travel writer, a fading poet whose efforts at fiction had failed embarrassingly, when James talked about Balzac and Flaubert. The joy of great friendship meant much to both, but perhaps the greatest joy and greatest importance of the relationship was that it gave both a chance to talk their minds out, to search deep and discover the thrill of knowing that fresh creative resources were there and beginning to well up with new impulses toward art. The great profit from the friendship was that from it each one learned better how to be himself.

Until the day of his death, Howells became James's devoted and unswerving admirer. James continued throughout their lives to be, from time to time, dependent on Howells' loyalty and judgment. It can be no mere happenstance that many of James's most passionate, penetrating, important, and quotable words concerning his own career and concerning the art they shared in common continued to be written in letters to Howells. At the same time, James's affection for Howells was deep, and he knew in his turn how to be both helpful and very generous. As he was in his most definitive statement (written for Howells' seventy-fifth birthday celebration) on their early relationship:

'. . . You held out your open editorial hand to me at the time I began to write with a frankness and sweetness of hospitality that was really the making of me, the making of the confidence that required help and sympathy and that I should otherwise—I think, have strayed and stumbled about a long time without acquiring. You showed me the way and opened me the door. . . . More than this even, you cheered me on with a sympathy that was in itself an inspiration. I mean that you talked to me and listened to me—ever so patiently and genially and suggestively conversed and consorted with me. This won me to you irresistibly and made you the most interesting person I knew—lost as I was in the charming sense that my best friend was an editor, and an almost insatiable editor, and that such a delicious being as that was a kind of property of my own. Yet how didn't that interest still quicken and spread when I became aware that—with such attention as you could spare from us, for I recognized my fellow-beneficiaries—you had started to cultivate *your* great garden as well; the tract of virgin soil that beginning as a cluster of bright, fresh, sunny, and savory patches close about the house, as it were, was to become that vast goodly pleasaunce of art and observation, of appreciation and creation. . . . Your liberal visits to *my* plot and your free-handed purchases there were still greater events when I began to see you handle yourself with such ease the key to our rich and inexhaustible mystery. . . . My confidence in myself, which you had so helped me to, gave way to a fascinated impression of your own spread and growth, for you broke out so insistently and variously that it was a charm to watch and an excitement to follow you.'

For in addition to everything else, Howells had indeed begun to cultivate his garden—most experimentally. *Italian Journeys,* which came out in December, 1867, helped consolidate his Italian reputation. Though he thought it better, it had nothing like the success of *Venetian Life* because its humor and evocation of place rested more on ironic weariness with travel than on the love which underlay the dryness of *Venetian Life.* Publishing it served principally to clear the decks for progress. And progress came hard. Only ambition, the exhilaration of life in Cambridge, and the toughness which came from a profound inward drive toward expression could have kept his creative growth alive in the face of all his other responsibilities. Many years later he nearly exploded into denial when Joyce Kilmer suggested to him the romantic myth that poverty is good for young writers. His own writing had suffered very much for lack of leisure, he replied. "I had to spend ten hours in drudgery for every two that I spent on my real work." And when he could work, there was the question of where to go, what to do. He was afraid he could not learn to write a novel, especially afraid that he could never learn to make fictional people talk well, never learn to write dialog.

Yet Fields was anxious to lighten up the "Emersonian and Whippletonian" magisterial tone of the *Atlantic* and expected contributions to pay for extra salary. And Howells remained ambitious. After casting about a bit, he discovered a new line in which his experience and talents had special play. He could travel at home, seeing Cambridge as if it were Venice, where a humorously objective eye could discover unsuspected interest in common, everyday life. Taking the horsecar into Boston, or sailing down the bay and back on a day's excursion could become Odysseys of pleasure and fresh perception when looked at through Howells' eyes. An ordinary negro cook, and especially the wandering peddlers, vagabonds, and musicians whom a home-keeping husband could meet at the door or find in his long walks around town, were meat for both fun and reflection. A journal he kept in 1869 shows how insatiably fascinated he became with the daily observation of people, their speech, manners, gestures, postures, tensions—everything which revealed their characters and suggested their histories. On one trip down the Bay he struck off perfectly a drunken sea captain and his angry wife, a prosperous Irish couple aggressively happy in their determination to enjoy their success.

Atlantic readers were charmed by Howells' power to sharpen their vision of their own most common lives—as he told, for instance of the saturnine Italian harpers whose playing drew a crowd of neighborhood children to his gate:

'It was a most serious company: the Neapolitans, with their cloudy brows, rapt in their music; and the Yankee children, with their impassive faces, warily guarding against the faintest expression of enjoyment; and when at last . . . the music began to work in the blood of the boys, and one of them, shuffling his reluctant feet upon the gravel, broke into a sudden and resistless dance, the spectacle became too sad for contemplation. The boy danced only from the hips down; no expression of his face gave the levity sanction, nor did any of his comrades: they beheld him with a silent fascination, but none was infected by the solemn undecorum: and when the legs and music ceased their play together, no comment was made, and the dancer turned unheated away.'

These pieces Howells did most tentatively. He was aware, as were Henry and William James, that they were small. But that was precisely because they were experimental. He was testing to see how his talents could be expanded and, especially, to see whether he could be as successful in treating American themes and subjects as he had been with Italy. The book which he gathered from his *Atlantic* pieces he called, with deliberate self-deprecation, *Suburban Sketches,* 1871. He was heartened and confirmed in his experiment by the magazine success of the sketches and the cordial welcome extended the book: "First Studies of American life," as he called it. The Jameses acclaimed the Americanism of his style and matter. And Lowell in the *North American Review* set the golden seal of official approval on *Suburban Sketches.* Though he was not ready to recognize the experimentalism of the pieces, Lowell was more than generous in praising their merits and left Howells with no doubt as to whether he was authorized to go ahead. "Truly these are poems, if the supreme gift of the poet be to rim the trivial things of our ordinary and prosaic experience with an ideal light," Lowell wrote. He compared the sketches to Chaucer's "gracious ease" and the "etchings of the old masters." The highest praise possible in that time and place went out to the author: "Let us make the most of Mr. Howells," Lowell commanded, "for . . . we have got a gentleman and an artist worthy to be ranked with Hawthorne in sensitiveness of observation, with Longfellow in perfection of style." What more could an experimenter ask?

Hints of realism or of what would someday become realism were very much in the air around Howells in that time. James and Norton talked it; Higginson and other *Atlantic* essayists wrote about it. American figures as diverse as G. W. Curtis, Bayard Taylor, and De Forest were working toward it. Intimations came from England in George Eliot and Charles Reade, from France in George Sand and Taine, and from Scandinavia in books of Björnstjerne Björnson. In his own reviews and talk, and in his writing, Howells was responding to all these. But he was as yet far from ready to become a "realist." He was interested in intellectual currents and especially in the developing, though hitherto almost non-existent, theory of the novel. Most of all, however, he was interested in becoming a writer with a method and a body of material that would let him do good work in his own way. Not until he grew to mastery of his own form would he be ready for doctrinaire realism, and even then his willingness to fight for it publicly and theoretically would be something not sought for but forced on him by the logic of events. For the time being growth was what concerned him, and the evidences of it filled him with joy and increasing power.

THE EDITOR OF THE
ATLANTIC MONTHLY: 1871–1881

EIGHTEEN SEVENTY-ONE WAS A GOLDEN YEAR FOR WILLIAM DEAN Howells; fortune smiled. He became official editor of the *Atlantic Monthly* on July 1. With the magazine issue of the same month he began to serialize another literary experiment, *Their Wedding Journey,* which turned out to be triumphantly popular. Socially, he and his wife tasted, with delight at first, prestige and international acceptance which brought them into contact with many of the most interesting people of their time. With America's leading magazine in his charge, with a growing audience for his writings on both sides of the Atlantic Ocean, with ready access to the famous and the mighty (including two Presidents of the United States during the seventies), with generally good health, rising income, and without serious personal shadows or perturbations during the decade, 1871–1881 was Howells' "good great time"—though it was in perspective still only preparation for the time of his greatness.

Much of the gayety of that time Howells shared with his journalist-contemporaries. Like Howells, they tended to achieve maturity and success earlier than the Cambridge intellectuals. And the most meteoric of them (both in his rise and fall) was Bret Harte. He was the flaming literary celebrity of the nation early in 1871, and when Boston and the *Atlantic Monthly* invited him from California to do him honor, the newspapers followed his progress across the continent like that of visiting royalty. Arrived in Boston with his wife and two children, Harte went to stay with the Howellses, and Elinor Howells had her first opportunity to give a really big party, inviting everybody who was anybody and doing it up in such gala style that Abby Fiske got out of a sickbed to cross the street and attend. It was "a very brilliant affair," everyone agreed—and a real social *coup.* Howells was charmed by Harte and his wit, even

157

though Harte masked his awe of the Cambridge celebrities by posing as a swaggering California literary badman. Howells remained charmed all the rest of his life, excusing Harte's feeble performance in fulfilling the ten-thousand-dollar contract to write for the *Atlantic* which Howells was instrumental in getting him, overlooking the Harte meannesses which so infuriated Mark Twain, and ignoring the fact that Harte, friendly to his face, was coldly poisonous behind his back. He did love Harte's humor, but perhaps he was most impressed by the memory of Harte's visit as an early milestone of the good great time.

That momentum given his happiness and reputation was speeded up in the middle of April when the Boston *Advertiser* announced, quite accurately, that it was "authorized to say that on the 1st of July next," Fields would retire from the *Atlantic* and be succeeded in the editorship by "Mr. W. D. Howells . . . and the literary taste and standing of Mr. Howells furnish sufficient guarantee as to the future of the *Atlantic* under his management."

Nothing more was needed to give him the confidence necessary to bring off the creative experiment at which he was working in the quiet morning hours in his little study on Berkley Street. As he showed in writing to his father, he knew exactly what he was doing: "At last I am fairly launched upon the story of our last summer's travels, which I am giving the form of fiction so far as the characters are concerned. If I succeed in this—and I believe I shall—I see clearly before me a path in literature which no one else has tried, and which I believe I can make most distinctly my own." The path on which Howells had set his feet, and along which he advanced significantly with this book, was more like a ladder of evolution, a series of metamorphoses, than a linear road. He had proved his ability to do excellent work with travel writing and with the essayist's trick of creating a voice, a literary personality, to slip reflections and impressions pleasantly into a reader's mind. Now he proposed to construct a book which would let him keep the benefits of his reliable skills and yet experiment with creating fictional characters and letting them talk. Good sales, good reviews, and warm private congratulations, instantaneous and international, assured him that his experiment had been a success in *Their Wedding Journey*.

In spite of doubt and the scars of earlier failure, Howells could know in mid-October, 1871, when he had put the last polish on the final installments of his book, that, while it was "My first attempt to mingle fiction and travel—fiction got the best of it." And of course that was all to the good. For though *Their Wedding Journey* has a certain footing in Howells' life, it is a work of fiction, a product of the artistic imagination, not simply reportage. He made good use of his newspaper travel letters from 1861, plucking out picturesque people and incidents from back files of the *Ohio State Journal* which Comly sent him. And he and his wife the previous summer had taken their first trip and first real vacation together since returning from Europe by making the same swing round Boston-New York-Albany-Niagara-Montreal-Quebec-Boston by boat and train which is the itinerary of the novel.

But the bridal couple of *Their Wedding Journey*, Basil and Isabel March, are not Will and Elinor Howells. They are products of Howells' imagination just as Hamlet was the product of Shakespeare's. We cannot know what the relationship of Hamlet as "fact" was to Shakespeare, and we know a great deal about the "fact" behind the Marches. Yet we must be just as wary of the "biographic fallacy," the temptation to assume a positivistic one-to-one relationship between biographic event as "fact" and literary usage as "fact," with Howells as with Shakespeare. Both were trying, and each in his own way succeeded, to create a structure of illusions which would make the words they placed upon the page stir the imagination of their reader. Both were forced to rely on their power to stir the imagination through illusion and so to entice or command that imagination to create experience within the reader's mind. Beyond reading, Shakespeare could rely on the illusions of the theater to help with the job; but in the end neither writer had anything but illusion to go on. In this sense, "realism" is neither more nor less "real" than any other kind of successful literary art, and certainly the characters of *Their Wedding Journey* are fiction. Further, much as Howells worked from observation and "experience"—a very slippery word—in all his fiction, one must never forget that it was fiction.

Once the success of characterization and dialog is recognized, perhaps the most important advance of *Their Wedding Journey* is in the direction of realism. Henry Adams noticed in it an "extreme and almost photographic truth to nature," a "faithful . . . picture of our American existence," and seemed puzzled to know why he was so pleased by material so "commonplace." Indeed, no reader could have failed to see that the author was explicit about his devotion to "poor Real Life." He digressed periodically to say that "the sincere observer of man" will try to see him in "his habitual mode," not his atypical moments of heroism or glamor. Irony was frequently mixed into these comments: "Do I pitch the pipe too low?" the author asked. "We poor honest men are at a sad disadvantage; and now and then I am minded to give a loose to fancy and attribute something really grand and fine to my people, in order to make them worthier the reader's respected acquaintance." Nevertheless he kept honest and kept the key low. He was, in fact, transferring to his fiction the lesson he had learned while writing about Venice. The rules, he warned his sister Annie a year later, were simple: *"Describe closely and realistically, keep the tone low,* and *let the reader do all the laughing."* One must avoid pomposity and romantic pretense. The important thing is the clear eye.

Thus realism began to become a matter of vision for Howells. He belonged truly enough to his time to be committed to the notion that the human eye could see "real" life as it was in itself if only the eye were clear enough. He was enough affected by the often unconsciously positivistic and scientistic assumptions of his age to take the possibility of accurate vision of objective reality for granted. For us who almost a hundred years later find it impossible to take that for granted, often impossible to believe in at all, the fact of Howells' faith in it is mostly useful as a way of understanding what he thought he was doing. The real problem, he wrote Ralph Keeler while finishing *Their Wedding Journey,* was to learn to look at American life with the clear, natural eye, not with some inherited instrument for optical illusion. See clearly, all the rest follows, Howells would have said.

For all that, he was a long way from writing what his later creed would have accepted as the realistic novel. How confidential and intrusive he is, how intimately conversational in the manner of the Irving-Thackeray-Hawthorne romancer's voice which tells anecdotes about Basil and Isabel, paints the scenery for us, tells us what is going on in people's minds, and every now and then breaks in with a piquant bit of philosophic or psychological reflection, or tells a joke. The blend of slick romantic technique with penetrating as well as very individual travel description and then with Howells' vision of "poor Real Life" makes a book still satisfying and entertaining today. But the common and near have subtly been made exotic, and the effects the author gets are unique, colorful, atmospheric, remote from the tone and key of everyday or representative existence. Henry Adams put his finger on the lasting virtues of *Their Wedding Journey* in calling it "essentially a lovers' book"—and adding in a typically Adams tone of voice: "And if it can throw over the average bridal couple some reflection of its own refinement and taste, it will prove itself a valuable assistant to American civilization." Down to and including Theodore Dreiser, the book has had thousands of admirers, perhaps the most extreme of whom was the historian James Parton, who despaired because he was not rich enough to settle a thousand dollars a year on Howells for writing it.

I

His prosperity Howells stood well, enjoying it and profiting from it without changing except in appearance. He kept the rather bushy haircut, parted in the middle and with bangs which easily became disheveled, and the walrus mustache which he had adopted in Venice and which seems to have been fashionable among literary people of his age—at least Twain, Aldrich and Gilder looked much the same in the seventies. But Howells lost the hungry, greyhound look of earlier years, developing a notable appetite for food and drink. He remains, wrote Godkin in 1871, "as sweet and gentle and winning in all ways as ever. . . . Howells *grows* steadily, I think, and in all ways, for he has become very stout."

In 1872–73 the Howellses had the thrill of designing (Mrs. Howells her own architect) and building a house at 37 Concord Avenue, close by their Berkley Street home. John Fiske, writing to his mother in 1877 in an effort to raise the money to buy it, was lost in admiration of Elinor Howells' design:

'The arrangement of rooms is unlike that in any other house I ever saw and extremely convenient and pretty. The library is finished in chestnut with frescoed ceiling. The dining room is fairly large and is finished in chestnut. There are hard wood mantelpieces, and open fireplaces in several rooms, though the furnace heats the house amply with 10 or 11 tons of coal, and Howells tends it himself and says it doesn't go out from November till May.

All the arrangements for cellar, kitchen, laundry, pantry, etc. are admirable. There are four bedrooms and one little room, besides bathroom, on second floor; and four in the Mansard; besides an attic store-room. That allows for practical use:

1 servant's room
1 nursery
1 guest-chamber
5 family bed-rooms

8

. . . The house is a kind of old friend, and it would be pleasant to live in it for the sweet associations. . . . It has a quiet tone about it, the indescribable quality which comes from its having been planned by a person of refined culture. . . .'

No doubt the Howellses meant to live forever in the Concord Avenue house, as they were later to move "permanently" to other domiciles without ever settling anywhere—until they became nomads whose only reliable address was their summer house. For the present, however, they could not have imagined their future and may have hardly been aware that their widening range of friendships and interests was subtly seducing them away from changing Cambridge.

The most seductive influence was a flamboyant Missourian who had settled in Hartford, Connecticut, Samuel Langhorne Clemens. Howells thought Mark Twain the greatest man of his time, the greatest of American writers, comparable to Shakespeare. And his friendship with "Clemens" was the most significant of his life. Twain's affection for him was easier, perhaps more natural and certainly less ambiguous, than that of Henry James. "Gaudy times," said Twain when they had been together, "Gaudy."

Howells was enchanted from the time he first met Twain in Fields's office in the fall of 1869. In Boston on a lecture tour, Twain had dropped in to say thank you for a cordial review of *Innocents Abroad* in the *Atlantic,* and they both had the good luck to have this one of the rare days on which Howells came into the Boston office. Always theatrical, Twain was resplendent in the sealskin outfit he wore to keep warm on back-country lecture stops. His fiery hair and eyebrows above his penetrating blue eyes made his slim, erect figure seem taller than Howells', though actually it was not. He was in highest fettle, gratefully celebrating his kind reception by the masters of the mighty *Atlantic,* and giving full rein to the drawling Western humor of which he was the greatest expert the world has known. Howells felt instantly at home. Their communication was thenceforth free and easy, often conducted in the man-talk of the Western village street, steamboat deck, and printing office; the letters of both (though Twain's more frequently) sprinkled with "hell's," "damn's," and "God damn's." It was in writing to Howells, and indeed picturing Howells as the author of it, that Twain invented one of the most magnificent oaths on record, making a dream-Howells call a servant "a quadrilateral, astronomical, incandescent son-of-a-bitch !" And now he endeared himself to Howells forever by likening his joy and relief at finding his iconoclastic book approved by the *Atlantic* to the river-town woman he had heard of—who was so *glad* her baby had come white.

Twain quickly associated himself with Aldrich, Ralph Keeler, and the others among Howells' journalist friends. And after Twain had settled in Hartford in the fall of 1871, forming with Mrs. Stowe, Charles Dudley Warner, and the minister Joseph Twichell a second and brighter galaxy of Hartford Wits, the stage was set for some of the gayest moments in the good great time. Prosperous from writing, some of it journalism, some literature, these new Hartford Wits had built houses together on a suburban development called Nook Farm. Their incomes were high—Twain made and spent one hundred thousand dollars in 1881—and they devoted themselves to an ideal of the good life shared by the business tycoons of Hartford. The new house Twain built was fabulous. Taking young Johnny down to visit, Howells told him he would see a palace just like Aladdin's. And the boy, who many years later would be the architect of Twain's last great house, was properly awed. Seeing George, the colored butler, fussing over the breakfast table in the morning, he ran back to whisper, "Come quick, Papa ! The slave is setting the table."

But when Aldrich came down, too, and Twain and Warner entertained them, the laughter was unquenchable. Never an intellectually significant friend, Aldrich was Howells' colleague and one of his most favorite quipsters. He could make Howells laugh until he begged for mercy. They could be unabashedly professional together. "I have bought a young Palace on Charles Street," Aldrich wrote him in 1870, "—cellar frescoed, coalbin inlaid with mother-of-pearl and the skulls of tax-collectors, and joyous birds, in gilded cages, in every room, warbling promissory notes to the tune of seven per-cent. !" Together they could indulge in outlander irreverence about Boston and Cambridge, and Howells could turn the laugh on Aldrich, too. There was the memory of Walt Whitman's solemn transcendental rebuke on being introduced: "Aldrich, Yes, yes, I've heard your little sheep bell tinkle." Naturally Aldrich was the butt of some of Howells' most famous *mots*. Had he heard how So-and-so had damned one of Howells' books? Aldrich asked one day.

"Do you think I have no bosom friends?" was the answer.

It was the absolute acid test of Howells' humor, not merely that it played an equal part in such company, but that, quite apart from Aldrich, Warner, Osgood, Twichell and the special, "gaudy" times, Mark Twain loved the humor and the man so abidingly. Howells was a good audience. Even in old age he had "the freshest, merriest, sincerest and most contagious laugh in the world." As the quick-witted Irish servant-girl, Katy Leary, recalled, the Clemens household "would all laugh from the time he come in till he went out." It was not just that Howells had from boyhood mastered the art of storytelling. He was creatively humorous, and the ordinary discourse of his mind reflected that. As when he warmly thanked Higginson for praise: "I felt proud and glad—until I remembered that I shall not survive the second glacial epoch, anyway." Or when the pompous Senator Ingalls entertained him with a cliché:

"If you want charity you must go to women."

"Yes," Howells drawled, with the Western technique, "Charity to the—actions—of—men."

Or even better, when cornered by a crashing literary bore who was fishing for compliments:

"I don't know why, Mr. Howells," said the bore, "but I don't seem to write as well as I used to."

"Oh, yes you do—indeed you do. You write as well as you ever did—but your *taste* is improving."

Best of all, of course, his humor came welling out through his writing, tasted and commented on with pleasure by readers from *Venetian Life* forward. And as he matured, his humor became more and more effectively an instrument for something more than fun, a critical, often a self-critical, instrument for conveying the subtlest meanings. It is in this regard most of all that the appreciation of Howells' work has suffered from hasty and superficial reading. Twain noticed that Howells' work was much more "deliciously humorous" when he read it for himself than when Howells read it aloud, and was puzzled to account for it. "Hang it, I know where the mystery is, now," he concluded. "When you are reading, you glide right along, and I don't get a chance to let the things soak home; but when I catch it in the magazine, I give a page 20 or 30 minutes in which to gently and thoroughly filter into me. Your humor is so subtle and elusive—(well, often it's just a vanishing breath of perfume which a body isn't certain he smelt till he stops and takes another smell). . . ." But not to smell it is not to grasp what the page has to offer, or, worse still, to get it all wrong.

"Humor," said Howells, "is the rebate on the heavy liability known as life." It was also his way of coming to terms with life, both within his own mind and in outside contact with the world of other minds. The natural expression of a quick, deep-thrusting wit, of a heartily self-critical consciousness, of a moral sensibility hardened to irony by suffering, Howells' playfulness— airy and gay, delightful as it seemed—was nevertheless a mask and a defense. He used it to sugar-coat his often devastatingly critical insights into manners and morals. But he also used it to keep destruction at arm's length, as a means of keeping his personality intact. In this he knew a deep, though almost hidden, kinship with Mark Twain.

So many writers have demolished the ancient canard that Howells somehow "poisoned" Twain's genius with an indefinable substance called "gentility" that it is no longer necessary to argue the point. Actually, their literary relationship, like their personal one, was stimulating to both men. Like almost every one of the dozens of writers who came into contact with Howells, Twain found his work strengthened and broadened, found himself encouraged—not to be like Howells—but to be his own best self. In the year of their first great intimacy, Twain finally found just the right inspiration and sent Howells the first of the *Atlantic* contributions for which the editor had been begging. Significantly, there was little humor in "A True Story," Twain's presentation in her own dialect of the powerful human integrity and pathetic life story of his ebullient negro cook. It displayed Twain's command of common speech and his flair for the dramatic, as well as that affectionate trust of the Negro which led Mrs. Clemens to propose to Mark a motto for his life's guidance: "Consider every man colored until he is proved white."

Although Twain's whole reputation was that of a funny man, Howells, who always saw deeper into Twain's genius, was delighted, made him a serious *Atlantic* author immediately, and called loudly for more. It was under the pressure of that call, especially for the approaching January number which it was *Atlantic* tradition to fill with greatness if possible, that Twain took his famous walk with Joe Twichell and unearthed the idea for some of his most memorable writing—the "Old Times on the Mississippi" papers which became the best chapters of *Life on the Mississippi.* Under no compulsion to be funny, or "commercial," encouraged instead to do serious work for the publication he most respected, Twain wrote his first unquestionably great literature—and uncovered one of the leads to *The Adventures of Huckleberry Finn.*

Twain heartily approved of the customary thoroughness of Howells' *Atlantic* editing of his manuscript. "Cut it, scarify it, reject it—handle it with entire freedom," he noted to Howells in submitting the "Mississippi" pieces. That anyone, and especially America's "recognized critical Court of Last Resort," as he called Howells, would take such trouble over his writing heartened Twain, who like many other writers found it difficult to tell the difference between the best and the worst of what he produced, and was honest enough to admit it. As he told Bliss Perry after Olivia Clemens' death, he was bereft of the best judge of what was fit for publication: "For I don't know, myself." And both he and Livy were glad to have Howells' help.

Consequently, when *Tom Sawyer* was ready, Twain asked Howells if he would read the manuscript for him. He was diffident in his approach because he was encroaching on a busy man's time and had to tell him from the start that, for economic reasons, the book could not possibly be offered for magazine publication. Howells read and marked it gladly, sitting up until one o'clock in the morning to get it done, and enthusiastically assuring Twain that his experiment with the boy-book had produced something new and important which was bound to be popular. Thereafter he read, either in manuscript or proof, *The Prince and the Pauper, A Connecticut Yankee at King Arthur's Court,* and *The Adventures of Huckleberry Finn.* Altogether Howells handled, before publication, most of Mark Twain's greatest writing.

What did he do with it? Really two things. He advised cutting out the sort of crude horseplay to which Twain's comic sense could descend when functioning at less than its best level and the scrapping of things like the original last chapter (possibly the germ of

Huckleberry Finn) which he thought threw *Tom Sawyer* out of symmetry. The other thing he did was, as well as he could, to edit out the sexual, scatalogical, and otherwise unacceptable references which his own taste and his hard-won *Atlantic* experiences with Reade, Holmes, and Stowe told him could offend the contemporary American audience. As Bernard De Voto's studies of the manuscript in *Mark Twain at Work* showed, Howells' objections were infrequent. His sympathy was so strong that, in a well-known instance, he forgot to object to Huck's saying in *Tom Sawyer* that at the Widder's "they comb me all to hell." Certainly Howells was not responsible for the war which raged deep in Twain's psyche between a prudish country boy and an expert smoking-car pornographer. Howells did try, and with considerable success, to shield Twain from the public effects (like the Concord, Massachusetts, Public Library's banning of *Huckleberry Finn*) of his "Elizabethan breadth" of parlance and his earthy imagination. He was trying to save him from Dr. Holland and all he represented. The need to save him and the character of the enemy from whom Twain needed to be defended is nowhere better indicated than in the letter which Richard Watson Gilder, Holland's successor as editor of the *Century* (earlier *Scribner's*) sent Twain after he had presented an adventure or two of the immortal Huck Finn to his readers:

January 8, 1886

My Dear Clemens:

I am going to venture upon an indiscretion. I have had a letter from a superintendent of public schools in a distant part of the West, and am sending you my letter to him. It was not written for your eye. I could go over it and make it much more complimentary to you and leave out something that sounds harsh, but I have concluded to send it to you as it is, as a sample of what often occurs here in the "Century." Here is the letter:—

"Dear Sir:

We thank you sincerely for your kind and frank letter. We understand the points to which you object in Mark Twain's writings, but we cannot agree with you that they are 'destitute of a single redeeming quality.' We think that the literary judgment of this country and of England will not sustain you in such an opinion. I ask you in all fairness to read Mr. Howells' essay of Mark Twain in the September number of the 'Century' for 1882. To say that the writings of Mark Twain are

*'hardly worth a place in the columns of the average country newspaper
which never assumes any literary airs' seems to us to be singularly un-
true. Mr. Clemens has great faults; at times he is inartistically and
indefensibly coarse, but we do not think anything of his that has been
printed in the 'Century' is without very decided value, literary and otherwise. At least, as a picture of the life which he describes, his 'Century'
sketches are of decided force and worth.*

*"Mark Twain is not a giber at religion or morality. He is a good
citizen and believes in the best things. Nevertheless there is much of his
writing that we would not print for a miscellaneous audience. If you
should ever carefully compare the chapters of 'Huckleberry Finn,' as we
printed them, with the same as they appear in his book, you will see the
most decided difference. These extracts were carefully edited for a
magazine audience with his full consent.*

*"Perhaps you know my friend Dr. George MacDonald, the celebrated
novelist, lecturer, and preacher. He is one of the most spiritually minded
men now living, and a most enthusiastic admirer of Mark Twain. Once,
when Dr. MacDonald was staying at my house, he spent some hours in
reading with great delight, one of Mark Twain's books, before preaching
one of the most profound, moving and spiritual sermons to which I ever
listened."*

The two letters, and especially Gilder's act of sending them for
Twain's "benefit," speak a volume.

The prestige of Howells' public and ceaseless support was of
inestimable value in Twain's painful fight for acceptance as more
than a comedian. Howells was quite willing to connive at this.
After reading *Tom Sawyer,* he told Twain that he would gladly
throw the weight of the *Atlantic* into intimidating the little critics
in its favor: "Give me a hint when it's to be out, and I'll start the
sheep to jumping in the right places." Howells felt no scruple
against this, for he was convinced that he was aiding one of the
greatest of Americans, "the Lincoln of our literature." Summing up
after seventy-five years, he placed Twain at the peak of his esteem
in carefully chosen words: "If I had been witness to no other sur-
passing things of American growth in my fifty years of observation,
I should think it glory enough to have lived in the same time and
same land with the man whose name must always embody American
humor to human remembrance." Twain reciprocated his esteem—
"fine thought and perfect wording are a natural gift with Howells,"

he said. And he studied Howells' books and allied himself to Howells' growing realism with unstinted admiration. As unlike as could be, the two greatest American writers of Howells' time, Mark Twain and Henry James, were Howells' close friends. Neither had any use for the other, yet he understood them both and conferred on both the greatest boon of friendship: he helped them be themselves more perfectly.

II

If as *Atlantic* editor Howells was able to help Twain as well as James (for whom he provided a reliable outlet and market as the early novels were developed), it is also true that as editor he needed them. He needed all that contacts, ingenuity, intuition, publicity, and even the product of his own pen could give him. For the counting room of the magazine went through stormy times during Howells' editorship. Financial disaster struck repeatedly. First there was the Boston Fire of November 13, 1872, which gutted the commercial center of the city and in effect tipped the balance of financial supremacy so that thereafter State Street slowly lost out to Wall Street. James E. Osgood, Fields's partner who had taken over at Fields's retirement and became until his own bankruptcy many years later Howells' boss, publisher, agent, and friend, suffered heavily from the fire. And when in 1873 one of the worst depressions in American history devastated the nation, Osgood was forced to sell the *Atlantic* off—and Howells with it, though he remained Howells' personal publisher.

Atlantic circulation had already dropped substantially from its wartime peak when Howells became editor. And all through his editorship after '73, the subscription list kept dwindling. Only the maintenance of the best standard Howells could achieve kept the *Atlantic* from sharing the death of Aldrich's *Every Saturday*. The shrinking number of people with cash to spare for magazine subscriptions was now being much more strongly competed for, and the *Atlantic* was subject to that journalistic version of Gresham's Law under which the existence of a first-rate magazine is threatened by imitators working at a slightly shoddier and more sensational level. The success of the *Atlantic* had brought changes in the policy of *Harper's*, to bring it into closer competition. In 1870 a new magazine, *Scribner's*, had been founded under the leadership of none other than Dr. Josiah G. Holland. Operating according to his standards, it was instantaneously successful. And for the intellectually marginal market, there appeared a new kind of publication— the illustrated magazine. Howells was in a fight all the way.

Hard labor was one of his resources. Boyesen was impressed in that time by Howells' "remarkable power of work." He could spend four or five hours at his desk in the morning, writing his own stuff —editorially as well as personally justifiable because he became one of his magazine's greatest drawing cards. And then he had energy enough to spend three or four hours in the afternoon reading manuscripts and proof and writing away at the many hundreds of letters, often gay and personally warm, which his editorship required. When he could get it, he hired competent help to ease his burdens. John Fiske read proof and contributed staff writing on science at least in 1871–72, and from 1875–77 George Parsons Lathrop, who had married Hawthorne's daughter Rose, was Howells' full-fledged assistant. Others were engaged to do reviewing and to conduct the departments which were among Howells' ideas for broadening the coverage and the intellectual significance of the *Atlantic*.

An increasingly successful literary experimenter, Howells was inclined to be inventive in his conduct of the magazine. It is generally agreed that he bettered the *Atlantic*, perhaps more significantly than any other editor after Lowell, by his experiments, even though they often flew in the face of Bostonian preference. For most of his regime he tried calling to the reader's attention the new scope of the magazine by instituting "departments." The January, 1872, issue unveiled departments of Recent Literature, Art, Music, Science, and Politics. Later Education and Drama also appeared. Though all these were scrapped from the format and absorbed back into the permanently enriched general table of contents in another change not long before the end of Howells' tenure, another of his inventions became one of the most attractive features of the *Atlantic* after the January issue of 1877. Offering ten dollars a page for lively expressions of opinion written in the style of conversation or personal correspondence, Howells begged all his friends for paragraphs for the Contributors Club. He and Lathrop had to write some of it at first, but when once it had caught hold, the Club columns became the first items read when a new issue came to the living room of many an *Atlantic* fan.

It was not, on the other hand, in character for Howells to have been the inventor of another new *Atlantic* venture of his time. More likely the *Atlantic* Dinners were dreamed up by some early public relations genius in the publisher's office. Though there had been earlier ones, a rather small affair held on December 15, 1874, to celebrate the purchase of the magazine by Houghton attracted such newspaper attention that repetitions were clearly in order when the right occasions offered. The Boston *Transcript* reporter "looked down the table, and saw . . . the accomplished editor, Mr. Howells, surrounded by such of his coadjutors" as Aldrich, Henry James, Perry, and Lathrop and "could not repress the reflection that the magazine was safe to be trusted as an exponent of American thought and literature in such hands." In 1877 came the Whittier Birthday Dinner, which appears to have been a grand success as an affair in spite of the personal disaster of Mark Twain's speech. He had imagined a travesty of three mining-camp tramps masquerading as Emerson, Longfellow, and Holmes. But nobody at a solemn, high Boston literary celebration laughed. Twain was crushed, and both he and Howells fearful that the demigods were insulted and the Boston public outraged. As it turned out, nobody but the two frustrated Midwesterners seems to have been much impressed by the affair. No retribution followed, and Twain's speech at the Holmes Dinner two years later was an entire success. As publicity-getting devices, the dinners worked well, and Howells performed manfully as speech-maker and master of ceremonies at them. They helped keep the magazine at the peak in public reputation; they gave honor to old contributors in their waning years; and of course they helped pass *Atlantic* prestige on to Howells' new contributors.

Dealing with writers, getting attractive and important contributors in and improving on what did come in was, of course, Howells' greatest problem, as it is that of any magazine not mass-produced and staff-written. And it is beyond question that in his time the *Atlantic* far outstripped other American magazines in the quality of its content, the genius of its contributors. Howells' correspondence of these years shows clearly how intelligently, sensitively, helpfully, fairly, yet firmly he dealt with them, whether his contributors were great names, close friends, struggling authors, or new and unknown.

Though many of the great New England reputations upon whom the *Atlantic* had been founded were Howells' friends, not all were, and there were potential difficulties with all. Perhaps repelled alike by Howells' Italophile reputation and his skepticism, Emerson was touchy and hard to deal with. And then there was the tradition of *Atlantic* proofreading. Could young Howells enforce its standards on the Old Guard as Lowell, one of them, or Fields, their publisher, had? After a few embarrassments he decided not to try, but to let the creators of the *Atlantic* guard their own reputations in its pages and keep those pages open to whatever they sent.

His own contemporaries and younger writers, however, he edited as responsibly as he could under the sometimes almost intolerable burdens the job of dealing with them brought him. There were tough problems of conscience which the hundreds of incoming manuscripts dumped on a tender-minded editor. To his horror he discovered that Lowell and Fields in turn had bequeathed him a heavy half-barrel of manuscripts, accepted and paid for but never published. It took him weeks to read them and discard with relief those whose authors had died in the meanwhile—but what to do with the rest? It was a kind of blessing when the barrel went up in flames, together with much of the rest of Boston's hoarded wealth, in the Fire of 1872. Then at least his sins of editorial procrastination were his own.

He learned how to dodge the irrelevant pleas of pathos and distress which "the poor fellows, and still more the poor dears" brought to bear, hoping to press him into accepting poor stuff. And he learned how to reject promising people or even established ones without alienating them. "Thank you for your funny, kind little note," said Sarah Orne Jewett, whom he had so carefully brought along, and she might have been speaking for many another author. "You take rejections so sweetly," said Howells to Lucy Larcom, "that I have scarcely the heart to accept anything of yours. But I do like 'Phebe,' and I am going to keep her." And he could deal with masculine authors on their terms, too, as we have seen in his negotiations with Twain. He could put Bret Harte in his place when he fussily refused to be edited. He squelched Bayard Taylor's revolt against consistent rejection of Taylor's till-the-sands-of-the-desert-grow-cold poetry by pointing out that as editor he passed not on the intrinsic merit of a manuscript but on what it would do for the magazine. Yet he also knew when to give way, and when Stedman protested effectively against the rejection of a lyric, Howells asked to have it back so he could print it and let the *Atlantic* readership judge between them.

Howells was a good editor, because he printed the best writers and developed as well as "discovered" a number of them. James's *Roderick Hudson* and *The American* appeared, together with most of his early short pieces, in Howells' *Atlantic* alongside De Forest, Boyesen, Aldrich, and Howells himself as novelists. He brought Twain, Harte, and Edward Eggleston into the magazine, and "discovered" Jewett, S. Weir Mitchell, Edith Jones (Wharton), Mary Murfree, Charles W. Stoddard, and John Hay, among many others. As his prestige increased, his unfailing kindness to young talent became more meaningful, until, as Edward Bellamy wrote him in thanks for his praise of *Dr. Heidenhoff's Process*, Howells' letter was "as refreshing to me as you may suppose a note from Hawthorne in commendation of one of your earlier efforts would have been to you."

In the long perspective, one of the most significant things Howells as editor did, Black Republican and abolitionist though he was, was to throw open the intellectual citadel of Yankeedom to the new writers of the South. And there was nothing grudging about his way of doing so, even though he could not accept the early poems of Sidney Lanier. Howells welcomed, where Fields had not, the poems of Paul Hamilton Hayne, took them so cordially and praised them in print so warmly that Hayne wrote him of "the high, & exceptional esteem wherewith I regard you; an esteem strengthened & sanctified by affection, (for your blended candor & kindness have touched my heart). . . ." Hayne confided his greatest secret (his heart trouble, which was concealed even from his wife) to Howells and regarded Howells' praise as one of the finest accolades of his life. In 1874 Howells went a step further and deliberately contracted with a Confederate soldier, George Cary Eggleston, for the writing of "A Rebel's Recollections," which began in the February, 1875, *Atlantic*. If that brought a hornet's nest of professional G.A.R. patriots about the editor's ears, the second wave of more genuine public opinion vindicated him, and Howells could tell Eggleston that the hornets had begun to sing hymns of praise in his ears. As acts of reconciliation these became significant far beyond their pleasant personal effect. They ushered the South back into the national cultural life and demonstrated to Southern writers that their wares were welcome in the North's highest and most typical

market. They helped pave the road to reunion, and they were a part
of the facts which justified Henry James in recalling that "the
new American novel . . . had . . . its first seeds . . . sown very
exactly in *Atlantic* soil, where . . . Howells soon began editorially
to cultivate them."

Under Howells' aegis, more than that of any other single man,
American letters became national rather than sectional. Not only
did he take in Southerners, he swung the cultural leadership of the
Atlantic completely about-face. Though Lowell had tried hard to
encourage the West (that was how Howells himself had first entered
the magazine), Fields had not, and public opinion was that the
Atlantic was a possession of Boston and provincial expression of
New England, where occasionally outland visitors were admitted on
sufferance. Fields's Anglophilia and the overwhelming predomin-
ance of New England, even Boston and its suburbs, in the list of
contributors gave strong support to that opinion. It was Howells,
said Bliss Perry, himself *Atlantic* editor, 1899–1909, who "trans-
formed a 'Bostonian' magazine into an American magazine," built
up subscriptions and contributions across the nation, and rendered
"Beacon Hill opinion of the *Atlantic* . . . negligible." Certainly
Howells himself was, though probably not deliberately seeking
such a result, conscious that on his *Atlantic* "we had become southern, mid-western, and far-western in our sympathies."

To recognize his two great friendships as symbolic, which in a
way they were, it is fair to say, however, that Howells became
national and American with Mark Twain without ceasing to be
international with Henry James. Continuing to take the *Atlantic*
seriously as "in some sort a critical authority in a country where
criticism is rare," Howells tried to see to it that every good American book had its due in the magazine. But his very first change in
Atlantic makeup was to introduce a department of "Recent Literature" which set out to acquaint Americans with what was happening in European literature, especially in France and Germany.
Seizing the opportunity of his seventy-fifth birthday dinner, Howells
deliberately, even defiantly, summed up the literary history of his
times by insisting that the best impulse came from the Continent,
not England, that American "fiction so far as it really exists is of
the European and not the English make, and the newer English
fiction, so far as it really exists, is not of the English make, but
of the European make, the American make." His tone was testa-

mentary as well as polemic as he insisted there in 1912: "Some of you may not know this, but I know it, for I am of the generation that lived it, and I would fain help to have it remembered that we studied from the French masters, the continental masters, to imitate nature, and gave American fiction the bent which it still keeps wherever it is vital." Polemics aside, he was looking back forty years to remember that he and his generation had turned away from Dickens, Thackeray, and their rather feeble British successors to Flaubert, Daudet and, especially in the seventies, Turgenev. He might have added that as *Atlantic* editor he had overtly promoted this result by establishing the Recent Literature department and commissioning Thomas Sergeant Perry to run it.

Long-time friend of the Jameses, Perry had become a member of The Club circle soon after his return from Europe to become a Harvard tutor in French and German in the fall of 1868. Perry was pre-eminently one of the *jeunesse dorée*, traveled, polished, witty, a little too high-toned ever quite to settle down in life. Howells thought him the best-read man he had ever known and gave him his full loyalty, apparently able to forgive in Perry the same jealous need for behind-the-back cattiness which sometimes possessed Henry James. For years Howells found Perry jobs, promoted his efforts to place books, defended, publicized, and encouraged him. And felt well rewarded by the distinction Perry's learning (though not his style) lent the *Atlantic,* by Perry's friendship and by the developing education in the new ideas and ideals of the novel Perry provided first for Howells and then, more generally, for the American public. The education of the public aside, the changes which gradually came over Howells' own work and literary thought as the decade of his editorship wore on were in no small way due to Perry and the 427 items he published in Howells' *Atlantic.* For the most part, however, the Perry-induced changes were literary and are best observed in connection with the evolution of Howells' novels. At least equally important changes were taking place in other parts of the editor's mind because he was playing a leading public and cultural role in what historians have pretty well agreed to call, after Mark Twain and Charles Dudley Warner's comic indictment of it, the Gilded Age.

III

There has been a great deal more agreement on designating the period as the Gilded Age than agreement as to just what is meant by the term and what attitudes one ought to take with regard to it. Objectively rather than pejoratively or defensively viewed, the Gilded Age may be said to be the period of the first full, dislocating shock upon American life of the greatest change in human cultural history since man ceased to be a hunter-nomad and settled down to the life of the agricultural village. The Gilded Age was the first period of the full industrialization of American life. From about 1850 forward, that process moved slowly from the East to the West, retarded of course by the last stages of the conquest of the frontier; and after the Civil War it moved from North to South, retarded by Reconstruction, the lack of Southern capital, and a crumbling but stubborn agrarian idealism. But it moved and it conquered all through Howells' active lifetime. It is symbolic enough that long before Howells' death the little brick house with its lovely peach tree where he was born were torn up and the site buried beneath the sooty thundering steel of the rail yards in Martins Ferry. The boy who had lived in a log cabin at Eureka Mills lived on through the ages of Iron, Steam, Steel, and Electricity into the first stage of the Internal Combustion Engine era.

The very essence of the Gilded Age was change and dislocation. Profoundly though the theoretical impact of science shook men's faith through Darwinism, the cultural impact of industrialization was yet more devastating. Eternal, accelerating change, dislocation, and hugeness were its badges. Howells was born into a farm, home, and village economy so simple that the village printer seemed an anomaly. Then came the reciprocating team of applied science, invention, and industrial progress. Heavy industry with heavy transport flung rails over the nation, iron ships on the lakes and at sea, and ore, coal, oil, lumber and a thousand semi-processed materials began to flow across the nation. Mills and factories sprang up at the center of disorganized industrial cities, jammed with people who had no customs to tell them how to cope with the terrible human problems their new environment piled on them. Consumer industries began to mass-produce textiles, shoes, meat—and publications—destroying demand for handicraft products, raising the productive output of labor and in the mass, at least, raising standards of living. There was often mass unemployment, yet there were not hands enough for the work to be done, and immigrants poured in from Europe and Asia by the millions. Though improved communication and mass marketing tended to standardize American life, the millions of new citizens created pockets of alien strangeness in language and custom, especially in the cities.

The new circumstances also created a new class, with a new outlook on life, the business men. In the old society there had been, for the most part, farmers, a relatively few people who provided services for them, and a very few patricians. Now came the business man, whose ability to acquire wealth and social power by means which would have seemed mysterious in the old society gradually brought him dominance over the new. He was possessed by the Business Mind. "The business of America is Business," President Coolidge is supposed to have said. "The Gospel of Wealth" Professor Ralph Gabriel called the conviction of the business mind that all of life— whether the qualities of personal living, and personal relationships, the arts, politics, or even religion—must go to serve the increase of business success. If what men had long thought higher and nobler things had to be suppressed or, better yet, corrupted to serve business, the business mind could salve its uneasiness readily: it believed that nothing on this earth really was higher than business and that God's smile and success were the same.

So long as the great postwar prosperity kept its buoyancy, all that went swimmingly. Moralists like Lowell and Godkin and Mark Twain, and their friend Howells, might be shocked by governmental corruption and depressed by the low, materialistic standards of manners and public morality, but there was always the chance (even Walt Whitman in *Democratic Vistas* was given pause by it) that the business men might be right. At least they were maintaining an unprecedented level of prosperity and expansion. But in 1873 all the dislocations and confusions came around into phase at once, and the roof fell in. With millions of unemployed, thousands of failures and bankruptcies, prices falling, wages disappearing, crowds of men dropping out of society and becoming hoboes, the sufferings of the slums made tragic, the frontier farmer reduced to beggary, workingmen goaded into strikes and open warfare while the surviving rich and well-to-do waxed stronger and more luxurious as their dollar grew bigger and bigger, the business man was put on the defensive. The corruptionist ceased to be a joke. The long depression went on year after year; for all anyone could tell it might be permanent. Sensitive and serious men—the early political scientists, moralists and amateurs like Henry George and Edward Bellamy, and editors and artists like William Dean Howells—began an increasingly concerned examination of themselves and their times to see if they could understand just what was going on and what might be the remedy for it.

Howells' experience and circumstances were such that his responses to the Gilded Age as editor of the *Atlantic* were first and naturally political, then more gradually socio-economic. In the light of his Ohio background, it is not surprising that one of the new departments he instituted in the *Atlantic* was Politics or that he got Arthur G. Sedgewick, a Liberal Republican brother-in-law of Charles Eliot Norton, to conduct it. Appalled by the corruption and barbaric ineptitude of the first Grant administration, Republican idealists, and notably those of Howells' Cambridge acquaintanceship, tried to bolt the regular party and nominate Charles Francis Adams on a good government, civil service, free trade, and reconciliation with the South platform in 1872. Howells was a Liberal Republican, threw the *Atlantic* behind the party and felt crushed when the Cincinnati Convention of the Liberals was captured by Horace Greeley, who then was also nominated by the Democrats. There was nothing to do but go back to Grant, and for the fall campaign he got his old partner Samuel Reed to write anti-Greeley pieces for the magazine. Keeping the prewar faith from the time when he and Reed in Columbus, like William Cooper Howells in the Western Reserve, had fought for the life of a party which would free the slave, the *Atlantic* editor was as Republican as he could be; but the logic of events was forcing him to doubt and waver. Soon he must seek a social idealism which could speak to the condition of the Gilded Age.

He had no such problems in the next election, however, for the Republican candidate was an old and trusted Ohio friend, the man most responsible for Howells' meeting his wife, Elinor Howells' cousin Rutherford B. Hayes. If not brilliant, Hayes was honest and able. He was strong for Civil Service reform and a self-confessed Liberal Republican who had been nominated by the party as a compromise candidate between the Regular and Liberal factions. For once in his life, Howells was utterly satisfied with a candidate. Having kept up with Hayes over the years, he could write him friendly congratulations on nomination and get a reply in his own tones of banter. So that when his publisher, H. C. Houghton, came up with the idea that Howells should take off as long as he needed and, for his *Atlantic* salary and a ten per cent royalty, write a campaign life of Hayes, the idea excited Howells and met with a ready, even a flattered, response from Hayes.

Howells mobilized Comly and other Ohio friends to send material, borrowed a half-barrel of family papers from Hayes, and in twenty-eight days, interrupted by a week's bout of summer dysentery, turned out his second (and last) campaign biography. Unfortunately, the book showed the haste with which it was done and was far from up to Howells' literary standard. Its market reflected the perilous state of Hayes's fortunes against Samuel J. Tilden, and it sold few more than two thousand copies. When, however, Hayes was at last declared the victor by the Supreme Court in 1877, the Howellses had a President in the family. They were at once invited to the White House, the Chief Magistrate's ear was cordially open to them, and they had an opportunity to reap a large harvest of personal publicity, political and personal advantage (ex-consul Howells might easily have had an Ambassadorship), as well as personal odium if they pressed their advantage.

Fortunately they had too much integrity and tact to do anything of the sort. With quiet discretion Howells found himself too busy to come to Washington or accompany Hayes on trips to the West until, toward the end of Hayes's term when it was clear that he was retiring after a single term and the gesture was no longer politically significant, he did accept one last cordial invitation for himself and "Nellie," as Hayes called his younger cousin, to visit for a week in the White House. For the rest he kept himself in the background, maneuvering skillfully to get Lowell made Ambassador to Spain and then to the Court of St. James, restoring Hayes's faith in Bret Harte enough to assure him a consulship in Germany, but failing to place De Forest and Stoddard in consulates. All offers for himself he politely declined, and when he did wish to help his father move from the consulate at Quebec to the one at Montreal (finally Toronto), he permitted Hayes to be approached on the matter only through "channels"—through Congressman James A. Garfield, who was already much indebted politically to William Cooper Howells. The *Atlantic* supported Hayes and his programs as it supported Garfield when he next ran for the presidency and won. But in both cases the friend of the Presidents who edited the great magazine kept his balance. He could have no qualms of conscience about the fact that his known forbearance aided the growth of his own public reputation and social prestige.

To think and act as a liberal Republican and to befriend Hayes and Garfield was for Howells only to act naturally in accordance with the development of his life's experience from its Ohio beginnings. But to begin to contemplate seriously the nature and structure of the public world of politics and economics in which he lived and saw his nation trapped in suffering and confusion—that was a new departure for Howells. It was not a radical or previously unthinkable event—after all he had grown up in a Utopian radical's household—but a new growth in a mind whose outreach had in recent years been mainly esthetic.

The articles on tariff policy and the money question which Howells solicited for his magazine may have been mostly politically motivated, but he kept the antipathy toward the railroad barons which he had shown in the *Nation*. In *Their Wedding Journey* he went out of his way to strike at "the shabby despots who govern New York, and the swindling railroad kings whose word is law to the whole land. . . ." And he saw to it that railroad arrogance and dirty machinations were exposed in the *Atlantic,* most effectively by Charles Francis Adams. Reflecting his family background as well as a new personal interest in the Shakers, among whom he had spent some of his summer vacations, Howells printed various articles exploring Utopian communities and their relations to a wicked world.

After 1875 the frequency of articles with socio-economic implications deepened the tone of the *Atlantic* noticeably. It was almost as if, half-consciously, Howells felt himself to be presiding over a public inquiry into the economic disease of his society. There are few clear indications of conviction on his part, and those which do exist are inconclusive. Howells' personal statements tended to reflect a mild conservatism, a tempered optimism—almost as if he were whistling in the dark. But the main trend of the articles he kept taking was in the opposite direction—toward declining assurance, toward doubt.

In 1880 he approvingly reviewed J. B. Harrison's gently conservative faith that everything was all right despite *Certain Dangerous Tendencies in American Life* (much of which had appeared in the *Atlantic* as articles). He also commended Aldrich's anti-labor *Stillwater Tragedy*—though of course even as a later Socialist Howells was to continue to disapprove of the strike. Yet that same December he printed parallel pro and con reviews of Henry George's

Progress and Poverty. The following March he brought the pioneering liberal sociologist, Richard T. Ely, into the *Atlantic* and in the same issue published one of the most explosive antibusiness articles of the entire Gilded Age, Henry D. Lloyd's "The Story of a Great Monopoly."

Lloyd's was by no means the first among the myriad books and articles which made up the literature of protest through which Americans of the age began to clarify their responses to the tremendous problems heaped on them by the great new cultural change. But it is probably fair to say that with it the decisive Muckrakers' movement was begun. So great a sensation did Lloyd's indictment against Standard Oil for its cutthroat railroad price collusion create that the *Atlantic* ran an unprecedented seven printings and there were many thousands of pirated reprints both here and in England. One of the great reform careers was launched, as the cultivated, well-to-do, morally passionate young Chicagoan proved himself able to reach the public with a propagandistic technique comparable to that of Thomas Paine. It had not been easy for Howells to make the decision to print Lloyd's piece. The *North American Review* had already decided not to risk it. But after consulting Charles Francis Adams about its factual reliability, Howells wrote Lloyd accepting it, not aware when he did so that when it came time that would be one of the last proofs he would ever read for the *Atlantic*. Not that there was any connection between his printing Lloyd and his leaving the *Atlantic* in 1881. There was none. But in the light of his future development, there was a kind of prophetic symbolism in Howells' exploding Lloyd upon the nation as a sort of salute to his own departure from the editor's chair.

It is thus clear that Howells received an important conceptual and emotional education from his *Atlantic* examination of the Gilded Age. He was far from ready to accept Lowell's black conclusion that America was the "Land of the Broken Promise." But he had moved away from John Fiske's eupeptic, Social Darwinian disregard for socio-economic problems. Howells had come, by as early as 1877, to reflect on "the lesson that humanity is above literature," and so had put his pilgrim feet on the road to Altruria. His deepening concern for the cultural crisis of his time began to percolate downward into his creative mind. Gradually he turned toward "problems" in his novels and then, with a truly creative flight beyond the previous range of his merely logical mind, found himself stirred by insights which impelled him into the production of a wholly new and important kind of novel. The result was that he had hardly achieved success and international acclaim with the novels of his second, Experimental Period, before he was off on his flight toward a third, Realistic Period.

IV

In the summer of 1869, when the Howellses were at the peak of their delight in their St. Lawrence vacation, they met in Quebec one of their newer Cambridge acquaintances, Thomas Sergeant Perry, who was traveling with a Harvard classmate. Home from Europe less than a year, Perry was not delighted by his trip. The scenery bored him; the vulgarity of his fellow passengers grated on his nerves; and he said so—thus unconsciously to both of them implanting the seed of a story in the fresh-plowed soil of Howells' imagination. In *Their Wedding Journey* Howells had done as much as he wanted to for the present with Basil and Isabel March. But he had only half developed (and left behind in Quebec) a fascinating creature, Kitty Ellison, a lovely, witty girl with free, Western manners and a small-town outlook. What if Kitty, isolated from the Marches, were to make her own journey down the river and meet someone—someone not really like Perry but fit to symbolize the gulf between a warm, natural way of taking experience and accepting people and the rather frigid way Perry had been taking his trip? What would happen should they accidentally meet—and fall in love? And what would the implications be?

In this new volume Howells was able to preserve all the charm of *Their Wedding Journey* and add the familiar piquancy of a love-affair plot, thus winning for *A Chance Acquaintance* (somewhat to his surprise and to James's ill-concealed disgust) a wide and durable popularity, particularly in England. Even though the love-plot ended unhappily with a broken engagement, "the very boarding-house patronized by Kitty" became a minor tourist attraction in Quebec, and that evidence of Howells' growing fame seemed important enough for international transmission as literary gossip. But much more important was the fact that, for the first time, Howells' imagination, his moral sensibility, his keen intellectual faculties had coincided to create a sharp, satiric vision of "commonplace" yet typical personalities engaged in a fictional action symbolic of significant tensions in American society. Apparently he began by seeing a contrast between Proper Boston and the West and then generalized his concept, as he explained to Henry James, as "the notion of confronting two extreme American types: the conventional and the unconventional."

Though Howells was quite willing to grasp the olive branch held out to him by Dr. Holmes and agree that Miles Arbuton, the gelid young gentleman who fails to make the grade as a hero in *A Chance Acquaintance,* was "*a* Bostonian and not *the* Bostonian," it is important to see that he deliberately constructed this early novel as the first of a long series of attacks on Proper Boston. An acute, retrospective critic observed in 1890 that a number of Howells' novels "might be arranged in a series appropriately entitled 'Boston Under the Scalpel,' or 'Boston Torn to Tatters,' or 'The True Inwardness of Boston.'" It is also true that each of these books has much to do with the "confrontation," or, more exactly, the conflict between the "conventional" and "unconventional" types. It was not that Howells failed of recognition in Boston. He was elected to the Saturday Club in 1874, and was later first president of the Tavern Club and a charter member of St. Botolph's. "It seems almost as if you had cheated some native Esau out of his birthright," said Dr. Holmes in complimentary complaint. Yet it was dying Brahmin Boston that Howells most admired, and even that he regarded with a detached, outsider's eye. Of Proper Boston, especially in his fiction, he always wrote, as Lowell objected, "as if some swell had failed to bow to him on Beacon Street." But it was not personal pique which inspired Howells, it was a Western, humanitarian, democratic, Swedenborgian moral judgment upon social snobbery.

He set the situation up carefully in *A Chance Acquaintance.* Reviewing Kitty Ellison, we learn that her family (not altogether unlike Howells') came from West Virginia but had moved North and West because of its strong abolitionist convictions. Her father had been slain as a crusading country editor in Bloody Kansas, and she had been reared by "Uncle Jack," the ardent operator of an Underground Railway station in "Eriecreek," near Lake Erie in Western New York. Uncle Jack's humanitarian idealism, authorized by the great Boston abolitionists, has conceived of Boston as the cradle of "everything that is noble and grand and liberal and enlightened" in American life. He is overjoyed, he writes her, that she will have a chance to visit Boston on her trip: ". . . and I cannot doubt that you will find the character of the people marked by every attribute of a magnanimous democracy . . . a city where a man is valued simply and solely for what he is in himself, and where color, wealth, family, occupation, and other vulgar meretricious distinctions are wholly lost sight of in the consideration of individual excellence." Now as Howells was at least partly aware, since he had by "excellence" struggled into the gentlemanly condition from poverty and obscurity, Uncle Jack was dealing in the terms of an ancient concept: the idea of the "natural gentleman" by means of which American theorists like Jefferson, Cooper, Emerson, and others had reconciled Western Civilization's highest ideal of human excellence, "the gentleman," to America's commitment to democracy. Kitty was, in the best tradition, a natural lady—as Howells' other "unconventional" and often Western people are natural gentlemen or ladies.

But in Miles Arbuton, the trained, cultivated, educated man of family, the "conventional" gentleman from Proper Boston, Kitty is shocked to find the two traditionally essential attributes of gentlemanliness lacking. He is traveled and well-read, superbly dressed and rigidly schooled in etiquette. He has a code of behavior and morality which he would die rather than break. But he is self-centered, exclusive, superior, unimaginative (almost to the point of stupidity) and, worst of all, being cold he lacks kindness and therefore true courtesy, being selfish he lacks magnanimity. In one generous moment he saves Kitty's life from a vicious dog (Howells' *bête noire*) and is carried out of himself long enough to confess his love and win Kitty's hand. In the next moment he "conventionally" allows himself to be trapped by a couple of scheming Boston ladies, joins them in snubbing Kitty, and leaves her with no recourse but to send him away. Afterward, commented the author, Arbuton "saw it with paralyzing clearness; and as an inexorable fact that confounded quite as much as it dismayed him, he perceived that throughout that ignoble scene she had been the gentle person and he the vulgar one. How could it have happened with a man like him !" Thereafter it became a fashion with certain Bostonian critics to assert that poor Howells simply did not know how to portray a gentleman.

But Thomas Wentworth Higginson, whose mind and heart belonged to Brahmin and reforming Boston, no matter where his name belonged, saw well before the end of the decade that Howells' "best scenes imply a dialogue between the Atlantic and Pacific slopes." By no means uncritical of Howells in general, he testified that the *Chance Acquaintance* theme "is really contributing important studies to the future of our society. How is it to be stratified? How much weight is to be given to intellect, to character, to wealth, to antecedents, to inheritance?" Authors he thought more enlightening on these questions than statisticians or politicians. Therefore, "to trace American 'society' in its formative process, you must go to Howells; he alone shows you the essential forces in action," and he does it not as a "philosopher" but as "a novelist, which is better, and his dramatic situations recur again and again to the essential point."

Thereafter Howells did recur many times to the conventional-unconventional conflict. Its rich implications stirred his imagination to come at it from a number of points of vantage, and some of his best mature books have it in view. Two more of his works in the seventies deal centrally with the problem. In 1877 he published his first book-length play, a farce called *Out of the Question*. It contains a rather boldly explicit working out of the conventional-unconventional conflict in the romance of a Midwestern inventor and engineer, Blake, and a Boston patrician belle, Leslie Bellingham. The theory of the natural gentleman in conflict with factitious social values of money, education, and social position occupies the center of the stage (considerably reducing the theatrical effectiveness of the comedy), but that is now less important than the fact that Howells invented the first of his Back Bay families—the Bellinghams, who reappear from time to time in later books—and sketched them so as to cock a derisive snook at the very heart of Proper Boston, its matriarchate.

The third major example of Boston under the scalpel and natural gentility in triumph came toward the end of the decade with the first of Howells' fictions to attain an independent life of its own, *The Lady of the Aroostook*. To this day one meets a well-read lady of sensitive mold who says, defiantly because she knows she is flying in the face of virtually all official literary criticism of the past forty years, that she treasures the memory of *The Lady of the Aroostook*. And a dispassionate rereading will discover the reason why. Howells had learned a great deal about the writing of fiction by the time he heard from the inventor Samuel Langley of the young American girl who had crossed the ocean all alone on a ship full of

men and found in the anecdote the germ of a novel. His characterizations of minor figures—the grandfather, Thomas the cabin boy,
Captain Jenness, Aunt Maria—are excellent. Miss Lydia Blood,
the "lady" who sails on the *Aroostook,* is handled with just about the
right degree of lack of definition. For she is as she must be, the
mystery of innocent beauty at the center of the circle of dark
sophisticated and masculine thoughts which surround her. This is
Howells' *Pride and Prejudice*—except that the pride and the prejudice are both in the mind of a half-unAmericanized Bostonian, Staniford, who begins by mocking and sneering at "Lurella," as he
imagines her, and ends by marrying her.

Howells' greatest triumph is his ability to characterize Staniford
through his own conversation and in the little dramatic scenes of
life on board ship. Staniford's pride, his contemptuous patronizing
of Lydia, was Howells' primary indictment of Proper Boston. It is
punished as it is cured—by the simultaneous development of Lydia's
admirable qualities of heart and talent together with Staniford's
love for her and his relinquishment of self-concern. Thus far the
situation is different from that of *A Chance Acquaintance* only in
its greater literary sophistication and in Howells' allowing Staniford
to be worthy of love and its reward where Arbuton was not.

There was, however, another dimension to *The Lady of the
Aroostook.* It was not of cosmic importance and would not have
lent itself well to sensational development, and yet it was in Howells'
time a question of both moral and cultural significance. To Lydia
as American, and to her sort of simple, freshwater folks, there was
nothing wrong with her traveling unchaperoned on the *Aroostook.*
But in Venice, indeed in Europe, where she is going, nothing could
be more scandalous. There it is simply to be assumed that without
a "dragon," given opportunity to sleep or be slept with by the officers
and passengers of the *Aroostook,* she has done so. Her reputation
is blasted. And Staniford's prejudice, from the penalty of which
love and love's generosity save him very hardly, is that, as Bostonian, he sees Lydia's situation with split vision. At first he is
disgusted by its intimations, not of immorality, but of impropriety.
As a young man in Venice, Howells had been shocked by the sudden
revelation of European sexual assumptions and their contrast with
those of American society. Now he used his perceptions of cultural
and moral difference to give depth to his novel, to add dimension to
the conventional-unconventional conflict, and to arouse in American

readers that sense of the meaning of their culture which the eye sees from abroad more easily than at home. *The Lady of the Aroostook* was not a great novel, but it was not a trivial one, either.

V

Howells had been learning, in theory as well as practice, a great deal about the novel. The book which came next after *A Chance Acquaintance* was, Howells wrote on the flyleaf of a copy of *A Foregone Conclusion,* 1875, "My first novel." Since of his previous two books one had been largely fiction and the other almost wholly so, it is worthwhile seeing just what he meant by that remark.

Obviously it could not be enough for a serious writer that he should have only an affinity for his materials (in Howells' case familiar and commonplace materials) and a developing sense of how to make art of them in his unique way; he also needed some sort of theory of what he was doing. And in the 1870's usable theory of the novel was scanty. The men of Howells' time were just beginning to set about producing the great body of sophisticated theory which would become a major part of their legacy to the modern novelist. Since even French theoretical development was still immature, the best resources were the rather embryonic ideas come out of the great pioneering British contributions to the rise of fiction in the late eighteenth and early nineteenth centuries. And their most useful concept had been the distinction between the novel and the romance. "The Novel," said Clara Reeve, summarizing in 1785, "is a picture of real life and manners, and of the times in which it is written.
'The Romance in lofty and elevated language, describes what never happened nor is likely to happen— The novel gives a familiar relation of such things, as pass every day before our eyes, such as may happen to our friend, or to ourselves; and the perfection of it, is to represent every scene, in so easy and natural a manner, and to make them appear so probable, as to deceive us into a persuasion (at least while we are reading) that all is real, until we are affected by the joys or distress, of the persons in the story, as if they were our own.'

A crude critical instrument, tending to confuse artistic success with formal intention, that nevertheless was an instrument to work with and one important to the possibilities of the emergence of realism. It provided justification for the work of Jane Austen, for example. And, perhaps in default of a better, the idea was picked up and refined in the Romantic era by practitioners as diverse as Scott, Cooper, and Hawthorne. Scott defined Romance as "a fictitious narrative in prose or verse, the interest of which turns upon marvellous and uncommon interests," and the Novel as "a fictitious narrative, differing from the Romance, because the events are accommodated to the ordinary train of human events, and the modern state of society." Comparing himself with Austen, Scott said ruefully, "The Big Bow-wow strain I can do myself like any now going; but the exquisite touch, which renders ordinary commonplace things and characters interesting from the truth of the description and the sentiment, is denied to me."

So *Ivanhoe* and *Emma* became in a sense the touchstones which differentiated between the two methods. It is important to note that while the romance was admitted to be a legitimate form, the tradition tended to disparage it in favor of the novel. Almost incredibly, Hawthorne lamented that nature had not favored him with the genius to be Trollope. And neither the candor nor the irony of his preface to *The House of the Seven Gables* quite conceals his regret that it is a romance. The Novel, he says, "is presumed to aim at a very minute fidelity, not merely to the possible, but to the probable and ordinary course of man's experience." The Romance "—while, as a work of art, it must rigidly subject itself to laws, and while it sins unpardonably so far as it may swerve aside from the truth of the human heart—has fairly a right to present that truth under circumstances, to a great extent, of the writer's own choosing or creation."

All Howells' life he was a true and great lover of Hawthorne and, indeed, after his own fashion, a follower. As early as 1865 he had used the romance-novel distinction in a review, and he was to continue to find it useful both in criticism and practice throughout his career. At the same time he accepted the tradition of the novel's ultimate superiority. Greater maturity and wisdom went into the production of the novel, he thought. His humor, as William Crary Brownell, a disciple of Matthew Arnold, noted, expressed itself in ironies "all death to romance." And the decadent corruption of the romance and the romantic attitudes behind it became unbearable to Howells. "The love of the passionate and the heroic . . . is such a crude and unwholesome thing, so deaf and blind to all the most delicate and important facts of art and life, so insensible to the subtle values in either," he complained.

The hand of Dr. Holland and his ilk lay heavily on the Anglo-American literary audience. Howells' correspondence echoed with the wrath of the friends, James, Twain, De Forest, who like him were trying to write honest novels, when a bit of women's magazine fakery called *Helen's Babies,* by John Habberton, became an international best seller in 1876. To the agnostic as to the artist it seemed necessary to fight for honesty. As Howells explained to Higginson on September 17, 1879,

'It may or may not surprise you if I say that while I despise the *Tendenz romanskt* as much as anybody, I should be ashamed and sorry if my work did not unmistakably teach a lenient, generous, and liberal life: that is, I should feel degraded merely to amuse people. But I am very often puzzled to know what is the truth, and that may account for the "stopping-short" which you notice. It is, however, also a matter of artistic preference.'

There was, in other words, nothing inadvertent about his calling *A Foregone Conclusion,* "My first novel."

If one's mind were going to explore comparisons—East *versus* West, conventional *versus* unconventional—there was an intriguing area for fictional exploration which Howells' travel books had treated only implicitly—America *versus* Europe. And so, only a year or two before Henry James produced first *Roderick Hudson* and then *The American,* Howells began to work on the international theme. Imagine an artistic young American consul in Venice, not Will Howells but "one of my predecessors,"—somebody like Larkin Mead, or a painter like W. J. Stillman whom Howells had beaten out in the competition for the Venetian post—and call him Henry Ferris. Then imagine a lovely, temperamental, red-haired American girl, a bit at loose ends because she is the child of a deceased Army officer and has been reared amid the confusions of constant moves from one post to another. Call her Florida Vervain and give her only her flighty but well-intentioned and semi-invalid mother to tie to. In Venice for the mother's health, the Vervains will naturally lean on Ferris, since Mrs. Vervain is accustomed to special treatment from government officials. Ferris, in spite of himself, will enjoy being imposed on because of Florida's beauty, and eventually he will fall in love with her. But then, complicate the situation with a uniquely Venetian phenomenon, a character based on a man known and closely observed in Venice—a priest, Don Ippolito, whose vocation is obscure, who is a theological skeptic, a hapless would-be inventor, and who ekes out his ecclesiastical pittance by giving language lessons. Let Ferris introduce Don Ippolito to the Vervains to teach Florida Italian and let the shaky Don be so smitten by his charge that he meditates deserting the priesthood and emigrating to America in the hope of being able to win her hand. How would it all work out? And what would happen?

Howells, faced for the first time with a problem of fictional construction which could not be solved by stringing things out on a line of travel, skillfully worked out the question of how what he first called "The Tragedy of Don Ippolito" would go. With great compression and economy he proved, in Henry James's words, that he could "embrace a dramatic situation with true imaginative force" precisely by making his novel "dramatic"—that is, by building it in a series of scenes during which the little cast of characters spoke, acted, and appeared to each other in ways which gradually altered their feelings and convictions and which communicated, directly or subtly, various meanings (true or false) to each other's minds. As his Diary for the period reveals, Howells worked over the background minutely, sending a questionnaire to his Venetian friend Brunetta covering priests from details of dress to daily habits and duties and even legal status. But instead of using settings and Venetian esoterica for their own sakes, Howells now made them serve the emotional atmosphere in which the psychological action of his plot takes place. Everything converges to the tragic moment when the full folly of the illusions in which all the characters have been moving, each bemused by his own, is revealed.

Misled by Florida's passion for truthfulness and her consequent urging that if he cannot be a true priest he should be none, Don Ippolito prepares to run away, an apostate to his vows. But just before he is ready to go, he confesses his love to Florida in the garden. She is shocked. "You, a priest !" is all she can say. And Ippolito's heart is shattered along with his illusions. Wrung with pity over the pain she had unwittingly caused him, Florida futilely stoops to embrace and console him if she can, and just at that moment Ferris steps, unseen, into the garden, sent by Mrs. Vervain to see what has become of Florida. And, of course, he misunderstands completely and is shattered in his turn.

Howells wanted to end his novel at that point, symbolizing the tragic inability of American innocence and guilty European sophistication to understand one another or bridge the gulf between them with anything but suffering. But, as he indicated to Charles Eliot Norton, the publishers wouldn't permit it. Public outcry might be overwhelming against so stark a tragedy (he had already disappointed expectation in ending *A Chance Acquaintance*). And, then, he was in danger of seriously offending Catholic readers. So, to satisfy Osgood, he took poor, broken Don Ippolito home to bed and put him through a conversion experience and a reconciliation with Ferris. He brought Ferris home, put him in the Union Army, and wounded him (all quickly and undramatically) and then arranged a final scene in which Ferris and Florida met at an art exhibition where Ferris' portrait of Don Ippolito was hanging and there had them reconciled and soon after married.

A Foregone Conclusion was a critical as well as a popular success. Henry James reviewed it twice and praised its originality and character drawing as well as its construction. Naturally, he had eye enough to see and object to the deficiencies of the ending. In England the book was lauded by George Saintsbury. Howells, said he, writes so well that one "takes up any work of his with expectations of pleasure"; but the "goodness" of this "quite surpassed our most sanguine anticipations." The characters were done "with unquestionable originality and . . . very great skill." Saintsbury confounded the Bostonian retort on Miles Arbuton by admiring Howells' portrait of Ferris as a gentleman and grasped his intent perfectly in remarking that the "finest thing about the book" was his skill in contrasting Ferris and Ippolito without "any glaring or theatrical discords." Very popular and extensively pirated in Canada and England, *A Foregone Conclusion* was translated into German in 1876 and published by Tauchnitz in 1879. It was dramatized and played in London and New York in 1885 and 1886. But the greatest compliment paid it, and indeed the high point of Howells' reputation in his Experimental Period was Saintsbury's review.

One new feature of the Howellses' way of life in the good, great time was the change in their summers. Always a sufferer from the heat, which had stifling associations with his ancient "hypochondria"—and now newly obese to compound heat's effect on him—Howells used his enhanced income and freedom from editorial routine to escape. In common with thousands of middle class Americans in the East, his family could debate whether to go to the mountains or the shore. But they could also look forward to a full summer, often extended far beyond the conventional dates between

Memorial and Labor Days, in which to make of the summer hotel or boardinghouse a summer way of life. They went to the White Mountains, Winnepesaukee, Champlain, the Adirondacks, Saratoga; or to one of the Nahants or the coast of Maine. And wherever they went there was ample opportunity for Howells to study Americans in motion, revealing their inward selves in action which was unwonted enough to call forth character yet normal enough not to distort it.

In the summer of 1874 Howells took his tribe to the "mosquitory bower" of a farmhouse in Jaffrey, New Hampshire, and was there observed, notebook in hand, studying the withering culture of the New England country village, with its "natives" who made ends meet by selling winey air, fresh vegetables, and picturesqueness to the summer people who brought colorful contrasts of idea, costume, and manners into the setting. Obviously, this afforded fine materials for an eye and mind long trained to explore fresh juxtapositions of character and culture. Consequently, there began to appear in the November, 1875, *Atlantic* a story composed the preceding spring after a winter's ruminations on the summer's observations, a fascinating and little-known Howells novel called *Private Theatricals*.

The reason why the book is so little known is still somewhat mysterious. It was not separately published until 1921, when it appeared as *Mrs. Farrell;* and literary gossip, first printed in 1910, has it that Howells suppressed the book because he was threatened with suit by the people who ran the "Mountain Farm" where he had stayed and who felt themselves caricatured by their erstwhile paying guest. It may be that Howells "suppressed" his book publication (surely *Atlantic* publication was anything but suppression) as the price of preventing a damaging public outcry. The greatest mystery about the whole affair is how it was kept from becoming a juicy morsel of newspaper gossip at the moment. It is hard to know, in the absence of evidence, whether anything of Howells' satiric portrait of Yankee folk gone to seed could have been construed as so personal to his landlord's family as to have been actionable.

The great loss to later readers of Howells' books has not, however, been the view of New England in the dry autumn of her greatness. That he drew even better in half a dozen later pieces. The loss is of what was perhaps the finest among his "idylls," for irony, for feminine analysis, for sunny freshness of setting and local color, and for dramatic movement so swift and intense it becomes at times the closest thing to melodrama a grown-up Howells wrote. Compounded with that is the loss of a whole group of new figures, some only preliminary studies for finer successes in their kind to follow, but one magnificently complete. "Your Mrs. Farrell is terrific—" wrote Fanny Kemble, the great American actress and woman of the world. "Do for pity's sake give her the Small Pox—she deserves it. . . ." And Mrs. Farrell is, indeed, a stellar member of the small, select company of Howells' bitches.

Farrell is Howells' only real *femme fatale,* and she is superb. Ravishingly beautiful, she also has the requisite temperament—the nature and sources of which Howells understood and portrayed with an accuracy which might have made some of his hostile critics of the 1920's take thought had they read him. She lives for "effect," for theatrical sensation, and must always be engaged in "something vivid, stunning," but without ever being able to be "engaged" in the Existentialist sense. She senses occasionally that she is perhaps an amoral emotional monster, entirely unable to feel in her heart the emotions she keeps glittering and thundering about her. She has a genius for creating the situations she craves by luring other, honest hearts to disaster. And Howells has his final ironic word on her when at last she tries to see if her talent and passion for excitement can be satisfied on the legitimate stage. For there she subtly fails, and the bystanding husband of a woman who had acted as a sort of Greek chorus toward the main action of the book has his moment in the light to remark drily that perhaps, after all, Mrs. Farrell's genius is for private theatricals.

It would not have been Howells if he had not had things to say about the *femme fatale* which no one had quite said before, about the moral climate in which she lived—and slew not only men's hearts and her own, but her soul and perhaps theirs as well. He makes her story a perfect vehicle for exposing the immorality of "romantic" morals (still current at the soap opera and Reno levels) about love, courtship, and flirtation. At the climax of the book, indeed, he manages to make his moral dialectic so intense, with charge, counter-charge, confession, confrontation, attack and retreat, that he strays over the line toward melodrama. Since these stormy, electrically emotional scenes are properly part of a romantic pattern he was destroying, since they do fit the ironic point about private theatricals, he may have felt justified. The later realist would have felt it necessary to incarnate his ideas in a dialectic of moral implication—which could be shared only by the good reader who was experiencing the imaginative action to the full. That reader would have to do the moralizing for himself, and that made immense demands on him as reader. The fully mature Howells would know that, no matter how great his skill, he ran the chance of losing the weak or careless reader; but he would persist in creating the book most consonant with his faith in the atmosphere and ethos of the realistic illusion, most consonant with his own perception of what was highest in the art of fiction. And that would move increasingly far from the lapse toward melodrama in *Private Theatricals*.

VI

Howells' early novels, said his friend Horace E. Scudder retrospectively in 1890, were "altogether delightful and did not disturb our sleep." By being delightful and innocuous, the early Howells won an enviable reputation and Anglo-American popularity. People raved over Howells the "idyllist." Henry James thought him "a master of the waning art of saying delicate things in a way that does them justice," and lauded his "charm," his light touch, his "taste and culture and imagination, and incapacity to be common." Celia Thaxter spoke for his great feminine audience: "How slight the fabric, yet how firm and flawless, how delicate and fine !" Yet the great dean of serious Boston critics, E. P. Whipple, judged him a worthy successor to Addison, Goldsmith, and Irving, and solemnly admired the "exquisite harmony" and "singular felicity of his style," the "delicious humorous element" in his work, and his "refined perceptions of character."

All this praise, and high rewards in fame and cash to match it, Howells owed to the work of his Experimental Period, the time in which he found a way for himself in literature and taught himself to write Howellsian novels. A less honest man, a less genuine and devoted artist, might have stopped there and simply continued to cash in by turning out more and more of the same. But there is no evidence that Howells so much as considered stopping. Grateful to his audience, he nevertheless continued to explore and to advance. In a very short time after 1875–78, in which his principal effort to cash in was by way of an abortive attempt at becoming a playwright, his personal development and the hidden logic of his creative mind's growth had carried him away from mere gentle delightfulness. His audience began to feel uncomfortable at the change which was coming over its idyllist.

Something puzzling, "often crotchetty, eccentric, radically wrong" seemed to be affecting Howells' literary judgment, Paul Hamilton Hayne confided to Bayard Taylor. "For example, what the Devil *does* he, *can* he mean?" in refusing to admire Sir Walter Scott and William Morris, Hayne demanded. When *The Lady of the Aroostook* appeared, Stedman wrote to express his mystification as well as his joy: "the gradual change in your work is a perpetual surprise to me," he said. "This tale is absolutely *realistic*. . . ." He praised the effects of "your confoundedly accurate eye and ear," but felt authorized to sound a warning. Remember, he pleaded, that you are a poet; don't "too rigidly prescribe certain limits to yourself"; blend in some idealism, too.

The point at which certain readers began to balk was exactly that at which "idealism" seemed to disappear from Howells' view of his characters. In the same columns where Saintsbury's praise had been so happy in 1875, another British critic received *The Lady of the Aroostook* coldly in 1879. Though inaccurate, his key comment was interesting in its direction. Howells' "mission," he concluded, "lies in a corrupt following of Dr. Wendell Holmes rather than of Zola or Balzac. . . . All those physiological, psychological and metaphysical vagaries playing round simple characters in an everyday story. . . ." The objection is that Howells has ceased to be delicate, light, slight, and charming. He is violating the romantic convention that characters must be unified, symbolic fixtures round which the action circles. His people—like Don Ippolito and Florida Vervain, and especially like Staniford, are psychologically fluid, or at least plastic. They are seen relativistically, developmentally, and with skeptical reservations. As W. C. Brownell said a year later, part of the trouble was that Howells did not seem to be personally engaged in his characters' fates. His people seemed "clinically studied," and the best a romantically inclined critic could say for them was the very left-handed compliment that "the peculiar charms of an unromantic bleakness, of a spiritual tenuity, of a thin gilding of the picturesqueness of the commonplace, have hitherto gone uncelebrated." The trouble was, in other words, that the delicate charmer threatened to become a realist.

Many impulses native to Howells and others native to his own land directed him toward realism. He denied categorically that any given literary passion or influence had made a realist of him and properly insisted on the centrality of his own inward development and experimentation in bringing him to realism. Yet it cannot be doubted that the opportunity to join in a great international movement toward a new and antiromantic way of creating novels was of major significance to Howells. Understanding it in his own way, he joined up gladly. His discovery of Björnson was exciting and illuminating. And largely under the tutelage of James and Perry, he went on to Daudet and Flaubert as well as Balzac, to Taine and then to Zola. But as it seemed to him in the seventies, "the man who has set the standard for the novel of the future is Tourgenief." The Cambridge sophisticates were wild about him, and Howells was, for the time being, thoroughly in accord. Spareness, brevity, condensation, and a certain agnostic dryness in dealing with character were evident in favorite Turgenev books like *Smoke, Lisa,* and *Dimitri Roudine,* and of course they suited Howells' own fictional inclinations very well. But the great principle which he learned from Turgenev was the ideal of the "dramatic method," the notion that neither the author himself nor any created "voice" or "personality" of the author should be permitted to intrude into the illusion offered the reader by the author—the illusion that a process of life was working itself out before the reader's eyes. To this end Turgenev—and Howells after him—concentrated on character presentation and psychological development, minimizing plot and sensational incident. They let value-judgment and morality remain implicit in the action and outcome of the fiction, depending on the reader to have his own reflections on the meaning of what had been selected to stage itself in the arena of his imagination. For Howells, who after the manner of Goldsmith, Irving, Thackeray, and Heine had made himself so expert at humorous and reflective intrusion into his writing, this was a stern ideal which it cost him the pain of a great discipline to follow—and even then he was sometimes unable to resist the temptation to break over, particularly in the less scenic portions of a novel. That he was willing to try, however, is a mark of his huge admiration for Turgenev.

A measure of that admiration, by the way, was returned by Turgenev. He owned and had read some of Howells' work. Henry James became Turgenev's friend in Paris and could relay to Howells the news that the great Russian liked his books. Higginson and

Boyesen both served as couriers, but it was John Hay who, as Hayes's Assistant Secretary of State, saw that Howells got word of Turgenev's supreme praise, and that by way of a letter from the President himself. "I have spent the night reading *A Chance Acquaintance,*" Turgenev was quoted as saying, "and now I should like to visit a country where there are girls like the heroine." Hayes wrote Howells that Turgenev spoke "of your writings as superior to those of any now living, and that he enjoyed them more than the works of anybody else." Even when one makes allowance for friendly hyperbole, that is a sizable compliment. It could not have diminished Howells' loyalty to the new school of novelists.

Consequently, his new concern for the novel joined with his new concern for ideas in making him move on, away from his first success, and into his third, Realistic, period. His last novel of the decade, *The Undiscovered Country,* showed how far he had come from *Their Wedding Journey.* Because of its difference, the British *Academy* reviewer dismissed it promptly: "It is a novel with a purpose," he said. "English readers . . . will . . . be disappointed."

The Undiscovered Country is not, in the ordinary sense, a purpose novel, and it is one which ought sometime to be carefully elucidated (as almost none of Howells' novels ever has been) by a well-informed critic. It is a somewhat groping novel, lacking the clear definition and firm grasp of earlier books and not up to the major works soon to follow. But it tries and in some ways succeeds in grappling imaginatively in fiction—not speculatively—with a number of interesting ideas. As Howells wrote his father, this one was no "mere love-story" but "serious work" that "treats of serious matters." In one way it is a variation on a theme by Hawthorne, as Higginson noticed in an early review, the theme being that of *The Blithedale Romance.* The spiritualism which Howells had encountered in youth in Jefferson and which was being revived (as he makes his characters surmise) in the seventies as a desperate substitute for theological faith plays a central role. Shakerism, scientific doubt, feminine psychology, are other considerations. Further, it represents Howells' first serious attempt to bring American life into imaginative focus below the travelistic level. With native-born Elinor Howells at his side to interpret (*The Undiscovered Country* was her "favorite"), his summers in the New England countryside had helped him soak up impressions of the people's ways, characters, problems, and fate. They were not so different from Western Reserve Yankees, but he studied absorbedly, trying to get them right.

And he must have done so, at least for his contemporaries, for, though he began really to lose his British popularity with this book, it made serious New England readers ready to accept him as their regional novelist. John Fiske was moved to tears by it. Higginson hailed its new moral weightiness, its Hawthornian lack of self-commitment, its rendering of nature and the countryside, its avoidance of Howells' "sub-acid vein" of skeptical "philosophizing" (what he did was to put such reflections into the mouths of his characters à la Turgenev). Brooks Adams, though typically digressing to descant on the infinite cultural inferiority of America to Europe, praised Howells for his courage in daring to be American and so lay the ground for the future rise of a native literature. Then he spent two pages proving that Miles Arbuton was no gentleman and giving Arbuton sound advice on how to be a man.

It was evident that this latest novel left many readers and critics puzzled and a little wary. Intelligent people saw that Howells was definitely committed to realism by *The Undiscovered Country*, but also that it was not going to be easy to classify him. That is "the kind of realism I like," wrote Tom Appleton, Longfellow's debonair brother-in-law who must surely have served as one of the models for Bromfield Corey; "but Zola would give us Ann St."—Boston's waterfront sailor's hell. Convinced romanticists began to see that here a formidable enemy was arising. Admittedly, said W. C. Brownell, *The Undiscovered Country* is Mr. Howells' most "important" book, as everyone is saying. But let the defenders of the "romantic imagination" take notice: "Mr. Howells's realism is . . . a definitely held creed." His "theory is apparently that this is an 'everyday' world full of picturesque and, if you like, tragic material; but that, however great the tragedy, it is after all and in the main an 'everyday world.' " Brownell was an acute and sensitive critic. That was probably a more accurate account of Howells' position in 1880 than he could have written for himself.

Chapter Nine

THE CHIEF AMERICAN REALIST:
1881–1885

THE RESTLESS GROWTH OF HOWELLS' MIND AND ART DURING
the late seventies accompanied a significant domestic move.
He left Cambridge in the late spring of 1878 to go out to
the heights of Belmont, in the country. There on a slope with a
magnificent view eastward over Cambridge and Boston, surrounded
by fields, apple orchards, and country estates, a wealthy friend
named Charles Fairchild financed the building of what was then a
very modern house, designed by Elinor Howells' brother, of McKim,
Mead, and White. From its unusual sloping red roof and the red
timothy grass all around, the Howellses called it Red Top and were
flooded with tranquility amid the country quiet, fresh air, sun-
light, and gardens. Howells bought his first horse and rig, making
fine comic capital of the attendant frustrations—in a magazine piece
of course. Indoors he had the finest of his studies, with a great fire-
place and hand-carved book shelves, and painted as a frieze on the
wall a typically Shakespearian quotation—meant to proclaim that
this was it, the final resting place: *From Venice as far as Belmont.*

Aside from the attractions of Fairchild's offer to settle the
Howellses on his estate, there were good ostensible reasons for the
move. The children were growing, and they needed, robust young
John particularly, to have country air and a chance at country experience. And the pressure of Society, with its incessant engagements
had begun to tell on the adults. Memoirs and letters of all descriptions from this period forward make it clear that no "distinguished"
gathering would do without the Howellses if they could be had. But
if they were had, with anything like the frequency with which they
were wanted, the effect on her nerves and on his capacity to work
became cumulatively devastating during a "season." Now that the

first gay delight of the good, great time was passing into satiety, Belmont offered the refuge of distance. Then, of course, Cambridge was not what it had been. Swift change made it no longer seem the perfect home for Howells' spirit. Lowell and James were abroad; Longfellow and Norton were growing old. And Howells' spirit had altered, too. Perhaps it had grown too large for Cambridge.

The physical move from Cambridge preceded another and even more significant event: emancipation from magazine editing. As Howells' creative work deepened during the late seventies, the burden of the *Atlantic* weighed increasingly heavy. Chores he had once performed gladly he now slighted when he could. They distracted him from more important tasks. In 1880 the distraction suddenly became acute when Houghton and Osgood, his publishers, split irrevocably and began to quarrel over the division of their assets— among them the services of W. D. Howells. Early the next year he severed connection with both and about February 1 definitively resigned his editorship of the *Atlantic,* to be succeeded by Aldrich.

Having thus purged himself of editorship, Howells accepted an arrangement which left him free to write novels yet gave him more income with financial security at least as great as that of his *Atlantic* job. James R. Osgood and Company offered to pay him a fixed weekly salary. In return Osgood got the right to ten thousand royalty-free copies of each of Howells' books. He apparently also acted as agent in placing serials and other writings with magazines, though what his financial arrangement with Howells was on such matters is not clear. It is reasonable to guess that Howells got about $7500 a year in salary for a novel a year plus smaller pieces, and that he picked up at least another $2500 from back royalties, occasional magazine pieces, reviews, and similar material. The absence of evidence about his part in serial rights makes it hard to estimate his total income; but in the light of his ten-thousand-dollar Harper contract in 1885, it is hardly likely that his previous income was substantially greater. In the early eighties that was far from being a tycoon's income, but it enabled a man to support his family in superior style, and Howells did so.

Thus he became at last a professional writer, primarily a professional novelist, successfully dependent for a living on his pen—a position previously achieved by few Americans. His skill and stamina in steady, large productivity were such that he need never fear drying up or running out of literary goods to sell. But every act of refusal to play a merely popular game, every paragraph or sentiment which might alienate readers or upset editors and publishers would require an act of courage, an act of faith in the rightness of his course and in his power to win over his audience in spite of itself. The quite amazing fact about an author who carried on his psyche the tender scars of disastrous neurotic breakdowns is that Howells immediately showed that he possessed deep reservoirs of just that kind of faith and courage. He held to the path of the natural growth of his artistic imagination and ethical sensibility, and when he was subjected to pressure to cease to grow or at least conceal or evade the significance of his growth, he fought back with vigor.

I

As a professional man of letters in his early forties he was now ready to establish the habits of life and methods of work which would carry him through the next forty years and sixty-odd books. With essential responsibilities narrowed to his family and writing, he had large vistas of personal freedom in control of his time, his energy, and his place and mode of living. Therefore daily, systematic, hard work became an essential part of his formula. It was one of the family jokes that Elinor Howells said he wrote novels like a man sawing wood. His health had been so good for a decade that he had almost forgotten to be hypochondriac; and his stamina had been proved. And his personal growth, as exemplified for instance in the difference between the mind recorded in the notebook he kept for *Italian Journeys* and *Their Wedding Journey* and the one he kept for *Indian Summer* and later works in the eighties, is really striking. The old self-consciously poetic hypersensitivity and temptation to pose are gone. In their place are a balance of mind and accuracy of perception and response reminiscent of Benjamin Franklin. He was nearing the insight he confided to his father toward the end of the decade—that his enforced self-education had been no disaster: "There are some self-made men in this country who would have done well to spend the time making almost anything else; but on the whole the men made by others are worse."

His work habits became professionally well-grooved, and work became a passion, almost a vice, for a man who loved what he did.

Consequently he became contemptuous of the flighty author who must wait on inspiration. Why might the Muse not wait as readily on the man who made a business of wooing her as on the man who mooned about yearning for a miracle? "I sit down at my desk and go to work as regularly as if I were in a mercantile or banking office," Howells said, ". . . you can work it out by patient and methodical application." The trick was to discipline oneself to free his time and energies for his best effort. Howells got in the habit of rising between seven and seven-thirty in the morning, sitting down to a substantial breakfast at eight, and being at work by nine. Then he wrote until about twelve, never past one o'clock, and had lunch, averaging a thousand to fifteen hundred words of finished production for the day. In a handwriting which deteriorated with the years, he liked to write in extra-large script on half sheets, leaving wide spaces between lines for revisions and piling up huge stacks of paper. He aimed to work three hours a day and sleep eight, and he came to be able to write in trains or hotels, on shipboard, or anywhere there was room. Afternoons he might read or correct proof, but there was always his long constitutional to be walked. Evenings might be given to the theater, to reading aloud with his wife, or to going out.

As Howells' celebrity increased, his public personality continued to be attractive but developed protections. People were surprised on first meeting him to see how quiet, simple, deliberately undistinguished he seemed. He was short, stout, round-shouldered, and peaceable. His "voice had a gentle softness, as though there were twins asleep in the next room." Everyone felt his true kindliness and "absorbent" quality—he seemed really interested in other people and liked to make them talk and unfold themselves rather than parade his own ego. That and his subtle, quick humor gave him great personal charm. But alert observers also saw that in a sense he was armored behind his wit and gentleness. He could not be taken advantage of or pushed into positions he did not like; he was hard to attack. "It is not the attitude of a man who does not think, but more like that of one who does not care always to think aloud," said one sensitive interviewer. "In general he reserves his deeper meditations for himself, as everyone has a right to do. The plane on which he oftenest meets people is one of sensible, considerate, well-balanced reflection on life and books, enlivened by humor and averse to the tediousness of argument." The "colorless Napoleonic face" was full of vitality, the glance of the blue eye exceptionally penetrating; the full mustache was beginning to frost with gray.

All the rest of his career Howells continued to produce plays, essays, poems, reviews, travel pieces—but there was no question about which form enlisted his strongest love. As a brash young interviewer, Van Wyck Brooks "asked him in which, as a man of letters, he took most delight. . . . 'Oh, fiction, fiction,' he replied with a good deal of warmth." Yet, for all his faith in the conscientious application of the seat of the pants to the chair, Howells was just as dependent on the stirring of the waters, on the mysterious and uncontrollable appearance of the creative impulse from the sublogical levels of his mind, as any other artist. Fortunately, he suffered from no such poverty of impulse as some other writers, and his method for dealing with the creative impulse toward fiction, when it came, was as well-grooved as his working day.

"My plan is to choose my topic, select the characters I want for the story, choose my locality and time, and then go to work. . . . I generally content myself with choosing the phase of life or the subject that I wish to illustrate, sketch out in mind the principal characters, and then plunge into the work. Most books write themselves when you are fairly started, and I trust to the plot unfolding itself as there may be need. With the portraiture of character it is quite otherwise, and a good deal of reflection is necessary . . ."— thus Howells himself on his method. His system was designed to control himself, not his materials. He was ready to trust his talent and imaginative processes to work out the substance of a book. Academics imagine too much deliberate design in authors, he once protested to Professor Brander Matthews of Columbia: an artist *feels* his way to success; he doesn't *map* it.

For realist Howells, the great thing about fiction was, of course, character. His people absorbed by far the greatest part of his attention and delight. But he rejected the notion that the author is or should be possessed by his characters and lost in his creations: "Never," he said. "The essence of achievement is to keep outside, to be entirely dispassionate, as a sculptor must be, moulding his clay . . ."—or a good actor. By this he did not mean that passion must be absent, but that it must be under artistic command. When the Boston author Robert Grant asked Howells, an old man revisiting the Saturday Club, "how firm a hold he used to have upon his characters," he got a quick, passionate reply: "The grip of a bull dog !"

With the characters thus firmly in hand, he could give them their settings and conjecture their fates and significance. All this he could project as a novel: "describe it in 8 or 10 lines, estimate its length, and give its purpose. . . ." But he could go no further except by the process of hard, daily work. He would ordinarily refuse to do that until a magazine editor had agreed to accept the final product; and he would steadfastly refuse to elaborate further. The editor had to take the novel in outline if he took it at all and trust the author's imagination and discipline as the author did.

Of course, Howells was begging part of the question of his creative method when he spoke so easily of "choosing" topic, characters, locale, and all the rest. That leaves untouched the question of how the choices became possible. If anyone in a moment of egomania ever pretended that he could create a work of the literary imagination by simple, arbitrary acts of will and logic, it was Edgar Allan Poe, not Howells. Full understanding of Howells' creative processes will require careful study of his notebooks and manuscripts, not all yet available. But it seems clear that his creative impulses came from an esthetic use of memory. Or that the image of the Well as the source of creativity given in John Livingston Lowes's *The Road to Xanadu* applies to Howells' case. Lowes portrayed Coleridge's creative imagination as a mystic Well into which ideas and images from his wide reading dropped as if they were individual fragments with little hooks attached. In the depths of the Well they somehow, often incongruously, became tangled together. Then, when the mysterious energy of creativity troubled the waters, they rose to the surface in new and unpredictable combinations to make themselves available to the conscious, shaping mind of the skillful artist.

Howells' theory was that "an author is merely one who has had the fortune to remember more . . . than other men. A good many wise critics will tell you that writing is inventing; but I know better than that; it is only remembering . . . the history of your own life." His own memory was, as we have seen, much keener than most people's. But his theory of creativity as memory makes sense (in theory and in conjunction with his own various statements about the creation of literature) only if one takes his "remembering" as roughly equivalent to Lowes's "Well." As Lowes saw Coleridge, he seems to have stocked the Well almost exclusively from reading; Howells stocked his from experience of life as well as books. While memory of specific people and events, or indeed direct observation with literature aforethought, gave him materials for his work, what he remembered or recorded was at least as much the response of his own mind and emotions to places, people, and events as anything "objective"—even supposing a man and artist can really see objects as they are. Urged at the age of forty-nine to write a novel of Washington, D.C., he demurred, "I am too old now. I could not stand the going into society to catch the spirit of things."

Leaving for later discussion the question of how a writer may be imagined actually to have placed a "transcript of life" on his page, one needs to avoid being caught in the trap of supposing that Howells did somehow actually reproduce "real life" as it existed around him. As a realistic theoretician he talked a great deal about doing just that. In practice he found his impulses to creativity just where James or Hawthorne found them—in the "germs," the extraordinarily suggestive moments of experience which could set his imagination in motion and eventually make a work of fiction possible. Some of Howells' effects in his work were importantly different from some of theirs, but that is all. His diaries and notebooks follow an interesting rule of preparation for writing. When there are extensive observations of scenes and people, heavily detailed, these are notes for travel books. The notes for serious fiction are records of inward impulses, stirrings of the creative life shaping the work within. The exception to this rule is the special "study" made to flesh out a structure already given but not complete.

When once Howells had "remembered" the basis for a book, he sometimes had to do research to fill in where memory could not serve. In order not to shatter the illusion of life he was creating by falling into anachronisms, he was often at considerable pains to get things "right." While writing *The Quality of Mercy* he felt he needed to know, for instance, just what the police department of a Canadian city would do about a tip that an American embezzler was living there under cover. So he went to Montreal, walked into police headquarters, and solemnly put a hypothetical question to the chief —who immediately pounded his bell and turned out his detective squad to get a first-hand report on the story and be ready to go right to work.

Or, for one more instance among many possible ones, at work in 1878 on *A Woman's Reason,* one of his weakest novels, Howells found himself tangled in problems about which he could "remember" nothing. He wanted to survey the economic fate of a young lady deprived of father by death and of fortune by depression in Boston during the seventies. She has a faithful lover whom she has capriciously turned away, and Howells intends to have him return and rescue her at last, but he needs to have the naval officer lover out of the way for several years in order to study the economic helplessness of a mere lady. So he sends the lover off to a naval station at Hong Kong and then gets him wrecked at sea and marooned on an atoll. But how to do all this and do it sensibly? He wrote letters to a naval officer who had submitted poems to the *Atlantic*, gathering specific bits of advice, and puzzled over finishing his romance for five years after starting. The lesson was that he had, indeed, somehow to "remember" in order to do good work. As the genesis of his first major novel, the first big achievement of his free-lance period, *A Modern Instance*, shows, however, he worked best when something had acted to fire his imagination to a very special kind of remembering.

II

Along with other signs of the new age, Howells was a great deal concerned in the late seventies with feminism, the place of women in the emergent society. From his fictional beginnings he had shown extraordinary power to portray women and trace the elusive paths of feminine psychology. The fine development of Kitty Ellison had led naturally enough to Lydia Blood of the *Aroostook*, both in characterization and theme. But Howells' first attempts to take up sociological aspects of "the woman question," as it was often lightly referred to at the time, were not notably successful. He hit upon popular enough themes. Everybody, given the state of women's education in the period, wanted to know what in the world a woman was to do if not a wife, a schoolmarm, or a drudge. Howells' picture of Helen Harkness' economic futility in *A Woman's Reason* was a perfectly accurate projection of the fate of a "lady-educated" woman in Gilded Age business life.

Even more timely was another feminist study for which Howells had temporarily put aside *A Woman's Reason*—the exploration of the career of a young "doctress" in *Dr. Breen's Practice*. Even before Howells resigned from the *Atlantic*, having scheduled *Dr. Breen* for the summer of 1881, Elizabeth Stuart Phelps Ward had told him about her similar theme for *Dr. Zay* and he had compro-

mised on engaging to have hers follow right after his serial. Then
came another such outline from a hitherto unknown girl, whom
Howells visited with his proofs in a book bag to convince her that
he was not stealing her idea. And shortly after that a real "doctress" proposed her autobiography to Aldrich—all in the space of a
few months. Despite all that timeliness, however, *Dr. Breen's Practice* was no great shakes as a novel. Grace Breen is easily dislodged
into marriage from her profession. She is a homeopathist apparently none too thoroughly trained (although the Howellses at about
this time became patients of a Boston homeopathist, to the disgust
of Dr. Holmes), and she has gone into medicine on the rebound
from a love affair. Accepting this as "given," we can accept the
fact that she succumbs too readily to masculine disdain, conventional feminine disapproval, and the homeo-allopathic feud in medicine and falls out of her profession as soon as she can fall into love
again. Howells managed to cast only oblique light on the real problem—which was essentially moral.

When in the same period he did firmly grasp the moral aspects of
a part of the woman question, however, his imagination flamed suddenly with a blaze of illumination which revealed depths of significance more profound than any he had previously known. He had
served his apprenticeship and learned the art of the novel. Now,
when a fine illumination came, he was ready to produce his first major novel, *A Modern Instance.*

Sometime before the summer of 1876, Howells attended a performance of Euripides' *Medea* in Boston. Naturally, he was moved
by it, but in this case moved in that mysterious way which consti-
tutes the "germ" of an artistic creation. As he walked out of the
theater, unbidden combinations of earlier thought, newspaper accounts of what was then equivalent to present-day Reno, and the
implications of the esthetic experience from which he was just
emerging fell unexpectedly into pattern. "I said to myself," he told
a reporter many years later, " 'This is an Indiana divorce case,' . . .
and the novel was born." He talked about it as a new *Medea,* and
even suggested that as a possible title while struggling to find the
right one just before publication. The happy and robust summer
before he took on the Hayes biography he worked on his idea. But
it was not until after his break with the *Atlantic* that he felt free
to give his "New Medea" the concentrated energy it required. Then
he worked on it as he had never been able to work before. He went

out to Crawfordsville, Indiana, to see a divorce go through the County Court, stopping off at Columbus, Xenia, and Eureka Mills to renew his contact with Ohio soil on the way. And up to a point he wrote it with the "great pleasure" and "sharp interest" of a man on the threshold of fresh creative powers. Therefore, the book became his greatest favorite until *A Hazard of New Fortunes* came along, and it always kept a high place in his affections.

The limitation on his pleasure, which resulted in the principal limitation on the greatness of his achievement, came from the fact that, at the very climax of his experience in creating this novel, he fell sick. He was dangerously ill with "a fever" for a month, and spent, as he told John Hay, "seven endless weeks" in bed, emerging "only two or three years older than I was four months ago." The tragedy of such a thing happening at a crucial point in the creation of a major work by an artist in the first flush of his finest powers is obvious. It was compounded by the fact that his story had begun to appear in *The Century Magazine* while he was in bed, and there was no time for a recuperative vacation before he had to pick it up with shaking hands and get his revisions done and his fable finished off. "I find that every mental effort costs about twice as much as it used, and the result seems to lack texture," he confessed to Twain. To his father he wrote at the onset of his fever: "It's the result of long worry and sleeplessness from overwork . . ."—normal enough tensions in a man doing the best he knows how with a major artistic enterprise. If he was correct in his diagnosis, he had probably run again into that psychic boundary to the expenditure of energy which had made itself evident toward the end of his Venetian period. No one now can really tell anything except that it was a long and critical sickness, that it drove the Howellses back into Boston for a few months, forever ending their Belmont stay, and that its effect was to damage the ending of *A Modern Instance*.

That flaw in the novel was essentially an artistic failure—in fully and clearly *presenting* the final states of being at which the main characters arrive—linked with an intellectual failure to *think through* to their last conclusions the ideas for which the main body of the novel's drama stood. That flaw prevents the work from achieving the true greatness it so nearly missed. Yet many elements of greatness are there: a potent illusion of personalities, settings, and action, achieved by fine artistry in the handling of symbols, tone, atmosphere, dialog, and the textures of description and style.

There is expert penetration to the abstract significance of social custom, moral condition, moral choice, and their effects on fate and character, and to the sense of a profound movement of cultural change revealed in the lives of people who bear it in their minds and bodies. These things are handled naturally as well as perceptively, communicated through visions of the postures and gestures of characters or, often, by means of irony. Finally, the major mystery of literary art is present almost everywhere: this illusion and these ideas are fused. They can only be known together as the wholeness of the experience induced within a reader's imagination by the words he sees on the page. The trouble is that at last the experience of a satisfying form into which that act of the imagination can shape itself is frustrated by the deficiencies of the ending.

As befits the work of a pioneering realist, the plot outline or "fable" of *A Modern Instance* is starkly simple and antiromantic. It revolves about Marcia Gaylord, a beautiful girl from the small town of Equity, Maine—a place carefully studied from Jefferson, Ohio, and Brattleboro, Vermont. Marcia, the new Medea, is a lushly emotional creature whom the decay of up-country religion into arid free thought (embodied in tough old Squire Gaylord, her father) has left with no resources of civilization to discipline or channel her passions. So that when she meets a self-centered newspaper editor named Bartley Hubbard (in some ways studied from William Dean Howells), she has defenses neither against her alternating gusts of love and jealousy nor against the cynical skill with which Bartley can play on those passions to inflate his own ego. The first phase of the fable, much given to dramatizing the cultural bankruptcy of Equity, tells how the dubious love of Marcia and Bartley runs a very rough course until they elope away, marry in haste, and move to Boston.

At this point, where in the traditional romance troubled love has come safely home to the haven of marriage and the tale is done, the realist's modern instance is only well begun. For, he is concerned to see whether irresponsible passion and amoral egotism can live happily ever after. And he is also anxious to see if "civilized" Boston—whether Proper or commercial—has resources to offer which can help the Hubbards make a go of their marriage and their lives. The second phase of the novel consists of a series of test experiences —most of them ending in failure—in which both Marcia and Bartley fail to cope with their problems. Marcia, exposed to the influences of Proper Boston through old Harvard friends of Bartley's, finds them unable to communicate any vital spark of civilization to her. They can make her yearn to be like them, but they are themselves too far from the creative sources of their own tradition. They are living in the afterglow of a genteel tradition and are powerless to give her anything real. Bartley, daily exposed as a smart-aleck newspaperman to business Boston, disintegrates and degenerates morally at a shocking rate. Ultimately, Marcia's revulsion from his rascality coincides with a flareup of her jealousy and with ego-lacerating business defeats over sharp practice by Bartley. Therefore, he runs away, has his pocket picked while meditating a return from Cleveland, and "nothing remained for him but the ruin he had chosen."

Up to the point at which the second phase closes (Chapter XXXI) and the third begins (Chapter XXXII), *A Modern Instance* is a powerfully dramatized novel, packed with insights and artistically skillful well past the point of relative perfection required of novelistic greatness. Had Howells not recovered from his illness, he would have left behind a truncated masterpiece. For, it must have been at just about that point—with Bartley ruined and Marcia deserted—that he fell ill of worry and overwork. He wrote Twain that he had finished 1466 of his little manuscript pages when he came down with his fever and had three or four hundred to go. Working backward proportionately from the end of *A Modern Instance* at page 514, one comes out somewhere between the middle of Chapter XXXI and the beginning of XXXII as the point of the break. Howells' known dissatisfaction with the ending, together with the really unsatisfying nature of that third phase of the novel, add up to the probability that his breakdown did occur there.

The great weakness in this last part of the novel is its tendency to wander, to refuse to come up to the point. Howells' technical problem was with time. Marcia could not simply go to Indiana as a modern movie star might to Nevada. It must be Bartley who sought the divorce, and that underhandedly, before the avenging fury of the new Medea could be unleashed and the climactic divorce scene staged. Subconsciously, Howells was probably also tempted to maneuver around in an effort to ease his way toward the painful fact with which he was determined to end his novel. He largely wasted four chapters in exploring the lives of his Proper Bostonians, sending poor crippled Ben Halleck off to South America in penance for his silent love of Marcia, letting a stuffy lawyer named Atherton debate the moral problems of the book in fruitless Swedenborgian meanders, and briefly summarizing the romance and marriage of Atherton with Clara Kingsbury, a fluttery Junior League type. Finally, the editors of *The Century* rebelled and put pressure on him to get it over with. And then, in two of the finest chapters Howells ever wrote, he exploited his Indiana trip in a hard-hitting set of Midwestern scenes and a climactic, almost melodramatic, court performance by Squire Gaylord. Then he closed his novel out with a workmanlike bit of anticlimax.

The theme of divorce was a daring one for a serious novelist with an important public reputation in that day. The word was taboo in many a family circle and handled only with opprobrium in most pulpits and at most respectable dinner tables. Divorced people, especially grass widows, customarily suffered from social sanctions. Howells therefore had the advantages of a sensational topic—and ran the risk of alienating his audience right at the outset of his new career. Yet the novel had been conceived of as a divorce study from the start, and he was not afraid of the theme or his ability to bring it off; for he could easily have abandoned it any time between 1876 and 1881. On the other hand, it seems probable that his breakdown in midcourse was, like the illnesses of his late adolescence, somehow psychosomatic. He could not live, in direct vital contact at the imaginative core of his psyche, with the profound suffering of Marcia or the sinful self-destruction of Bartley—and that fact accounts for *A Modern Instance*'s lapse from greatness: not fear of the world so much as inability to bear the stress of self.

Yet the very great strengths of Howells' novel never had much to do with what was once sensational about his theme. Robert Louis Stevenson, who furiously broke off a promising friendship with Howells after reading *A Modern Instance*—because Stevenson had just married a divorced woman—would have been better advised to read the book carefully. For, as Horace E. Scudder, whose contemporaneous review is still the best critique of the novel in print, said, "It would be unjust to regard *A Modern Instance* as a tract against the divorce laws . . . it is a demonstration of a state of society of which the divorce laws are the index."

Howells had great trouble naming his "New Medea." His usual method of finding a title was to make out the longest list he could (for *The Son of Royal Langbrith* he had twenty) of acceptable names and send them to the publisher as suggestions, later thrashing the question out with an editor. A favorite way of finding titles was from a Shakespeare quotation, using a concordance if necessary. Along with *The New Medea*, Howells proposed seven other titles to Gilder for this novel, without seeming to ring the bell. Gilder's best try was *Marcia: A Modern Tragedy*. Then, at the last possible moment, the phrase about the fat, pretentious justice of *As You Like It*, "full of wise saws and modern instances," drifted into Howells' mind, and he telegraphed his title to Gilder. There was a typical self-deprecating irony in the Shakespearian allusion, and yet Howells also meant his novel seriously as a modern instance, as a means for earnest exploration of the moral condition (and its cultural underpinnings) of his time.

It is, says Professor Lionel Trilling, "upon the degree and quality of moral integrity that all esthetic considerations of the novel depend." And judged on these terms, *A Modern Instance* is entitled to high rank. Inescapably a moralist, Howells was also a realist. Therefore, he incarnated his moral problems in his characters, and he achieved moral intensity through the tight drama, carried by the vehicle of his art's illusion of life and of his characters' relationships—with their inward selves, with each other, and with their environment. He had, quite suddenly, been struck by a new vision of the familiar conventional-unconventional conflict. Here was a new *Medea*, a tale of sin and tragedy. Looked at from that angle of vision, the bloom of Jeffersonian innocence and purity of heart are gone from the "unconventional" person and her environment. Marcia has grown up with "no principles, no traditions" in Equity—where, after the death of rural religion, the withering of New England village culture, there is neither equity nor any of the idealistic promise of the American small town left. "Squire" Gaylord, her father, is the gnarled, arid chief of a people really ruled by vulgarity, triviality, and backbiting.

Therefore, she has no adequate resources either for controlling her own passions or for coping with Bartley Hubbard—who is smart, stylish, somewhat handsome, but with "no more moral nature than a baseball." In Marcia's eyes, Bartley has the glamor of the "conventional" man. He comes from the outside. He has been educated at Harvard. But he is something very different from Miles Arbuton. In an urbanizing and business-minded world and at class-conscious Harvard, Bartley has really been "educated" in snobbery and corruption, confirmed in vanity, self-indulgence, and cynicism. In Swedenborgian terms, he is swiftly making himself into an agent of hell. By the time blind pride and passion in Marcia combine with self-pity and malice in Bartley to make them elope, Howells' study has moved through and beyond simple considerations of morals and moral psychology. The ensuing study of marriage is subtle, at points profound, and therefore valuable in itself, but Howells has moved beyond that, too. He turns his novel into a uniquely early imaginative exploration of the rising cultural obsolescence of New England and so, by extension, of the modern world. For having once joined to begin their descent toward tragedy, the Hubbards can find nothing in that world to stay their doom.

The standing American clichés about Boston dictated that there Marcia and Bartley should find the resources of religion, ideality, and civilization which would save them, vindicate the romantic conventions about love's security in marriage, and make them able to live happily ever after. The one viable reality they find there, however, is further corruption. The hustling, money-minded, commercial town with its vulgar, dishonest journalism is perfectly designed to complete Bartley's ruin. And the Proper Bostonians they meet are helpless, their civilization crippled by uncertainty and irrelevance and fading fast into the obsolescence of a genteel tradition. Some, like the Hallecks, are kind, others are snobbish; they are all dim. And in that, precisely, lies the true tragedy of *A Modern Instance*. Bartley dies with his boots on in Whited Sepulchre, Arizona, unable at last to outrun the bullet of an avenging victim of his tricky pen. Marcia returns to Equity, shrinking and withering to the acrid hardness of her father and her town. Sin and suffering, death, destruction, and life-in-death are the penalties visited upon passion and self-love. An Indiana divorce case is a good modern instance of this truth; but it also instances the much more shocking fact that modern life nowhere offers the vital resources to save the Hubbards from themselves or each other.

Just why, in his waverings toward the end of the book, Howells chose to make Ben Halleck, the best and most Christian of the Bostonians, have to suffer the tongue-lashings of his icily Swedenborgian friend Atherton is not clear. What is clear is that Atherton should not be taken as a *raisonneur*, as Howells' moral spokesman, in his stratospheric condemnations of everybody else. Howells was too devoted a realist to use such a device; he believed too thoroughly in unmoralized morality, in not sermonizing. And, whatever his not wholly expressed intention for Halleck and Halleck-Atherton, it is most significant that even the previously cocksure Atherton is reduced to agnostic doubt by the tragic events he is forced to contemplate and in the end is driven to utter the last, despairing words of the book: "Ah, I don't know ! I don't know !"

Much can be learned about the significance of *A Modern Instance* and about Howells' new mastery of his realistic art by a quick examination of his use of symbols in this his first major novel. For the most part these are not easily noticeable. They are quiet, never protruding from the flow of narrative and dialog, never held up for display. Only the reader who takes care to miss nothing is likely to notice that they are symbols. One reason for this is that, unlike the symbols of a Hawthorne or Melville, these have no referents outside the immediate field of the novel. They do not point to abstractions of general validity or significance. They function only to give heightened imaginative power to the particular work. They are covert and serviceable, the symbols of a realist.

Typical of Marcia as a passionate woman is the fact that at moments of stress she blushes, or flushes, with striking color: "the rich jacqueminot-red flamed into her cheeks and burnt there a steady blaze to the end." It is this force, uncontrolled, that makes her Bartley's victim. And that fact is symbolized at Bartley's several moments of victory, when he has "got around" her, by his pinning her arms in an apparent hug of affection and holding her, helpless, while he laughs and laughs, "till it seemed he would never end." When the marriage has disintegrated, however, all this is changed. Marcia's face is drained white, and she will not let Bartley touch her.

A more subtle key to their relationship is suggested in a series of images Howells probably got from Swedenborg, whose mystic visions often record the foul effluvia generated by the wicked. Especially when Bartley's cynicism is becoming confirmed in the early parts of the book, his thought is associated with smoke, coal gas, foul "vapors." When he sits deciding to salve a wounded ego in the balm of Marcia's pathetically undisguised passion for him, he is forced to break off his meditation because "the acrid little jets of smoke which escaped from the joints of his stove from time to time annoyed him; he shut his portfolio at last, and went out to walk." At the same time, one of the tokens of Marcia's emotionality is her inability to catch her breath. Under stress she pants, she gasps for air; and this is, of course, not what Bartley can supply. These are blended triumphantly in the short Chapter XIII, where Bartley takes Marcia to see *The Colleen Bawn* on their honeymoon in Boston and finds her abstracted when they get back to their room:

'Bartley looked at her a moment, and then caught her to him and fell a-laughing over her. . . .

"And you thought—you thought" he cried, trying to get his breath,— "you thought you were Eily, and I was Hardress Cregan! Oh, I see, I see!" He went on making a mock and a burlesque of her tragical hallucination till she laughed with him at last. When he put his hand up to turn out the gas, he began his joking afresh. "The real thing for Hardress to do," he said, fumbling for the key, "is to *blow* it out. . . . That finishes off Eily, without troubling Danny Mann. The only drawback is that it finishes off Hardress, too; they're both found suffocated in the morning." '

This is a beautifully executed dramatic (that is, functional) composite symbol and also, of course, an effective evil omen where the romantic cliché demanded doves and roses. It ends the beginning section of the novel perfectly and prepares the way for the explosive but characteristic fight which, at the outset of the second section, embitters both the young marriage and Bartley's only genuine impulse toward honest success and marital generosity.

The middle section of the book, concerned with the downfall of the Hubbards' marriage from innate causes and from the inability of Bostonian civilization to afford them help, reflects these factors in the symbolic features of the two male antagonists—Bartley and Ben Halleck. Bartley, whose apparent success in journalism goes hand-in-hand with deepening selfishness, takes to drink (in a small way) as a sign of self-indulgence and becomes fat—the more immoral, the fatter. Halleck, the utterly civilized man, morally tender and scrupulous, is significantly crippled. He is unable to do anything for the Hubbards—his lending them money and introducing them to Proper Bostonians only compounds their troubles—because it is a streak of romanticism that has saved him from his environmental snobbery and materialism, and the same romanticism makes him fall helplessly in love with Marcia. His limp comes to the fore at every crisis in his relations with Marcia. And at the climax, when Bartley and Marcia have had their final falling out, he takes her back home and thrusts her in, saying, "No man can be your refuge from your husband !" Then, "He turned, and ran crookedly down the street, wavering from side to side in his lameness, and flinging up his arms to save himself from falling as he ran, with a gesture that was like a wild and hopeless appeal."

On the other hand, Halleck was fighting and, at whatever human price, winning a moral battle. He would not give in to his desire to snatch Marcia away from her tragic marriage even though he had to watch it destroy her as a woman and a person. And as Bartley waxed fat and smug—and fatter and smugger yet after his catastrophe—Halleck grew gaunt, frail, and desperate. Still fighting at the end, he is still suffering. This, again, was the realist's demonstration against the cliché of sentimental, respectable morality, but it appears in passing and is never spotlighted or editorialized.

III

A Modern Instance made Howells an openly controversial figure— but in the good sense that people felt something new and strong in it and reacted strongly for or against its author. Gilder at the *Century* was delighted at the celebrity—and the audience—which the novel drew. It sold well, for the period, in book form, and lent Howells a new, larger stature as an American man of letters.

The whole experience of producing it left the author exhausted, but it also emancipated him from all troubles but those of his family circle. And these were such that a trip to Europe seemed practically mandatory. Free of editorial responsibilities, he had at least momentarily satisfied Osgood's expectations. He and his wife had sometimes suffered real pangs of homesickness for Italy. Recurrent European travel, if not extended sojourns there, had become commonplace among their associates. The Howells children had come to an age where they were not only comparatively self-servicing but ready to profit substantially from living abroad. Having left Belmont to rent an apartment at 16 Louisburg Square during Howells' illness, they were free of household ties. And, of course, in Europe Howells could hope for leisure to recuperate, for isolation in which to get *A Woman's Reason* done, and could count on getting fresh literary materials, if only for another travel book.

There was another, more distressing, reason for the appeal of a trip abroad. For all the abounding love and close fellowship of the family circle, Winifred Howells, tall, sensitive, gifted, and sixteen years old, was showing symptoms of what seemed to Howells painfully like the troubles of his own adolescence. In the fall of 1880 she had been set to exercising in a gymnasium by way of therapy. When that failed to cure her, and other symptoms appeared, she was put to bed in the "rest cure" which Dr. S. Weir Mitchell in Philadelphia had been making famous. At last, in the spring of 1882, she seemed quite herself again, ready and able to make the best of the year abroad which doctors also often prescribed for such maladies. In July, therefore, the whole family went up to Canada to visit William Cooper Howells and the Fréchettes, and then sailed for England from beloved Quebec, to be gone a year.

For the Howellses to arrive in England in the summer of 1882 was, however briefly, to renew the good great time. Winifred felt better almost at once. And London seemed swarming with cordial American friends. Lowell was American Ambassador—and owed the fact largely to Howells. Henry James was overjoyed to see them and took a large, paternal interest in getting them housed and comfortably settled into London life. Howells, James, Osgood, Aldrich, John Hay, Clarence King, the famous writer-explorer-geologist, Edwin Booth, Charles Dudley Warner, and Bret Harte all met for dinner—an event which, as Harte observed, would have been extraordinary anywhere in the States—and they formed various shifting, skylarking tourist combinations all about the island during the rest of the summer. Delightful as that was, in London the Howellses discovered a new, and at least momentarily intoxicating, experience. They'd had their fill of American celebrity, but now they tasted directly for the first time Howells' foreign, his international fame. And for an American of the Gilded Age there was no foreign acclaim to compare with that of Britain.

The Howells of the Experimental Period had gone over exceedingly well with English readers, from *Venetian Life* through *The Lady of the Aroostook*. He was to keep a substantial British audience at least through the 1890's, though his popularity with the transatlantic "literary public" began to fade as soon as the trend to serious ideas in his fiction became evident. In 1882, however, his British popularity was at its height. Oscar Wilde was touring America, ostentatiously praising Howells and James to the reporters of one city after another. Howells' books had not only been pirated in Britain but were now being brought out both in cheap paperbacks and in an attractive uniform set by the Edinburgh publisher David Douglas, who paid Howells a royalty. Herbert Spencer, Mrs. Gladstone, and even, as it transpired the next year, Queen Victoria's daughter, the Crown Princess of Germany, were among his devoted readers. According to Professor Clarence Gohdes' figures, Howells between 1880 and 1900 had forty-five British editions or issues of his books, being surpassed only by Hawthorne, Mark Twain, and Lowell among American writers.

Seeking out the new American celebrity, London literary, artistic, and social lights found him, as the minor critic (not then Sir) Edmund Gosse put it, "affable, gentle, and exquisitely responsive," filled with a special charm of humor, "an aëry playfulness, a sort of roguishness. . . ." He was liked so well, in fact, that he could get little or no writing done for the press of invitations. He ducked out of London in mid-September to take up residence in Switzerland for a few months, determined to finish *A Woman's Reason* at last. And it was while he was living and working quietly in Villeneuve that a literary time bomb he had all innocently planted before he left Boston burst with a roar and cloud of dust which permanently altered his relations with literary England and in effect set him on the way to becoming a champion of doctrinaire realism.

With the death of Dr. Holland and Howells' leaving the *Atlantic,* the stage had been set for the able team of Roswell Smith as publisher and Richard Watson Gilder as editor to snatch the leading position among American magazines for the *Century.* And this they proceeded to do by more or less cornering the output of James, Twain, and Howells in the early and mid eighties. To publicize this fact, perhaps even to gloat a little, Gilder commissioned Perry (letting Howells choose his man) to write an illustrated article on Howells for the March *Century,* and then had Howells leave behind him essays on Twain and James. There is no doubt that these estimates were meant to be favorable—Gilder was careful to see that his critic in each case was favorably predisposed—but they were also meant to be, and in fact were, serious critical valuations, weighing pro and con, by reputable literary critics. Perry's was the best and most judicial study of Howells' career which had yet appeared. Howells' paper on Twain was an earnest plea for public recognition of his friend's true literary genius, again the best, if not the only, piece of serious literary criticism on Twain then in print. His essay on "Henry James, Jr." was equally sober and sincere. He had so little notion of being sensational or other than merely fair and factual with it, that when it turned out to be a bombshell he had to write to Gosse for a copy of the November *Century* to see what in the world he could possibly have said to stir up so much fuss. It is a most significant indicator of how unconsciously radical his literary principles had become that he was so surprised at the reaction to his matter-of-fact statement of them.

It may well be, in fact, that it was his very sobriety, his cool matter-of-factness, that so unsettled his attackers—though there were probably additional reasons for their fury. What Howells had to say would nowadays be accepted as literary commonplace, as indeed it was long before his death. All he said was that there was then a new movement afoot in the writing of the novel, that it was Continental rather than English, that it had introduced new principles of artistic responsibility and higher standards of artistic skill into the production of the novel, that Henry James had become the finest master of the new method then writing in English, and that his artistic achievement in the novel therefore made the artistry of Scott, Dickens, and Thackeray seem crude and obsolete. The reaction of the British newspapers and then of the mighty, man-eating *Quarterlies* was such that Howells might just as well have committed a public nuisance in the Poet's Corner.

As William Archer said in the *Illustrated London News* almost ten years later, "The habitual insolence with which Mr. W. D. Howells is treated by a certain school of English writers was for long a marvel to me. I could see nothing in his work, whether imaginative or critical, to place him without the pale of humanity." Andrew Lang, the fairy tale expert, himself one of the worst offenders, confessed in 1895 that Howells had been essentially right but "was met by yells and cat-calls" in the British press. Gosse, alarmed at the first newspaper reaction to the British edition of the *Century*, wrote Howells and then put an unauthorized promise in the *Athenaeum* that Howells would amplify and explain away his remarks—a promise never kept simply because when Howells reviewed what he had written he saw no reason to alter it. And in January the event Gosse had apparently feared—perhaps he had heard rumors of its coming—happened. The two great old baresarker *Quarterlies* of British literary warfare stripped down for action and went after Howells.

Somebody named Titus Munson Coan anonymously wrote a distorted and personal attack, entitled "American Literature in Eng-

land," for *Blackwood's*. Howells had, he intimated, written to prove
that he himself was a finer artist than the best of English novelists
(Thackeray). Therefore, the exquisite courtesy and hospitality with
which American writers had hitherto been treated in Britain must
no longer shield him from justice. Then he proceeded to mete out
justice in a series of snide and supercilious analyses of Howells'
books and of the man behind them. Coan's opposite number in the
Quarterly Review has remained anonymous, though his style and
"logic" suggest Andrew Lang. With greater literary effectiveness
than Coan, this reviewer devoted himself more directly to the defense of the romance and to that inverted chauvinism so popular
with nineteenth-century European critics which held that what was
wanted from American literature was the truly American—i.e.,
Indian—romance, not feebly imitative stories about ordinary civilized people. Howells and James, "the Transatlantic aesthetic reformers," he says, are simply "dull unspeakably dull"—nothing,
after all, but a "select circle of *puffistes littéraires.*" They are far
inferior to Cooper, Brockden Brown, and Harte, to say nothing of
demigods like Dickens and Thackeray. Nobody reads them in
America, and they have hitherto been supported only by groups of
deluded British readers. This last act of insolence (Howells' article) has made it necessary to call a halt. Therefore, he hopes he
has made "clear the distinction . . . between the real [romantic-
picturesque] and the spurious [realistic-psychological] American
novel."

The effect of this and its vengeful reverberations both in England
and America (where the Boston *Transcript* transcribed the *Quarterly Review,* for instance) was to wound but not dismay Howells.
He understood that national arrogance, startled romanticism, jealousy over the international fame of "Howells-and-James," and
probably personalities played their parts, that only some Englishmen
and not all were in cabal against him. He was sorry to have hurt
James rather than have helped as he intended. With his earlier and
partly inherited suspicions of Albion, he could not have been much
surprised. It must have been a relief to find that Gilder was delighted by the combined roar of fame and notoriety caused by the
simultaneous appearance of *A Modern Instance* and the James article in the *Century*. James and his other friends stood by him
staunchly, and Curtis devoted an issue of his prestigious "Editor's

Easy Chair" in *Harper's* (also published in England) to a firm paternal spanking of the *Quarterly Review.*

Yet, there arose a school of anti-Howells prejudice in England, much of it based on the Coan type of mean misrepresentation of Howells' words and motives. In a long stretch of time after 1882, in fact, there seems to have been only one candid effort—by J. M. Robertson in the *Westminster Review* in 1884—to understand what Howells was saying and to evaluate it rationally. In the end, however, the net effect on British thinking was salutary. Howells' James article, followed by his later "Editor's Study" pieces in *Harper's,* played a decisive role in stimulating British novelists to think theoretically about their craft in the 1880's and early nineties as they had perhaps never done before. Howells himself was forced by the outcry against ideas he had quietly taken for granted to accept more boldly the fact that he had become a literary radical and that the need to formulate his creed and fight for it might soon be imperative.

For the time being, however, he was content to go quietly about the job of cultivating his European refresher course. Somewhat to his astonishment, his experience proved disenchanting. The old, golden glamor of Italy was gone. He could find grace and esthetic solace in Florence; but amid the squalor and hopelessness of the people—and even in the face of the Italian past with its awful histories of bloodshed and betrayal—he experienced dismay and disillusion, as much with his younger self as with Italy. At any rate, Henry James's question as to whether an American novelist did not have to live abroad and deal with international society, a question which had remained in abeyance with Howells during his years of magazine service, was now definitely answered. America was his place.

He worked in the chill of a Florentine winter and wandered about gathering materials for what became *Tuscan Cities,* another travel book, suffering from the brash dependency of the young illustrator, Joseph Pennell, whom Gilder sent him. Pennell, who seems to have reacted against Howells as against a substitute father (Howells had to bail him out of trouble several times) took his revenge in noting that Florentines called the great man "Wowsley." Winifred had a relapse in Florence but was better in Venice, where ten-year-old Mildred produced the child's reactions to Venetian painting which Osgood soon published as *A Little Girl Among the Old Masters*. In June the Howellses returned to London, where Lowell saw to it that he was cordially introduced about London society. He went out to Hay to look up his father's birthplace and the plain Welsh origins of the "Quaker Howellses," and, in considerable relief at the last, sailed for Quebec on the fifth of July.

IV

Returning from his year abroad, Howells rented a house again in Louisburg Square, number four this time, and thus began the relatively brief period in which he was ever truly a Bostonian. His residence for a year in Louisburg Square, in a special way the heart both of Brahmin and Proper Boston, was symbolic, however. For he was now taking status as the representative figure of what had hitherto been very rare in the United States—the genuinely professional American man of letters. All too often American authors had been truants from other professions, or inspired amateurs. In Howells' generation, truly professional writers came into their own, and Howells became the man toward whom youngsters coming up could look as the image of success. He was the more welcome in Boston because the generations of native authors were thinning out. The time had all too clearly gone when a meeting of the Saturday Club brought a majority of the nation's literary stars together at the Parker House. Even more disconcerting was the fact that no young New Englanders seemed rising to the stature of Emerson, Hawthorne, Holmes, or Lowell.

Therefore, public Boston was quite ready to take Howells in as "the chief lineal heir and successor to the genius and distinction of the great New England group. . . ." He got along happily with intellectual and reforming Boston, with men like Edward Everett Hale, for instance, and of course with literary and Fourth Estate Boston, as his club memberships and his primal presidency of the Tavern Club indicate. But Proper Boston remained a problem. Howells' social charm and geniality covered insecurities stemming from his impecunious, obscure background, which made him sensitive to the snubbings Proper Boston apparently could not help administering. He had neither the toughness nor the competitive drive which had carried Dr. Holmes to the higher reaches of Society. And so he tended to maintain his independence, appearing where he felt at home "a genial, downright, matter of fact, and withal satirical person—just now in the very fullest possession of his means, writing and talking with the utmost neatness, without the slightest effort," as a visiting Englishman saw him. Or, as in the eyes of young Henry Cabot Lodge, "He had a very quiet and gentle manner, coupled with a great deal of dry humor, and very strong and definite opinions on many subjects . . . marked radical tendencies which I found most interesting and suggestive." Where he did not feel at home, he had always the well-trained resource of his youth—strategic retreat into quietude and irony.

The reasons why he did not retreat physically from Boston earlier than he did were various. There was, after all, no much better place to go (though he proposed to Twain in 1884 that they both move to Washington). Most of his best friends still lived in the vicinity, and interesting young men began to group around him. His business connection with Osgood centered in Boston. There was the possibility that if Boston life were given a fair trial it might turn out well—and his work was so mobile that temporary escape was easy. Most important of all, however, seems to have been the determination of Mrs. Howells that their contacts and prestige should be exploited for the children's benefit. They must belong to the society to which their name and good rearing gave them natural access. Most immediately, Winifred must be prepared for her debut in Boston.

Consequently, in August of 1884 Howells bought a house at 302 Beacon Street, two doors away from Dr. Holmes, and had it renovated to suit the family taste. And so he moved once more into a "permanent" home and entered upon life as a Boston man. As a journalist friend saw it, his house now was "plain and wide, of red brick, three stories and a mansard. . . . There is a little reception-room at the left of the hall, and the dining-room is on the same floor. You mount a flight of stairs, and come to the library and study, at the back, and the parlor in front . . . what a flood of light in this study !" The windows were famous for their view of the Back Bay and Charles River basin, and for their command of the sunsets flaming over Cambridge and the water. But visitors noticed something different from the rather pretentious touches of the Belmont study. Now in the flooding, clear daylight there was no bric-a-brac, no fussiness, only a few mementoes, some good painting, and the books and furniture of a working writer.

Though Howells was to do some of his finest writing in this room, he had in the year since his return from Europe probably already finished his creative imagination's gleaning from the trip—another major novel, *Indian Summer*. *The Rise of Silas Lapham* began in the *Century* in November, 1884, eight months ahead of *Indian Summer*'s appearance in the July, 1885 *Harper's* (and so *Lapham*'s book publication in 1885 was dated a year ahead of *Indian Summer*'s), but it is important to an understanding of both novels to recognize that *Indian Summer*, perhaps even begun in Florence, was written first.

The germ of *Indian Summer* was obviously the extended meditation on his own psyche which the experience of returning to Italy forced on Howells. His first coming as a young man had been like gliding into a dream of solace and joy. All the yearnings of a small-town, Midwestern youth for beauty and culture had been satisfied, and the effects of his Italian sojourn had opened the doors of opportunity as wide as his wildest ambition could have hoped. But now, on the other side of achievement, arrived in life, with youth and success behind and beneath him, he had come back to Italy to discover his middle-aged self. It is typical of Howells' moral wisdom and his maturity that, though profoundly moved, perhaps even shocked by his discovery, he found he could accept (with irony) both the youthful self revealed by his new perceptions and the middle-aged self revealed by inference from the act of perceiving his youth.

In the finest, tight-knit Turgenev manner, he took an imaginable figment of himself, named it Theodore Colville, and surrounded it with a few other figures. There are in *Indian Summer*, in fact, only three "round" figures—Colville, Mrs. Bowen, and Imogene Graham —and two "half-round" figures—Effie Bowen and the Rev. Mr. Waters—who have important roles as "reflectors" to the main characters of insights about themselves. The rest of the characters are so "flat," and indeed peripheral to the picture, as almost to lack existence.

As in most of Howells' best work, this extreme concentration on characters is matched by the brevity and simplicity of the narrative fable. Colville is, in one way, exactly what Howells might have become had he gone back to Columbus and the *Ohio State Journal*. He is the journalistically successful editor of the Des Vaches, Indiana, *Democrat-Republican* who has sold out his paper in disgust after having been tempted to run for political office on a reforming impulse and been trounced. Now he has returned to Florence, where in youth he had dreamed of becoming an architectural historian in the mode of Ruskin, attempting to revive again the esthetic soul of his youth. In another way, also, Colville reflects something out of Howells' past. In Florence in his twenties, Colville had thought himself utterly in love and then been thrown over by his lady. He has lived a bachelor ever since, nursing in Ik Marvellian sentimental melancholy the embers of his "tragic" passion. In Howells' Columbus years, and even before, he had cherished the dream image of a melancholy jiltee, a sensitive plant wounded by cruel love, and had planned a romance—which got no further than a sketch published in 1861—featuring this Byron-Marvel hero and his sufferings. Now, in Colville, he saw this hero very differently.

Once in Florence and struggling with the problems of middle age seeing its youth in the past and then seeing itself as middle age reflected in the mirror of youth, Colville runs into two women who symbolize his thoughts. On the Ponte Vecchio he encounters Mrs. Bowen, a widow his own age, who had been his friend in the old days and the confidante of the girl he loved—and who, indeed, had probably been the girl he should have loved had he been sensible enough. Mrs. Bowen is traveling with, and chaperoning, a beautiful girl almost young enough to be Colville's daughter—Imogene Graham. The rest is fairly simple, though most effectively bodied forth in Howells' subtle command of speech, Florentine settings, and the social activities of the foreign colony in Florence. Colville and Imogene, each fatuously misled by personal illusions, fall into an engagement which both find intolerable until they finally discover a means (which Howells had almost desperately to invent in order to save their moral characters) of breaking it off. Then Colville, mind cleared by suffering and disillusion, lays siege to Mrs. Bowen, manages to outmaneuver her wounded pride, and triumphantly marries her.

Howells first thought of calling his book "September and May," for the contrast of middle age and youth was the theme on which his imagination originally began to work. And he handled his theme excellently in the drama—inward for each main character, and outward in their relationships with each other—of his novel. The conclusion to which *Indian Summer* works out had then and still has great value as wisdom for Americans who too easily become obsessed with the advantages of resilient tissue and physical euphoria—with youth. Accept your age and act it, says the novel. Contemporaries go best with contemporaries: Howells gets fine comedy out of the agonizing efforts of Colville and Imogene to fit into each other's worlds. Yet middle age is really better than youth, anyhow. As the elderly Rev. Mr. Waters puts it:

'At forty one has still a great part of youth before him—perhaps the richest and sweetest part. By that time the turmoil of ideas and sensations is over; we see clearly and feel consciously. We are in a sort of quiet which we peacefully enjoy. We have enlarged our perspective sufficiently to perceive things in their true proportion and relation; we are no longer tormented with the lurking fear of death, which darkens and embitters our earlier years; we have got into the habit of life; we have often been ailing and we have not died. Then we have time enough behind us to supply us with the materials of reverie and reminiscence; the terrible solitude of inexperience is broken, we have learned to smile at many things besides the fear of death. We ought also to have learned pity and patience. Yes . . . it is a beautiful age.'

As Howells began to work with his triangle of characters and their problems with youth and age, however, he began to see deeper into them and to perceive that, in addition to their ideas and emotions, the most important thing about them was their illusions: illusions about themselves, each other, age, love, duty, and, especially, about the moral psyche. The fact which must be seen before *Indian Summer*'s major importance—its profound moral and psychological insight—can be grasped is the fact that the final reconciliation, the "happy ending," is the vehicle for a perfect irony. Where the ending of *A Modern Instance* is flawed, that of *Indian Summer* is a triumph; and that makes it perhaps the most technically perfect of Howells' novels.

Given the ending, the entire action of the novel operates satirically to expose the romanticistic follies, the *igni fatui*, of the characters, to chastise them through suffering and the deflation of pride, and to correct them by leading each figure into a right action. It is true, as has usually been observed, that Colville's sentimentalities about youth, about love, about his emotions, and about his past are exposed as follies. When he can recapture his youth as symbolically bodied forth in lovely and aggressive Imogene (male fantasy to perfection), he finds that he neither wants nor can stand it. He is happier far with mature and civilized Mrs. Bowen. With her he can act his age and enjoy the pooling together of far richer resources of mental life.

Colville's humiliation and enlightenment come earliest, but they by no means exhaust the ironic possibilities of the novel. Each of the women has her salutary disillusionment to complete as well. Next comes Imogene. She has played an essential role in Colville's trouble. She has thrown herself at him, maneuvered him into an engagement, convinced herself and him that she is passionately in love with him. Actually, she is deluded by a romantic fantasy about her duty as a woman to mend his long-broken heart and soothe his ancient pain by casting herself away in a melodramatic act of self-sacrifice. Her discovery, however, is that love and engagements simply are not what the sentimental romancers have made them out. She can only momentarily stand, "flushed and thrilling with the notion of her self-sacrifice." Engagement to Colville is all too peaceable. She laments:

'Oh, what I dread is this smooth tranquility! If our lives could only be stormy and full of cares and anxieties and troubles that I could take on myself, then, I shouldn't be afraid of the future! But I'm afraid they won't be so—no, I'm afraid that they will be easy and quiet and then what shall I do?'

Coming to face up to the realities and to see how she had trapped herself, and Colville, recognizing that the inverted pride of romantic excess really underlies her self-sacrifice, this is the beginning of wisdom for Imogene. As Howells memorialized himself in his notebook, "Imogene shd (*sic*) typify the fatuous egotism of youth. She never imagines Mrs. B. in love." And so Imogene passes out of the book, leaving Mrs. Bowen with her unsolved problems, among them Colville. For Mrs. Bowen has been responsible, and in large measure, for the troubles of both Colville and Imogene. She has understood them both from the start, been in confidential contact with both, and complicated rather than eased their situation by her words and actions. The truth is that she has been infected with grand illusions, with an almost monstrous romantic *hubris*.

In the first place, she has, most mistakenly for an American woman, allowed herself to fall prey to the European idea of her relation to Imogene. She dramatizes herself as the blameless matron, the perfect duenna, antiseptically mounted above the reach of the human emotions to which the girl in charge is subject and from which she must be protected. Along with this goes the mature illusion which is the counter to Colville's fantasy of recapturing his youth. The mature person who knows he cannot return to youth may feel immeasurably superior to youth and to the youth illusionist. He may fall into the opposite illusion of possessing perfect understanding, and Mrs. Bowen succumbs to her vision of herself as the perfect strategist, the unmoved mover.

When, therefore, she discovers that she is indeed moved, that she cares for Colville, that it is agony to see him in danger of compounding his earlier folly, that, indeed, she wants him for herself, Mrs. Bowen tries to take refuge in another variation of the same disease of pride as that infecting Imogene. In the name of "sacrificing" herself she absolutely bars them from access to her knowledge of their real situations and conceals her feeling for Colville behind an apparent contempt. Her self-sacrifice is simple, absolute, and intensely egotistical. Only when Colville in his hard-won self-knowledge combines with Effie in her innocent realism to conspire against Mrs. Bowen, can her monstrous logic and pride be broken down. And then she submits to reality only "in the self-contemptuous voice of a woman who falls below her idea of herself."

Howells' notebook reveals how carefully he worked over the problem of that ending. And also shows how his imagination grappled with such problems. He worried the ending about from almost the earliest of his entries: "It must be Effie who brings C. and Mrs. B. together at last, with a burst of grief at C's going away." Settling upon that device was, however, only the beginning of a solution the meaning of which had gradually to be elucidated for the author before he could body it forth in fiction for his reader. First he proposed to himself that "C. and Mrs. Bowen she finds have driven I. into her fever. It must be at this as well as her sense of having been mistaken and humiliated and driven into a full [false?] position which makes her persist so long in refusing him at the end." Then, more fictionally if still somewhat tortuously he could hear them talk:

'C. to Mrs. B. in last talk. "If you thought she was deluding herself in supposing she cared for me, why not tell her?"

"Because I cared for you too. I couldn't." (without a consciousness of being interested that would prevent). This perhaps appeals to C's sense of humor.'

Finally he began to get it more nearly "right" and could hear the voices talking clearly in character:

'Mrs. B. to C. "You made it hard for me to be true to her; you know that I loved you." '

Or again:

' "I saw you didn't love her, and I should have gladly broken it off—for her sake. But for my own sake, that was different." '

And then, almost finally:

' "I despised myself for caring for a man who was in love with me when he was engaged to another. Don't you think I saw it? I tried to make you—and I hated myself for that."

"You didn't have to try hard."

—Mrs. B. and C.'s last talk.'

The ultimate irony, the one Howells probably most enjoyed, was that he was able at once to satisfy his audience's craving for a conventionally happy ending and to preserve his artistic integrity, to give the shallow reader a pleasant surface and still keep the depths of his work true to his best perceptions. He was particularly conscious of such matters as he wrote *Indian Summer*, embedding little barbs for his English critics just below the surface of conversation in the novel by putting ostensibly playful jokes about James and himself in characters' mouths. He enjoyed writing the novel, always remaining fond of it. And perhaps what he most enjoyed was his success at creating what would seem to the ordinary magazine reader a return to the charms of his earlier materials and manner but would have, for the mature and responsible reader, the rewards of rich human insight and moral wisdom which make up the best of Howells. No one, perhaps, ever appreciated that best in *Indian Summer* more than William James: ". . . it has given me about as exquisite a kind of delight as anything I ever read in my life, in the line to which it belongs," he wrote Howells. "How you tread the narrow line of nature's truth so infallibly is more than I can understand. Then the profanity, the humor, the humanity, the morality —the everything ! In short, 'tis cubical, and set it up any way you please, 't will stand."

V

And now as Howells worked he moved a great audience with him. Each new novel became a national event. Once he reminded his father how he had yearned in 1861 to be published in the *Atlantic;* but "now if I were two W.D.H.'s I could not supply the magazines' demand for that writer in England and America," he said. He was becoming a part of the American way of life, in an age when the novel was still the prime resource of domestic cultural life. "When I was a little boy," wrote a nostalgic lover of Howells in 1913, "I used to spend a good deal of time at my grandfather's. There, in the long, cold, quiet evenings of winter, we would play backgammon, we would read aloud, and at ten we would have a collation . . . of cold ham and chicken, cider and mince-pie." And the author most vivid and important to that circle, he remembered was Howells. Hamlin Garland found *The Undiscovered Country* in a frontier store in Osage, Iowa, in 1881 and discovered a new mode in literature. In 1884, when he reached the East, he saw that "all literary Boston was divided into three parts, those who liked [Howells] and read him; those who read him and hated him, and those who just plain hated him."

His next novel, the writing of which may very well have even interpenetrated that of *Indian Summer,* made him still more "controversial." First accepted by Gilder as "The Rise of Silas Needham," *The Rise of Silas Lapham* stirred up a tempest of debate and even abuse when the *Century* began to print it in November, 1884. The Laphams became part of the national consciousness. Out in Indiana, fifteen-year-old Booth Tarkington lay feverishly in wait for the mailman, pounced on the *Century,* devoured the latest installment of *Lapham,* and had to run away to hide his tears when forced to tell his sister that Silas had gotten drunk at the Coreys' dinner. People began to notice that certain rich men looked or acted like Silas Lapham. Tourists in Boston asked to be shown his house. A paint company (unsuccessfully) begged permission to use his name on its product. A Methodist clergyman in Indianapolis was disciplined for daring to preach a sermon about him.

In the light of the eighty years of literary and cultural history since, it requires an act of the historical imagination to see why *Lapham* should have stirred up so much fuss in its time. In larger scale than any of Howells' previous novels, with the same intense moral and cultural penetration as *A Modern Instance* and with much of the technical virtuosity of *Indian Summer,* it is an excellent and important work of fiction. But it has disappeared from its prominence as required reading in the high schools for several reasons— one of them the reduced general literacy of the population, which too seldom requires a high school graduate to have read *any* book all the way through. Its fine evocation of time and place has ceased to have relevance except as social history; and, as is usual with Howells, it takes the mature effort of a good reader to grasp the depths of the novel.

On the surface of *The Rise of Silas Lapham* things seem rather tame. The main plot concerns an up-country farm boy come to Boston as an incipient millionaire from his devoted exploitation of a paint mine on the ancestral farm. In the struggle between his conscience and the immoral requirements of competitive success in the business world of the Gilded Age (the novel's time is 1874), Silas at first succumbs to the strong romanticism of the Business Mind and devours a partner. Ultimately, however, he is able to fight and suffer triumphantly against a series of temptations to save his wealth and business by still shoddier practices. In restoring his conscience he loses his million—and this is the (moral) rise of Silas Lapham, Horatio Alger upside down.

The subplot, yet another variation on the conventional-unconventional conflict, shows Howells' lover's quarrel with Boston-Under-the-Scalpel again. The energetic son of an otherwise decadent Brahmin-Proper Boston family, Tom Corey, comes to work for Lapham. This introduces him to Penelope and Irene Lapham, Silas' daughters, and he falls in love with Penelope. This, in turn, introduces the families, bringing the New Man, the Business Man and his wife, into polite conflict with the Bostonians, and giving new dimensions to the familiar conflict. "Make Lapham vulgar but not sordid," Howells advised his notebook; and again, "Make sure of the fact that the Laphams don't know what to do with their money." Since Irene is blonde and pretty and Penelope dark and bookish, the Laphams make the unBostonian assumption that Tom has come courting the blonde rather than the brain, and this provides Howells with another go at a romanticism he had already hammered in *Indian Summer*—the sentimental feminine quixotism of self-sacrifice.

The Rise of Silas Lapham was a big and a controversial book because it spoke directly to the condition of its time. In creating the first important literary projection of the American business man, his mind and his morality, Howells provided symbols of the greatest importance for minds seeking to grasp the new culture. His picture challenged the comfortable optimisms of the Gospel of Wealth and of Social Darwinism—which made it the more important. While unsettling readers with its challenge to the new, however, the book also made its contribution to the advance of the newness. Its author was openly out to demolish what he regarded as the false emotions and outworn clichés of the obsolescent and irrelevant romanticistic past. "The most fiercely debated question in many clubs," reported Garland, was " 'Are Howells's heroines true to life or are they merely satiric types?' and most of his feminine critics were fiercely indignant over his 'injustice to women.' 'He never depicts a noble woman,' they declared.

" 'Well,' retorted his male admirers, 'he's just as hard on us. He is not concerned with nobly perfect individuals—he is depicting men and women as they are.' "

Indeed, nothing about Howells seems to have stirred up quite as much dust in his own time as his effort to shatter the "chivalric" fiction of woman's helpless nobility and set women free to become simple, equal participants in modern culture. His enemies rejoiced in the chance to express their "positive resentment" of his "libels . . . upon American womanhood"—and mainly on the ground that "there is not a *noble* woman among" all his many feminine characters. It did Howells little good to explain, even when he did so in good humor.

"What have you to say to the charge that you create no noble women?" a reporter asked him.

"This criticism always seems to me extremely comical. I once said to a lady who asked me, 'Why don't you give us a grand, noble, perfect woman?' that I was waiting for the Almighty to begin."

Then he pointed out that, as he saw it, the portraiture of "ideal" characters was artistically "offensive"—"and as far as morality goes I believe that when an artist tries to create an ideal he mixes some truth up with a vast deal of sentimentality and produces something . . . extremely noxious as well as nauseous." But the people who clamored for the ideal females of the sentimental-chivalric tradition ("sappy as maples and flat as the prairies," as Lowell said of Cooper's women) were also the opponents of realism in general. They went on damning Howells' "curiously and indeed exasperatingly inadequate portraiture of American womanhood." Noble American ladies pictured as "only one remove from idiocy . . . silly and flighty"—why, the man was guilty of "treason to American woman !" And even those who sympathized with realism and granted the healthfulness of Howells' criticism were sometimes ap-

palled. J. W. De Forest, who had suffered much from the unwilling-
ness of the public to accept his portraits of women wrote:

'I   admire
. . . your honesty and courage. How dare you speak out your beliefs
as you do? You spare neither manhood nor womanhood, and especially
not the latter, though it furnishes four-fifths of *our* novel-reading public.
It is a wonder that the females of America . . . do not stone you in the
streets.'

Henry James and many others admired the originality and force
of Howells' presentation of "the delicate, nervous, emancipated
young woman begotten of our institutions and our climate, and
equipped with a lovely face and an irritable moral consciousness."
Each in his own way, Howells and James made the American girl
internationally famous. But the impact of Howells' early heroines
and then of "Daisy Millerism" died away and left both men with a
commercially dangerous reaction to avoid as they went about developing maturer phases of their careers. Instead of slacking off his
criticism of American women, however, Howells intensified it, as we
have seen, in *A Modern Instance* and *Indian Summer*. In *The Rise
of Silas Lapham* he brought it one step further. He studied the
marriages of the Laphams and of the Coreys carefully, drawing out
in each case the strengths and weaknesses of the wives to show
what contribution they made to Silas' fall and rise. Even more
carefully he worked over the courtship to reveal the tangle of love,
egotism, feminine logic, and quixotism which contributed so much
unnecessary agony to it.

Profoundly aided by his extraordinary partnership with keen-
witted Elinor Howells, he was fascinated by the feminine psyche and
the (from a male point of view) illogical but often sagacious processes of feminine thought. He believed women to be morally and
esthetically superior to men and very much wanted them, in every
aspect of life, to be stimulated to give the best of their gifts to a
sorrowfully needy world. Bad education and foolish romances encouraged women to be childish, he thought, and he aimed to use his
access to the feminine novel-reading audience to correct that. A
feminist in the best of all senses, he wished to help women become
freer psychologically and intellectually, more honest, more mature,
more realistic, healthier.

What seems to have worried Howells most about women was their susceptibility, when their nervous intuitiveness was childishly undisciplined, to quixotism, especially the quixotism of self-sacrifice. Naturally enough, he took marriage very seriously; he "might almost be called the apostle to the married," said one critic. And he hoped for the emergence of a modern ideal of marriage which would forever displace the ancient notion of Patient Griselda—who nobly triumphed over every evil and spite from her husband by an unutterably sweet and passionately passive endurance. His new ideal would be "that of a sort of Impatient Grizzle, who achieves through a fine, rebellious self-sacrifice all the best results of the old Patient one's subjection. It is the wife who has her will only the better to walk in the husband's way."

The key word, the dangerous word, there was "self-sacrifice." Howells became permanently concerned about that state of "emotional anarchy" in America, as one of his keenest contemporary appreciators put it, in which "an emotion is so sacred a thing that not only no outsider but not even its possessor may presume to undertake its regulation," leaving us thus "a society without an emotional code." From Swedenborg by way of his father, Howells believed that the sacrifice of self to moral right and the good of others was essential. All good came from self-abnegation, all evil from selfishness. But the clarity of his moral vision perceived that, in a state of emotional anarchy, a sentimental quixotism of self-sacrifice was a peculiarly insidious and destructive form of egotism. The roots of this kind of self-abnegation were subjective emotional debauchery and ego-loving pride. Evidently, he thought American women susceptible to that vice, for he portrayed them suffering in its toils and threatening to destroy the lives of others with it repeatedly, and established the Rev. Mr. Sewell in *The Rise of Silas Lapham* apparently mostly for the purpose of preaching against it.

Thus Howells' mind was becoming thoroughly and seriously, not merely literarily, antiromantic. And the freshest part of *The Rise of Silas Lapham*, the criticism of business, showed the effect of that change. Seeking to grasp the psychological meaning of the emergence of the business mind, Howells concluded that it was founded on a new kind of romanticism. "Money," says Bromfield Corey, ". . . is the romance, the poetry of our age. It's the thing that chiefly strikes the imagination." Nothing is clearer about Silas Lapham than the fact that only his business has romance in life for him. Mrs. Lapham charges him bitterly with having made his paint his god, but she, as usual, has only half understood him. His paint business and his success are much realer to Silas than God. Only when he is living and talking paint does Silas truly come alive. There his treasure is and his heart also, and he is even more deeply in need of a cleansing shower of cool, moral realism than the most quixotic of women.

The Rise of Silas Lapham is the testament of a realist who wishes his reader to see directly the moral confusion into which the new times have fallen. He also insists that the reader see critically how false, feeble, or irrelevant are the moral resources of the past, especially when those resources are obsoletely romantic. In doing this he is renewing and extending the insights of *A Modern Instance*. And much as Marcia Gaylord was a kind of Maine Medea, Silas is a businessman Faust. Wealth, and more meaningfully the pride of power in life which comes from money success in the Gilded Age, have poured in on him. By trampling under his partner Rogers, Silas has elevated himself at the opening of the book to a position of sinful pride. Then the question becomes: what shall it profit a man to gain the whole world and lose his own soul? But with it goes the question: what kind of world—American world—was it through which Silas moved to his victory-in-defeat? The moral-spiritual rise of Silas Lapham was a worldly descent from arrogance to doubt to struggle and at last to repentance. There can be little question that Swedenborgian-trained Howells knew from the start what his conclusion was going to be; but the intensities and the implications of some of the insights Howells discovered within his own mind day by day, as he worked out the dramatic presentation of Lapham's rise-fall, shocked him.

Lapham is not really either a comedy or a tragedy—insofar as analogies from the techniques of the drama are useful in understanding it—but a mixed form, what play analysts of Howells' time called a *drame*, a free mingling of the comic and tragic. In one sense *Lapham* is a comedy in that there are striking and sometimes very funny satiric and ironic scenes and moments throughout it. In a different sense it is "comic" like Dante's *Divina Commedia*. It ends well: as Christian faith has always insisted the cosmic drama and the drama of human history will end—in victory for God and goodness; or as the drama of any individual life may end—in the hard-won triumph of grace and conscience over sin. In a striking image Howells failed to transfer from his notebook into the novel, he once envisaged the final situation as analogous to "the young trees growing out of the falling logs in the forest—the new life out of the old. Apply to Lapham's fall." But in other ways *Lapham* is tragic. Like Christianity, it intimates that man's love of his prideful ego, its immunities and power, its aggressiveness and treachery, must lead to destruction. Either it will harry him into disaster, or it must be self-suppressed and humiliated. Even more, Howells' theoretical, Swedenborgian "knowledge" of the self-damnation—the worldliness—of the world became acutely real as it was dramatized in the texture of his novel. Who would have supposed the worlds of Boston—all of them and therefore the contemporary world everywhere—were so undone?

In his book, Silas Lapham moves through a series of morality plays, meeting persons clothed in the realistic texture of commonplace life, all of whom tend to corrupt rather than save him, in all of whom moral deficiencies and cultural inadequacies are organically united. In himself there is Colonel Sellers' irresponsible business romanticism united with what John Woolman called "the spirit of fierceness," the arrogant economic individualism which says: you shall serve and suffer; I shall take, exult, and perhaps enjoy. This was the root of the Business Mind, the essence of the System: Every man for himself, and the devil take the hindmost. Root, hog, or die ! Stronger and fiercer as well as luckier than many, Silas was able to crowd out his rather vague partner, Rogers, and then to know in the face of the predatory Railroad later on what it was like to be under the wheel.

The Lapham daughters and, for much of the time, Mrs. Lapham are so caught in the meshes of female quixotism on the one hand and social competition on the other that they simply obscure Silas' vision and confuse his mind even more. That aside, however, there are two other large movements in this rich book which profoundly reveal the deficiencies of Silas' world. One of these centers on Mrs. Lapham, the other on Bromfield Corey and his family. Taken together in their major implications, these constitute a sweeping criticism of the New England of Howells' day—and therefore of the civilized world.

At first blush Mrs. Lapham might be taken as the moral *raisonneur* of the novel, Howells' spokeswoman. She sees and condemns Silas' treachery to Rogers; she understands and condemns his motives and emotions. She represents the stern Puritan tradition of the Vermont countryside from which the Laphams have come. For a long time she is Silas' conscience, unsparing, caustic, pessimistic. But the country culture from which her Puritan hang-over comes Howells had long seen to be riddled with dry rot. All the Lapham boys had gone West, Silas only returning to the farm for a few years before the War and his exodus to the city. The vitality of cultural relevance is gone from Persis Lapham's morality (no longer rooted in religion) as surely as it was gone from Marcia Gaylord's Equity, Maine, or from the old farms going back to brush in *Private Theatricals*. Consequently, Persis cannot avoid becoming trapped in the sins of conspicuous consumption and yearning to help Silas and her daughters compete with the Coreys. She cannot avoid giving in to the code of respectability and so forcing Silas to be secretive in helping the wife and daughter of his old comrade-at-arms and so betraying both herself and him in flying into a fury of misguided wifely outrage when a malicious note intimates that Silas is really keeping Zerilla as a mistress rather than a typist. Consequently she falters and fails Silas completely when the crisis of his struggle for righteousness comes. In that crisis he is left entirely alone, deserted by the dry-rotted culture of his past as by the wife who embodies it.

The least well-digested part of *Lapham*, indeed, is Howells' vision of slum Boston, given briefly and more or less incidentally in glimpses of Zerilla (Millon) Dewey and her plight. Obviously, Howells' concern for "the other half" was deepening. Silas' refusal to deny help to Zerilla for the sake of respectability and his insistence on taking personal responsibility for keeping her from being lost in the morass of Boston slum life make him morally superior to his wife as well as to the frivolous Lady Bountiful humanitarianism of Clara Kingsbury and her ilk. But it is also clear that Howells himself, though troubled, was not yet ready to come to grips with that problem.

He understood much better how to handle Bromfield Corey, the perfect blend of Brahmin and Proper Boston, who had made a failure of being a painter and a great success of "gentlemaning as a profession." One could take the four houses in *Lapham*—the Vermont farmhouse where Silas begins and ends, the Lapham's vulgar Nankeen Square house, their fine but doomed, architect-built, Beacon Street house, and Bromfield Corey's home—as the organizing centers for an understanding of the esthetic-cultural (as on the whole distinct from the moral-cultural) core of the book. Corey is a gentleman *par excellence*. He is utterly cultivated and all but utterly civilized. He knows how to appreciate the best in Silas, and he has, at least potentially, the resources to teach Silas how to enjoy his wealth through beauty. Corey has the generosity and even the imagination to see where he, his family, and his son really stand in modern society and therefore the magnanimity to encourage Tom to go into business with Silas, even to marry Penelope Lapham if he really wants to. He sees that it is good for Tom, since he honestly can, to throw himself into the mainstream of modern life and restore the living relationship to it which Bromfield's "India Merchant" father had enjoyed and dilettante Bromfield lost. He knows, but cannot himself overcome, his own "sterile elegance."

Bromfield Corey can rise above the snobbish hostility which makes Penelope say, as she drives away with Tom on the way to live in Mexico after her marriage: "I don't think I shall feel strange amongst the Mexicans now." But his condemnation and that of his class is that they can offer Silas no help in his moral warfare. Their elegance is better than his vulgarity, but they and their culture also leave him isolated in his struggle with good and evil.

At the crucial moment in the novel, Silas can still save himself and his wealth if he will connive at a deal cooked up by his old partner Rogers. A pair of rascally Englishmen will buy Silas' Western property, paying a large sum by way of defrauding a wealthy British humanitarian fund, regardless of the fact that the property will shortly be squeezed out of all value by the tyranny of the Great Lacustrine and Polar Railroad. Silas has only to wink. Rogers and the Englishmen will do the dirty work. In two quick, deliberately underwritten scenes of great emotional power and moral implication, Howells then achieves the climax of his novel. Silas has shut the door upon Rogers after Mrs. Lapham has failed him completely:

'His wife called down to him from above as he approached the room again, "Well?"

"I've told him I'd let him know in the morning."

"Want I should come down and talk with you?"

"No," answered Lapham, in the proud bitterness which his isolation brought, "you couldn't do any good." He went in and shut the door, and by and by his wife heard him begin walking up and down; and then the rest of the night she lay awake and listened to him walking up and down. But when the first light whitened the window, the words of the Scripture came into her mind: "And there wrestled a man with him

until the breaking of the day. . . . And he said, Let me go, for the day
breaketh. And he said, I will not let thee go, except thou bless me."

She could not ask him anything when they met, but he raised his dull
eyes after the first silence, and said, "I don't know what I'm going to say
to Rogers."

She could not speak; she did not know what to say, and she saw her
husband, when she followed him with her eyes from the window, drag
heavily toward the corner, where he was to take the horse-car.

He arrived rather later than usual at his office, and he found his
letters already on his table. There was one, long and official-looking,
with a printed letter-heading on the outside, and Lapham had no need
to open it in order to know that it was the offer of the Great Lacustrine &
Polar Railroad for his mills. But he went mechanically through the
verification of his prophetic fear, which was also his sole hope, and then
sat looking blankly at it.

Rogers came promptly at the appointed time, and Lapham handed him
the letter. He must have taken it all in at a glance, and seen the im-
possibility of negotiating any further now, even with victims so pliant
and willing as those Englishmen.

"You've ruined me!" Rogers broke out. "I haven't a cent left in the
world! God help my poor wife!"

He went out, and Lapham remained staring at the door which closed
upon him. This was his reward for standing firm for right and justice
to his own destruction: to feel like a thief and a murderer.'

The Jacob image, so natural to Persis Lapham's Puritan heritage,
functions very richly as a symbol in this context. Jacob, a far from
attractive man, became the father of his people after wrestling all
night with an angel and refusing to let him go "except thou bless
me." Whereupon the angel both blessed him and crippled him for
life. The popular clichés—all too popular in the best-selling fiction
of Howells' day—demanded that chimes of blessing resound in this
world and the next at a deed of moral heroism. Silas' deed is stum-
bling, not dramatically clean-cut, and it is heroic mainly in the consequences he has to bear. No heavenly music warms his lacerated
spirit. He is crippled, and in worldly terms his blessing seems negative. He relinquishes the material gain, the loot, of his sin. He rises
—but only out of the pit—up to the heights of humiliation, left
there to work out the rest of his salvation with the blessing of the
clarified vision his victory has won him. This is the way an agnostic
moralist and literary realist will have us see the world. He has not

written a novel against business, but against a world in the bonds of selfishness. The modern world had left behind such anomalies as feudal classes and slavery, but Howells wished to make it see that it had reclothed the spirit of fierceness in the business mind and in the gospel of wealth. *The Rise of Silas Lapham* remains important to us as one of its age's supremely suggestive aids to the historical imagination in its vivid presentation of the life of a lost era. As drama of the moral imagination, however, it is relevant now, at least as meaningful to an American of the second half of the twentieth century as to one of the nineteenth.

It is fruitless to argue that *Lapham* is or is not the best of Howells' novels. That the question is arguable is high tribute to the excellence of the comparable works, for this one is unchallengeably major. It has endured with great vitality the decades of ignorant and often malicious anti-Howells prejudice, and it may be expected to prosper further in readers' attention now that prejudice has begun to subside. Many of the reasons which favor that expectation were summed up by Hippolyte Taine in recommending the translation of *Lapham* to a French publisher:

'Je l'ai lu en anglais avec le plus grand plaisir et avec beaucoup d'admiration; c'est le meilleur roman écrit par un américain, le plus semblable à ceux de Balzac, le plus profond, et le plus compréhensif. Silas, sa femme et ses deux filles sont des types et nouveaux par nous, très solides et très complets.'

VI

Reactions to *The Rise of Silas Lapham* were mixed, as might be supposed. Various sensitive observers saw at once that this was Howells' best novel yet and were overjoyed. Romanticists showed their acumen by fighting it bitterly, and thus made the author a figure more controversial than ever. And within Howells himself the backlash of his effort to see his novel through as nearly to the bottom as he could triggered off a reaction which altered the entire course of his life, thought, and art.

There had previously been signs of alarm enough at Howells' realism and some of its implications. The little tempest in England had emboldened some romanticists to come out openly against him. Julian Hawthorne, the great romancer's son, praised the "texture" and artistic "fineness" of Howells and James but lamented their susceptibility to science and "the new order of things." They tended to put on "the modest and humble doubter," the "agnostic," and succumb to "discreet and supercilious skepticism," he said. He wished, however, to remind them, in Goethe's terms, that "Art is creative; but Mephistopheles, the spirit that denies, is destructive." Therefore, he called them back—from what he saw as an agnostic interregnum to the old standard of ideality.

But when *Lapham* came out, the romantic-idealists found it time to strip off their kid gloves and go to war with Howells. Interestingly, though perhaps not surprisingly, the two most intemperate assaults came from the *Catholic World* and from the *Andover Review*, the stronghold of Calvinist, evangelical orthodoxy. The anonymous Catholic writer penned a downright polemic. Howells, he said, was a cold and soulless man, a "Puritan" who "despises art" and makes fiction a science, and his novels were "a degradation." The scenes with Zerilla Dewey horrified the reviewer. There Howells, "for hopeless depravity both in author and subject, out-Zolas Zola," he said. After all his pouring out of soul, it must have astonished Howells to be told that his "moral tone" was "so unpleasantly bad." The whole trouble, as the *Catholic World* saw it, was the connection backwards from realism to Darwinism. Howells' turning as realist to "the commonplace," Catholic readers were warned, was a subtly dangerous reductionism: "the progress from man to the apes, from the apes to the worms, from the worms to bacteria, from bacteria to mud. It is the descent to dirt."

That was hard-hitting and could have done little for Howells' sales to whatever Catholic readership he had. But it was, after all, obviously no more honest than sophisticated. Much more dangerous was the extended essay, tough, solid, and lucid, written by a young but distinguished literary critic for the intellectually prestigious *Andover Review*. Hamilton Wright Mabie, a gifted man, took the trouble to estimate Howells accurately and fairly. Most unusually for a neo-romantic opponent, he understood Howells beautifully, knew exactly what he disagreed with and why, and made his points with candor as well as force. Mabie began his review of "A Typical Novel" by recognizing that *Lapham* was Howells' "best and most characteristic work," sensitively, artistically, earnestly done. "As an expression of personal power and as a type of the dominant school of contemporary fiction in this country and in France, whence the special impulse of recent realism has come, this latest work of

a very accomplished and conscientious writer deserves . . . study,"
he said, and proceeded to study it. He saw that Howells had grown
to full stature as an artist and revealed "a deepening movement of
thought" in his work. *Lapham* treats "a stage of social evolution
with which everybody is familiar and in which everybody is interested . . . it is real, it is vital, and it is not without deep significance." He felt that Howells had been able to impart dignity and
consequentiality to his characters without failing in his earlier
humor—altogether, the author was entitled to "very high praise."

Having given Howells all he could, Mabie then made ready to
destroy him. For, in spite of all praiseworthiness, he said, *Lapham*
was "an unsatisfactory story; defective in power, in reality, and in
the vitalizing atmosphere of imagination . . . cold." Then he proceeded to give his reasons for that condemnation. Howells he
thought too detached and analytic. A "subtle skepticism pervades
his work," and there is no "mist of tears" over his eyes, no spon-
taneous "great force" of emotion overflowing his heart as he writes.
Instead, like James, he is "analytic" and tries to understand his
characters "not by insight, the method of imagination, but by observation, the method of science." Mabie objects to realism's social
vulgarity. Instead of giving us the "large, typical characters" of
the old school, realism infringes (on our feelings of respectability,
he means but does not quite say) by bringing us close to "commonplace people; people whom one would positively avoid coming in
contact with in real life." It must, he thinks, be either "a mental
or a moral disease which makes such trivial themes attractive to
men of real talent."

And then having sufficiently stirred up the beasts of Victorian
prejudice in their cages, he prepares to strip away Howells' immunities and invite the Calvinists to throw him naked into the arena.
The important thing about realism is not something esthetic but
something metaphysical: "The new realism is not dissent from a
particular method; it is a fundamental skepticism of the essential
reality of the old ends and subjects of art. . . ." Once upon a time
Realist had meant Idealist. "The older art of the world," said
Mabie, "is based on the conception that life is at bottom a revelation; that human relations of all kinds have spiritual types behind
them; and that the discovery of these universal facts, and the clear,
noble embodiment of them . . . is the office of genius and the end
of art. . . . But modern realism knows nothing of any revelation in

human life; of any spiritual facts of which its facts are significant; of any spiritual laws to which they conform in the unbroken order of the Universe. It does more than ignore these things; it denies them. . . . It is, in a word, practical atheism applied to art."

"Skepticism," "dirt," "poison," "vulgarity," "atheism": these were very dangerous words to have flying about the head of a man whose livelihood depended on popular favor for his pen. Controversy over a public man is good so long as it adds more to his fame than to his notoriety, so long as it makes him interesting rather than odious. There are some men who thrive on controversy and delight in steering it to their own ends. But William Dean Howells was not really that kind of Rooseveltian man. Should he retreat? Knuckle under? Go back to writing *Foregone Conclusion*'s? It wasn't just the name-calling; Mabie had called the turn on him, had pointed the issues clearly and exactly. War had been declared on Howells, and he either had to run or fight. There can be no higher praise of the man than to say that he followed the logic of his development rather than the desire of his wounded psyche and prepared to fight. He kept on advancing, and he declared war himself.

At the same time it is important to recognize that his coming open warfare with the principalities and powers of the later Gilded Age in America was accompanied by a decisive inner conflict which would bring about the last major change, the final act of growth in the development of his mind and personality. Sometime before Howells finished *Lapham*, which he did about the first of March, 1885, he experienced the kind of psychic event for which the Swedenborgians had a peculiar and fitting word—"vastation." As a friend recounted the story more than ten years later, Howells felt set upon by "grave questions . . . compelling attention, refusing to be curtly dismissed. They made their demands—these questions and problems—when Mr. Howells was writing *Silas Lapham*. His affairs prospering, his work marching as well as heart could wish, suddenly, and without apparent cause, the status seemed wholly wrong. His own expression, in speaking with me about that time, was, 'The bottom dropped out.' "

We still use in common American speech that phrase—"the bottom dropped out"—but we have almost forgotten what it graphically meant to an age when many people lived along canals built by rather primitive engineering and were dependent on them. The canal had been one of the most fascinating parts of Howells' boy's town, and he knew all too well what happened when the bottom dropped out. A channel appeared suddenly, a break not in the banks of the canal but in the bottom and undermining the bank. Suddenly, treacherously, the water burst and flooded out of a whole section of the canal between two sets of locks, leaving mud and desolation behind. All travel stopped. Boats caught in the devastated section were stranded in the muck. With the water-pressure gone from their sides, banks, and even the buildings standing on them might collapse and compound the disaster. Every nerve had to be strained to patch the hole and get the water back in the canal before almost irreparable damage followed.

When "the bottom dropped out" for Howells while he was daily confronting in his imagination the drama of *Silas Lapham*, something fateful happened. Since he apparently left no clear account (perhaps could not readily have made one), one can only roughly infer what happened. Certainly, Howells had been experiencing new perturbations of soul in that period. The long agony of watching Winifred pass into permanent invalidism was increased by one turn of the screw every time she rallied and then relapsed a little deeper into a medically mysterious (and apparently misdiagnosed) malady. When Gosse came over from England in 1884, they had long walks and intimate conversations in which Howells, perhaps misguidedly, permitted Gosse to see below the surface into his fears and troubles. As he told Osgood in the spring of 1884, his view of life was becoming increasingly "tragical," and the effect was likely to show up in his work. Perhaps to get literary material, perhaps to test himself, he subjected himself to the experience which had been so shattering in Cincinnati—a night in Police Court. "Perhaps it was because, in my revolt against unreality, I was in the humor to see life whose reality asserts itself every day in the newspapers with indisputable force." It seems not to have shattered him again, but "the sight and the smell" stayed with him for a long time.

Also, he underwent a series of moving, symbolic experiences in his grand, new Beacon Street house. Simply to be there alone, in relative comfort in the huge, empty house on the water's edge in the heat of August made him feel guilty. "How unequally things are divided in this world," he wrote his father. "While these beautiful, airy, wholesome houses are uninhabited, thousands upon thousands of poor creatures are stifling in wretched barracks in the city here, whole families in one room. I wonder that men are so patient with society as they are." And worse things than sunsets over Harvard appeared from time to time outside the wonderful study windows. Once he and Twain saw a woman climbing down the embankment to commit suicide in the water, and rushed out to help prevent her. Then Howells had to stand and argue with her while she "crazily grieved at her rescue" while Twain went for a policeman. Still another time young Owen Wister came to visit Howells and was told:

'I had a sort of religious experience this afternoon. People down there in the alley along the water kept climbing on my back fence to see the rowing; and a policeman was busy making them get off. I sent for him, and thanked him. After he had gone, it came over me, what better right had I than they to sit comfortably in this room when they were out on the fence?'

Whatever else was happening, Howells' conscience was becoming acutely sensitized. The psychic event which occurred to make all this true is essentially unknowable. But one can infer without risking serious error that what it meant was that Howells' old leap of faith, at the threshold of his career, into the religion of healthy-mindedness had been compromised and his more native tendencies to melancholy, pessimism, and religious "exercise" had been uncovered again by the psychic, reflective, and creative as well as objective events he had been passing through. As William James, that best chronicler of psychological events in Howells' generation, put it:

'The method of averting one's attention from evil, and living simply in the light of good is splendid as long as it will work. . . . But it breaks down impotently as soon as melancholy comes; and even though one be quite free from melancholy one's self, there is no doubt that healthy-mindedness is inadequate as a philosophical doctrine, because the evil facts which it refuses positively to account for are a genuine portion of reality; and they may after all be the best key to life's significance, and possibly the only openers of our eyes to the deepest levels of truth.'

It is very likely that James here furnishes us the key to the significance of the fact that "the bottom dropped out" for Howells in the midst of his composing *The Rise of Silas Lapham*. Certainly, this moment of crisis which came at the first full peak of his development marks the end of his unfolding years and the point at which the uniquely significant years of his maturity as a major American artist and man of letters began.

BIBLIOGRAPHICAL NOTES

THE STANDARD REFERENCES ON HOWELLS ARE: DELMAR G. COOKE, *William Dean Howells, A Critical Study,* 1922; Oscar W. Firkins, *William Dean Howells, A Study,* 1924; Mildred Howells, *Life in Letters of William Dean Howells,* 1928; William M. Gibson and George Arms, *A Bibliography of William Dean Howells,* 1948; Clara and Rudolph Kirk, *William Dean Howells, Representative Selections,* 1950; and Everett Carter, *Howells and the Age of Realism,* 1954. Agree or not, admire or cavil, one cannot help being indebted to these books, as to many other studies in and out of print, for large elements in his thinking about the author. For reasons of space and because excellent bibliographies exist, there appear in these notes only references to the debts owed by the author to essential sources of information, and references to the supporting evidence for facts or interpretations which might strike an inquiring reader as calling for documentation. It has not seemed necessary to list the hundreds of other books, or periodical, newspaper, and manuscript items which have been handled in the course of research for this volume.

Chapter One

John James Audubon, *Ornithological Biography,* 1831, I, 31–32.

I

For background on Joseph Howells see William Cooper Howells, *Recollections of Life in Ohio, 1813–40,* 1895; Howells to Bertha Howells, January 15, 1914 (Library of Congress) says nothing was known about the family beyond his father's information. Also: Mildred Howells, *Life in Letters of William Dean Howells,* 1928, 2 vols., hereafter referred to as *Letters;* W. D. Howells, *A Boy's Town,* 1890, and *Years of My Youth* (hereafter *Youth*), 1916; "A Day in Howells' 'Boy's Town,'" *New England Magazine,* May 1907, 289–297. On Welsh names for children, see M. D. Conway to

Howells, October 7, 1863 (Harvard). The Mohawk Howells-John-sons were children of the marriage of a young Mohawk chieftain (and namesake, if not descendant, of Sir William Johnson of Revolutionary fame) and one of W. C. Howells' cousins who had come to Canada from Wales with her sister, the wife of an Anglican clergyman. Cp. Hector Charlesworth, *Candid Chronicles*, 1925, 98–99, and interview with Howells, *New York Times*, February 25, 1912.

II

On William Cooper Howells' life the prime document is his *Recollections*. Also W. D. Howells, "The Country Printer," *Scribners*, May 1893, 551. Excellent background material is in Arthur E. Bestor, *Backwoods Utopias*, 1950. Unfortunately, I have been able to find no file of *The Gleaner* or *The Eclectic Observer and Workingman's Advocate*.

III

On Mary Dean: Lida R. McCabe, "Literary and Social Recollections of William Dean Howells," *Lippincott's*, October 1887, 547; also W. C. Howells' *Recollections*, W. D. Howells' *Youth; Letters*, especially II, 44. Henry Howe, *History of Ohio*, 327, prints a neat sketch, drawn by W. C. Howells himself, of W. D. Howells' Martins Ferry birthplace, torn down around mid-century to make way for railroad tracks. Good general background for this chapter as a whole is in the volumes by Utter and Weisenberger in *History of Ohio*, II and III, 1941; and W. H. Venable, *The Beginnings of Literary Culture in the Ohio Valley*, 1891.

Chapter Two

On the move to Hamilton see *Recollections* and *Youth;* also W. C. Howells to Mrs. Lloyd Dock, March 1, 1894; W. D. Howells to Mira Dock, January 28, 1909 (Library of Congress); on Hamilton in general, Alta H. Heiser, *Hamilton in the Making*, 1941; Cone, *Biographical and Historical Sketches of Hamilton and Its Residents*, 1896; Earhart interview, *New England Magazine* (*supra*).

I

On peach blossoms and crippled man see *A Boy's Town,* 7–9; also Rood, "William Dean Howells, Some Notes of a Literary Acquaintance," *Ladies' Home Journal,* September 1920, 154. Cp. Howells to Bayard Taylor, December 19, 1876 (Cornell).

II

Otherwise undocumented facts about W. D. Howells' Hamilton years are taken from *A Boy's Town, Youth,* or *My Literary Passions,* 1895.

The first W. C. Howells number of the *Hamilton Intelligencer* was Vol. IX, no. 14, February 27, 1840. I have, of course, made full use of the extant files of the *Intelligencer* and *The Retina.*

III

On Cincinnati Swedenborgians see C. D. Smith, "Adam Hurdus and the Swedenborgians," *Ohio State Archeological and Historical Quarterly* (hereafter *OAHQ*), April–June 1944. The record of Howells' baptism by the Rev. Mr. M. M. Carll is in the University of Cincinnati Library.

IV

For description of Will and Joe see Earhart, 291. There the names of many of the boys in *A Boy's Town* are given. Henry Howe, 268, prints a sketch he made of the Hamilton covered bridge about 1841, and says that Joe, then nine, is one of the foreground figures.

Mitchell to Howells, n. d. (Harvard); Howells to Mitchell, April 2, 1891 (S. Weir Mitchell Papers, University of Pennsylvania).

A Boys' Town records Howells' "ague." In *Ohio State Journal* for September 1, 1860, he recalls that John L. Harvey's "The Fever Dream" was "one of the horrible delights of our boyhood." For Victoria's death see *Biographical History of North East Ohio,* 263. On malaria in Ohio in general see Utter, 343.

V

On Ohio antislavery see Weisenberger's volume in *History of Ohio* and especially Annette C. Walsh, "Three Anti-slavery Newspapers," *OAHQ*, April 1922; on the collapse of the Whig Party in Ohio, Roseboom, *History of Ohio*, IV.

VI

Besides the usual autobiographies and *Letters*, sources for the Dayton period are the files of the *Dayton Transcript* (somewhat damaged by the flood of 1914) and *A History of Dayton*, 1889; Curwen, *Sketch of the History of Dayton;* Dowry, *A History of the City of Dayton;* and Steele, *Early Dayton.*

Besides *Conjugial Love*, see Swedenborg, *Heaven and Its Wonders, and Hell*, and the excellent biography by Signe Toksvig, *Emanuel Swedenborg, Scientist and Mystic*, 1948.

VII

For Howells and his mother see especially Howells to Harriet Taylor Upton, March 9, 1910 (Western Reserve Historical Society), only partly reprinted in H. T. Upton, *History of the Western Reserve*, 1910, 577.

Chapter Three

I

The Columbus months in 1851–52 are revealed in the earliest of the manuscript Journals preserved in the Houghton Library, Harvard, a source Howells himself used for relevant sections of *Youth*, flinching a little from these glimpses of his previous self about seventy years after. For materials in this section not in *Youth*, I am indebted to that early Journal.

II

For Howells on the Jefferson Yankees see "The Country Printer," *My Literary Passions*, and *Youth*. For Giddings, Howe, 269; Roseboom, 203. Runaway slave comment is in *Ashtabula Sentinel*, May 25, 1854, 4. For brief general account of the *Sentinel* in the mid-fifties see Cady, "Howells and the *Ashtabula Sentinel*," *OAHQ*, January–March 1944, 39–51.

III

The records of the Howells family's financial transactions in Jefferson may be read in the registers of Wills and of Deeds and Mortgages in the Ashtabula County Court House, Jefferson. Howells adds light in the *Scribner's* article already cited and in *Youth*, which also supplies insights into the tensions with his mother and Joe. But the letter to Mrs. Upton is supported by several in *Letters* and by a number of the family letters at Harvard, which show, incidentally, that Howells contributed continuing and substantial amounts of money to the Jefferson family for many years, not only to his father but to brothers and sisters as well. On poor Henry Howells there are, of course, many troubled letters among the family papers. See especially notations on the back of a photograph at Harvard and *Letters*, I, 111, which give slightly variant accounts of the original accident.

On William Cooper Howells' latter years see W. D. Howells to Dr. Smith, October 3, 1861 (Comly Papers, Ohio); *Biographical History of North East Ohio*, 263; *Cleveland Leader*, May 18 and 24, 1867; Charlesworth, 99; and W. C. Howells to ?, May 2, 1862 (Anthony Papers, N.Y. Public Library). Cp. Howells to W. C. Howells letters at Harvard.

The names of Howells' Jefferson girl friends he gives in *Letters*, II, 251. Special sources on Jefferson include newspaper columns by, but more especially conversations with, Mr. E. C. Lampson, editor of *The Jefferson Gazette and Ashtabula Sentinel*, successor to "J. A. Howells and Co." (see especially *Jefferson Gazette*, August 4, 1953); Annette Fitch Nelson, "The Coming of the Howells Family to Ashtabula County," an unpublished radio script (Ohio); interview with Joseph A. Howells, "The Place Where William Dean Howells Began His Literary Career," *Ohio State Journal* (hereafter *OSJ*), February 9, 1902, illustrated section, 5; the *Ashtabula Sentinel* (Howells family file in Ashtabula Public Library, Ashtabula, Ohio); and *The Casket*, see William M. Gibson and George Arms, *A Bibliography of William Dean Howells* (hereafter "Gibson and Arms"), New York, 1948, nos. 53-1, 2, 5, *et passim*. For humor, see *Youth;* Howe, *John Jay Chapman, and His Letters*, 1937, 254; Howells to W. C. Howells, July 6, 1890 (Harvard).

For detailed discussion of *The Independent Candidate*, including identification of it as Howells', see Cady, "Howells and the *Ash-*

tabula Sentinel." Dating of venture into law study in "1852" Journal.

On Heine see *My Literary Passions,* 128–129; Howells to "Dear Cousin," September 9, 1852 (Harvard); and Bainton, *Art of Authorship,* 335. I am indebted to Dr. Alfred Marks, *Hawthorne and Romantic Irony,* unpublished dissertation, Syracuse University, 1953, for insights into romantic irony; and also to William Stirling, translator, Heine, *The North Sea and Other Poems,* 1947; C. G. Leland, translator, Heine, *Pictures of Travel,* 1901; Louis Untermeyer, *Heinrich Heine,* 1937; and H. Walter, *Heinrich Heine,* 1930.

IV

The evidences of Howells' breakdown are legion. See Cady, "The Neuroticism of Howells," *PMLA,* March 1946, 229–38. Also *Youth* and interview with Joseph A. Howells in *Critic,* December 1899, 1022–28; Howells to Mary Dean Howells, July 12, 1868 (Harvard). For religion, see Owen Wister, "William Dean Howells," *Atlantic,* December 1937, 713.

V

On Jefferson see *Letters,* I, 89; II, 80; Howells to Victoria Howells, January 2, 1859; March 29, 1861 (among others at Harvard).

Chapter Four

This earliest of Howells' portraits was frequently reproduced in newspapers and periodicals during his lifetime, but the best print is in *Letters,* I, 10.

George H. Porter, *Ohio Politics During the Civil War Period,* 1911, 18.

I

References to Howells' early writings depend, with a few exceptions, on identifications made by Gibson and Arms. For Howells' early addiction to politics and clever political journalism see Louis J. Budd, "Howells' 'Blistering and Cauterizing,' " *OAHQ,* October 1953, 334–47.

II

The main objective information available on this phase of the Cincinnati experience comes from F. C. Marston's discovery of the April 10 letter in the collection of William Dean Howells II now in the Rutherford B. Hayes Memorial Library, Fremont, Ohio and his publication of it with illuminating comment in *American Literature*, May 1946, 163–165. Marston identified Babb and provided the only secure evidence for dating the episode. Howells' account appears in *My Literary Passions* and *Youth*. Cp. Howells to W. C. Howells, April 19, 1867 (Harvard).

My identification of "City Intelligence" as Howells is not supported by Gibson and Arms. Letters to William H. Smith shed some retrospective light on the *Gazette* episode, especially Howells to Smith, January 31 and February 7, 1860 (Ohio). *Youth*, 142–43, tells of reporting sermons, graduation exercises at a young ladies' seminary, and the drunken woman in police court.

The dating of the January 1858 breakdown rests on Marston's work as supplied to Gibson and Arms, 78–79.

III

On efforts to "get a basis" in 1858 see Howells to Dr. G. Bailey, September 21; and Howells to M. D. Potter, October 9 (Harvard).

The *Cleveland Leader* is quoted in the *Ashtabula Sentinel*, November 25, 1858, a rare event, for W. C. Howells' policy was to keep the family name out of the news columns of his own paper.

On Howells and Ohio politics, see Roseboom, 200–01, 300; on Cooke, Parrington, *Main Currents in American Thought*, III, 32–42.

On "The Poet's Friends," see Lida R. McCabe, "Literary and Social Recollections of Howells," 549. For "hippo," see "Journal for Vic," April 19 [1859?] (Harvard). The banking story is told both by Mrs. McCabe, 549–50, and by Alfred E. Lee, *History of the City of Columbus*, I, 479.

On "Old Brown," see Gibson and Arms, 83.

IV

For "heyday" see *My Literary Passions*, 146, 138. The impression Howells gives here is strongly borne out in a series of warm letters to old Columbus friends, dating from 1861 to 1898, in the Comly Papers (Ohio) and in letters to Victoria Howells (Harvard). The after all rather small issue of where Howells met Elinor Mead has been confused by an offhand remark of Moncure D. Conway (*Autobiography*, I, 308) that they met at the home of Miss Nourse in Cincinnati. Since Conway was a close friend and supporter of Howells in the Columbus years and intimate with the Howellses in the Venetian years, and since Elinor had originally come to Ohio to visit her cousin Rutherford B. Hayes in Cincinnati (C. E. Williams, editor, *Diary and Letters of Rutherford B. Hayes*, I, 565–66, *et passim*), it is possible that Conway is right. Yet, there are small inaccuracies of one sort or another in Conway's other accounts of Howells, and it seems more likely that Howells' own testimony in *Youth* backed up by that of Miss Mildred Howells (*Letters*, I, 12), should be taken instead of Conway's. Perhaps some weight should be given to the fact that, on this kind of detail, women's memories are more likely to be accurate than men's, and Miss Howells' witness is independently supported by that of Mrs. Lida McCabe, *op. cit.*, 551, who is also the source for the story of Elinor Mead's caricature of J. Q. A. Ward. The conversation with Laura Platt is in *Letters*, I, 24. Cp. R. Gray, "Howells, the Last," *Fortnightly Review*, January 1921, 155.

On the Meads, the Noyeses, and the Hayeses, see *George Hayes of Windsor*, 1884, 40–41; C. R. Williams, *Rutherford Birchard Hayes*, 1926, *passim*, and Hayes' *Diary*, especially I, 532. Mary R. Cabot, *Annals of Brattleboro*, 1681–1895, 1924, especially 542 ff.; *A Yankee Saint*, 1935, 94; and *Letters*, I, 10–12, 24, 61. The Fiske statement is in Ethel Fisk, editor, *Letters of John Fiske*, 321. Also Howells to W. C. Howells, July 17, 1887, July 22, 1862 (Harvard).

V

For full, and thoroughly reliable, bibliographical information on *Poems of Two Friends* (as on any of Howells' books), see Gibson and Arms. The publishing circumstances, sales, and reviews of the book are surveyed, with many unique details, in Rudolph and Clara Kirk, " 'Poems of Two Friends,' " *Journal of the Rutgers University Library*, June 1941, 33–44.

The date of the *Saturday Press* review (January 28, 1860) makes improbable W. H. Venable's (121) claim that Conway's Cincinnati *Dial* (March 1860) review was the "first printed notice of his work that Howells ever saw," even though Venable hinted that Howells himself was the "authority" for the statement. Lowell's review was *Atlantic*, April 1860, 510–11; and Howells himself confined a review entirely to Piatt's part, *OSJ*, December 26, 1859; see also Cleveland *Herald* quoted in *Ashtabula Sentinel*, January 4, 1860. Howells' effort to get the Cincinnati *Gazette* to reprint the *Saturday Press* encomium was thwarted by a personal enemy—Howells to W. H. Smith, January 31, February 7, 1860 (Ohio).

For cheese and wine see Howells to Comly, July 20, 1873 (Ohio) and "Letter En Passant," *OSJ*, July 23, 1860. Conway, *Autobiography*, I, 309. Cf. pocket notebook for 1860 (Harvard). Howells to W. C. Howells, April 21, 1860 (Harvard).

The Lincoln biography is ably surveyed in Benjamin P. Thomas, "A Unique Biography of Lincoln," *Bulletin of the Abraham Lincoln Association*, no. 35 (June 1934), 3–8, and in his introduction to the facsimile edition of Lincoln's annotated copy of *The Life of Abraham Lincoln*, by W. D. Howells, 1938; and in Ernest J. Wessen, "Campaign Lives of Abraham Lincoln," *Papers in Illinois History and Transactions for the Year 1937*, 1938, 187–203. See also Gibson and Arms; and Helen Nicolay, *Lincoln's Secretary*, 1949, 34–5. Howells' estimate of his income from it is in *Biographical History of Northeastern Ohio*, 1893, 185.

VI

For the *Cincinnati Gazette* "Glimpses of Summer Travel" and the *OSJ* "En Passant" letters of Howells' summer pilgrimage see Gibson and Arms.

In *Literary Friends*, 46–47, the "Harvard Senior" was the future Justice Holmes. Cf. Howells to Mrs. Smith, September 28, 1861 (Comly Papers).

The New York visit stirred up some genuine animosity. When Howells had written about it, William Winter, in one of the choked-up reminiscences which earned him the sobriquet of "Weeping Willie," attacked Howells as having come to Pfaff's "a prig"—"a respectable youth in black raiment" and gone away to lie about it (see *Old Friends*, 1909, 89–92). He was answered by F. M. Colby, *Bookman*, October 1908, 124–126, in round fashion: "Mr. Winter would naturally dislike Mr. Howells. Talent in a contemporary writer is offensive to Mr. Winter, physically offensive."

On Whitman see *OSJ*, February 9, March 28, 1860; Whitman essay appeared first in *Ashtabula Sentinel*, July 18, 1860, as review of *Leaves of Grass* and then in *Saturday Press*, III (August 11, 1860). Cp. Gibson and Arms, 60–25, p. 84. See also Howells' review of *Drum Taps*, in *Round Table*, November 11, 1865; Stedman to

Howells, December 2, 1866 (Harvard); Howells to Stedman, *Life and Letters of E. C. Stedman*, May 8, 1880, II, 106. Horace Traubel, *With Walt Whitman in Camden*, 1906–14, especially 1888–89; Clara Burrus, *Whitman and Burroughs, Comrades*, 1931, especially 173; P. Baker, "Walt Whitman and the *Atlantic*," *American Literature*, VI (November 1934); R. Huback, "Three Uncollected St. Louis Interviews of Walt Whitman," *American Literature*, XIV (May 1942). Clara Burrus, editor, *The Life and Letters of John Burroughs*, 1925; *The Heart of Burroughs' Journals*, 1928; Burroughs, "Mr. Howells's Agreement with Walt Whitman," *Critic*, February 6, 1892. Lowell to Howells, Aug. [5,] 1860, C. E. Norton, editor, *Letters of James Russell Lowell*, 1894, I, 305; Bigelow, *Recollections of an Active Life*, 1910, I, 299–300. Cf. Howells to Fields, August 22, 1860, *Letters*, I, 29–30; Price to Howells, November 28, 1868 (Harvard).

VII

On Ohio at the opening of the war see Porter, 49–50, and Roseboom, 385; Sandburg, *Lincoln: the War Years*, is particularly good on Chase, *passim*. Howells to Fields, September 29, 1861 (Fields Papers, Huntington Library). Howells to Mrs. Smith, September 28, 1861 (Comly Papers); Howells to Salmon P. Chase, June 10, 1861 (Penna. Historical Society). Cp. Roseboom, 154. Howells to Mary D. Howells, May 26, 1861 (Harvard). In addition to *Youth*, see *Life and Letters of Edmund Clarence Stedman*, I, 248–9; Howells to Mrs. Smith, September 28, 1861—the Comly Papers show that Howells was not merely a faithful friend to the Smith family for the rest of his life but, more than thirty years later, insisted kindly but firmly that they take gifts of money as "unpaid debts" (though he had long since repaid Dr. Smith's $150 loan) when, after the doctor's death, they needed cash. Ingratitude was not one of Howells' faults. On Nicolay and Hay see also Howells interviewed by T. C. Crawford, *New York Tribune*, June 26, 1892. On New York search cf. Henry Rood interview with Howells, *New York Times*, February 25, 1912.

The fact that Howells was able in December 1862, after a year out of the country, to persuade the Meads to permit Elinor to come to Europe to marry him makes it highly probable that his courtship had arrived at a point at least virtually equivalent to an engagement before he left and that the intensely family-minded Meads had seen him and approved; his letter to Elinor's father announcing the fact of their marriage is couched in terms of Will's very best playful humor and remembers himself to everybody in a familiar way (to Larkin G. Mead, Sr., December 24, 1862, *Letters*, I, 62).

The sea-voyage "Letter from Europe" is in *Ashtabula Sentinel*, January 22, 1862; the "Letter from Europe" also appeared in *OSJ;* see Gibson and Arms.

Chapter Five

Besides the general autobiographical volumes (*Youth, My Literary Passions, Literary Friends and Acquaintances*) and the introduction to W. C. Howells' *Recollections*, Howells' "Ohio" books are *A Boy's Town, My Year in a Log Cabin, New Leaf Mills, The Coast of Bohemia, Stories of Ohio, The Kentons*, and *The Leatherwood God*. Other volumes have the Midwest and Midwesterners centrally concerned: viz., *A Hazard of New Fortunes, The World of Chance, Indian Summer, Out of the Question*, etc. To take a few instances, Howells characters as varied as Kitty Ellison (*A Chance Acquaintance*), Mrs. Erwin (*The Lady of Aroostook*), and Silas Lapham are said to have had Ohio originals (McCabe, 55); also Lindau (*A Hazard of New Fortunes*), cf. Kirk and Kirk, 39, among other sources; and Putney (*Annie Kilburn*), M. S. Hellman, editor, "The Letters of Howells to Higginson," *Twenty-seventh Annual Report of the Bibliophile Society*, 1929, 45–46.

For "Buckeye" see Howells to J. R. Peaslee, thanking the school children of Cincinnati for planting a tree in his name, May 1, 1892 (Ohio) and cp. Howells to Mira Dock, April 16, 1916 (Library of Congress); "liberty and equality," *Youth*, 81, 209. In addition to previous materials on Howells and the frontier, see his having been able to cite, from memory, for the historian Don Seitz the date on which the Wyandotte Indians were shipped from Ohio to Kansas because, as a boy of six, he watched them go through Hamilton on the canal (Rood, 157). Also Howells to Comly, April 16, 1868 (Ohio).

"Town pump," "Letter from Europe," *Ashtabula Sentinel*, May 14, 1862.

On romantic regionalism see "Some Western Poets of Today," *OSJ*, September 25, 1860; Howells to Lowell about the Coggeshall book, August 25, 1860, *Letters*, I, 31–32; Howells to Lowell, December 14, 1860 (Harvard). Excellent background on this question can be had from Benjamin T. Spencer, in Merrill Jensen, editor, *Re-*

gionalism in America, especially 221–22, 225–29; and "A National Literature, 1837–1855," *American Literature,* May 1936.

I

"Three Days in London" and "Still in Europe," *Ashtabula Sentinel,* February 5, 12, 1862. "Overland to Venice," *Harper's,* November 1918; "At the Sign of the Savage," *Atlantic,* July 1877; Howells to W. C. Howells, December 7, 1861, *Letters,* I, 41–44.

"An Old Venetian Friend," *Harper's,* April 1919. As anyone who works with the subject must be, I am indebted in various ways in this chapter to James Woodress, *Howells and Italy,* 1952. Cp. Cady, "Howells in Italy: Some Bibliographical Notes," *Symposium,* May 1953, 147–153.

Particularly significant is the Venetian letter to Sister Vic, *Letters,* I, 56–59; also to W. C. Howells, 52–55; see "A Young Venetian Friend," *Harper's,* April 1919; "Tonelli's Marriage," *Atlantic,* July 1868. Identifications of Brunetta, Perissinotti, and Libera were made by Woodress.

II

For Moran, see E. Samuels, *Young Henry Adams,* 125. Mrs. Howells' view of the affair has been relayed by Mrs. Thomas Bailey Aldrich, *Crowding Memories,* 89–90, who was over-impressed by the elements of pathos built into the story to point up its humor. The character is Col. Kenton of "At the Sign of the Savage," *Atlantic,* July 1877. The tale is done as if the Howellses had made his original trip through Germany to Venice together. Howells' personal letters teem with tributes to his wife, though he shunned exposing her to the publicity which beat down on him through most of their years together.

"By the Sea," *Poems,* 1873, 97. Howells to Mary D. Howells, April 18, 1862, *Letters,* I, 68. W. James, *The Varieties of Religious Experience,* 1902, 90. Moncure D. Conway, *Autobiography,* I, 426–27.

Elinor Howells to Lucy Keeler, February 7 [1905?] (Hayes Library). On Larkin Mead's courtship see Woodress, 23. On Mead in general see *Annals of Brattleboro;* Van Wyck Brooks, *Scenes and Portraits,* 920.

Among many sources on the Howellses see H. H. Boyesen, "Howells at Close Range," *Ladies' Home Journal,* November 1893; Rood, *loc. cit.*

III

Lowell reviewed *Venetian Life, North American Review,* October 1866.

"Canoe," Frank B. Sanborn, "A Letter to the Chairman," *North American Review,* April 1912.

Foster to Howells, October 3, 1863 (among seven illuminating letters from Foster to Howells at Harvard).

Browning to M. D. Conway, August 1, 1863 (Harvard).

Howells to Stoddard, November 25, 1864 (Anthony Papers, New York Public). There is a confirmatory valedictory note in Howells' comments about the 1873 edition of his *Poems,* e. g., Howells to Bayard Taylor, especially November 5, 1873 (Cornell).

Cady and Clark, editors, *Whittier on Writers and Writing,* 1950, 166.

Letters of the time show that Howells was clear in his own mind about the immediate aim of his new experiment with travel writing. See Howells to S. P. Chase, October 3, 1863 (Penna. Hist. Soc.); Howells to Hale, October 25, 1863, *Letters,* I, 77; Howells to Harpers, February 20, 1864 (Harvard).

Venetian Life, 1866, 157. Cook and Wedderburn, editors, *The Works of John Ruskin,* VIII, 139, 142; X, 225, cf. 215–25.

IV

"Carlo Goldoni," *Atlantic,* November 1877; cp. "Real Conversations . . . ," *McClure's,* June 1893; *My Literary Passions,* 155–157; Woodress, 170–186.

V

Howells to Aurelia Howells, n. d., *Letters,* I, 82; to W. H. Smith, May 12, 1864 (Ohio); to Mary Dean Howells, October 28, 1864. *Letters,* I, 91–92.

Norton, editor, Lowell, *Letters,* I, 338.

Howells to W. C. Howells, August 25, 1864, *Letters,* I, 87–91; cp. Joseph A. Howells to W. H. Smith, July 20, 1864 (Ohio). Garfield to W. C. Howells, February 9, 1865 (Garfield Papers, Library of Congress).

B. Booth, editor, *Letters of Anthony Trollope,* Trollope to Howells, July 13, 1863.

Venetian Life, 344. Lowell, review *Venetian Life,* 612.

Chapter Six

"Our Consuls in China and Elsewhere," *Nation*, November 2, 1865. It was just as well that Howells decided not to stay. Piatt, trying to succeed him, found the Venetian consul's salary whacked in half, *Hesperian Tree*, 1903, 374.

Howells' own best account of his return is in *Literary Friends*, 101–07. There is a fine cycle of letters, mostly to family, *Letters*, I, 94–103; also Boyesen, "Real Conversations, I . . . ," *McClure's*, June 1893; C. Johnson, interviewing Howells, "The Writer and the Rest of the World," *Outlook*, March 31, 1894; in Comly Papers (Ohio) see Howells to W. H. Smith, November 12, 1865; for Joe's song envelope see McCabe, 548; "newspaper man," see John Mead Howells interviewed by Hannah G. Belcher, "William Dean Howells, Magazine Writer," unpublished dissertation, Michigan, 1942, 34, *inter alia*.

I

"Strangeness," see Howells to Don Lloyd Wyman, September 5, 1865 (UCLA); "Real Conversations, I . . . ," 8.

Frank E. Foster to Howells, October 3, 1863 (Harvard); Henry James, *Atlantic*, July 1915, 21; cp. Benjamin T. Spencer, "A National Literature: Post-Civil War Decade," *Mod. Lang. Quart.*, March 1943, 71–2; *Literary Friends*, 215, 226. Howells to S. P. Chase, November 1, 1862 (Penna. Hist.) well expresses his mid-War gloom. See H. H. Clark, "The Nationalist," xxxvii–ix, Clark and Foerster, *James Russell Lowell*, 1947, and *Literary Friends*, 226; Malcolm Marsden, *Charles Eliot Norton: An Intellectual Biography*, unpublished dissertation, Syracuse, 1951, especially 180–260.

II

Nation: Howells to Comly. January 8, 1866 (Ohio); *Letters*, I, 103–04, II, 241–42; Rollo Ogden, *Life and Letters of E. L. Godkin*, 1907, I, 240; and Howells' review, "A Great New York Journalist," *North American Review*, May 1907, especially 48–49; Howells, "The Turning Point of My Life," *Harper's Bazaar*, March 1910, 165–66; also Gustav Pollak, *Fifty Years of American Idealism: The New York Nation, 1865–1915*, 1918; Louis Budd, *William Dean Howells' Relations with Political Parties*, unpublished dissertation, Wisconsin, 1947; Marsden, 237–39; J. H. Harper, *I Remember*, 1934, 152. For Howells' writings in *Nation* and *Cincinnati Gazette* see Gibson and Arms, 90–93. I think some of the late "Minor Topics" columns suspect, perhaps not by Howells.

III

Lida McCabe, "One Never Can Tell," *Outlook*, May 1898, 132.

Venetian Life publication: see *Letters*, I, 94–98; "Real Conversations . . . ," 7–8; *Literary Friends*, 101–02; Woodress, 50–66, has an excellent general account of the event. Stedman, I, 367; II, 536. Howells' New York friends were frequently praised in his *Cincinnati Gazette* letters.

Holland: see H. H. Peckham, *Josiah Gilbert Holland*, 1940, especially 70–71, 111–12, 115; Rood in *N. Y. Times*, February 25, 1912; Joyce Kilmer, interviewing Howells, "War Stops Literature," *N. Y. Times*, November 29, 1914; cp. *Literature in the Making*, 1917; Stedman, I, 526–27.

Lincoln's hand: see *Literary Friends*, 107; *Letters*, I, 102; Stedman, I, 368.

IV

Fields conversation, *Literary Friends*, III. *Atlantic* negotiations: *Letters*, I, 104–06; James C. Austin, *Fields of the Atlantic Monthly*, 1952, prints new letters by both men.

Chapter Seven

Bowles: *Literary Friends*, 113; Howells to Stoddard, March 12, 1866 (Anthony Papers, N.Y. Public); C. F. Browne to Howells, March 12, 1866 (Harvard).

I

This is the theme throughout *Literary Friends*, which for the most part concludes with Howells' leaving Boston in the late eighties, bringing his autobiographical coverage to an end at about that period. See also Howells to Mrs. Annie Fields, December 13, 1896 (Huntington).

Greenslet, *Thomas Bailey Aldrich*, 78.

"Flash Age," James L. Ford, *Forty-Odd Years*, 1921, 60; cp.

Letters, I, 168–69; *Literary Friends*, 129 (also 116, 131, 141, 146–47, 200, 287); *The Quality of Mercy*, 1892, 271; F. Greenslet, editor, "A Group of Aldrich Letters," *Century*, August 1908, 496.

Cleveland Amory, *The Proper Bostonians*, 1942, 39–40, 53, 67; for "Brahmin" see Cady, *The Gentleman in America*, 1949, 149–50, 17, 23, 184; *Literary Friends*, 147; G. P. Lathrop, "Literary and Social Boston," *Harper's*, May 1881, 393–94.

Boston apartment: Howells to Messrs. Church, February 24; March 13, 1866 (N.Y. Public); *Literary Friends*, 152; Holmes to Motley, October 10, 1865, G. W. Curtis, editor, *Correspondence of J. L. Motley*, 1889, 212; Howe, editor, *Memories of a Hostess*, 1922, *passim;* Howells to Mildred Howells, January 1915, *Letters*, II, 349; Henry James, "Mr. and Mrs. James T. Fields," *Atlantic*, July 1915, 29; Annie Howells to Mrs. W. H. Smith, April 5, 1866 (Comly Papers, Ohio); Richards, *et al., Julia Ward Howe*, I, 244–45; cp. Whitney, *Kate Field*, 185.

"Pill-box": Aldrich to Howells, October 25, 1895, *Life of Aldrich*, 191–92; *Literary Friends*, 178–79, 161; "Charles Eliot Norton," *North American Review*, December 1913, 839; *Letters*, I, 106–09, II, 239; Howells to Norton, March 1, 1866 (Huntington).

II

Letters, I, 107; *Harper's Bazaar*, March 1910.

Howells' *Atlantic* career has been well written about: *Literary Friends, passim,* and "Recollections of an *Atlantic* Editorship," *Atlantic*, November 1907; James C. Austin, *Fields of the Atlantic Monthly*, 139–63, *et passim;* M. A. De Wolfe Howe, *The Atlantic Monthly and Its Makers*, 1919; F. L. Mott, *History of American Magazines, 1850–1865*, 505–06; Robert E. Butler, *William Dean Howells as Editor of the Atlantic Monthly*, unpublished dissertation, Rutgers, 1950.

Susan M. Francis, "The Atlantic Pleasant Days in Tremont Street," *Atlantic*, November 1927, 716–20; J. T. Trowbridge, *My Own Story*, 1904, 318–19.

A good deal of Howells' correspondence, incoming and outgoing, both published in *Letters* or elsewhere and unpublished, was naturally concerned with his technical editorial duties. It seems unnecessary to try to list it here. See *Literary Friends*, 138–39; "Recollections of an *Atlantic* Editorship," 605. See Gibson and Arms, 93–94. George S. Hellman, editor, "The Letters of Howells to Higginson," *Twenty-Seventh Annual Report of the Bibliophile Society,* 1929 (hereafter "Hellman"), Howells to Higginson, December 24, 1869; on Howells as *Atlantic* reviewer see Austin, 152–55. For Howells' theory of the review in this period see his review of Purnell, *Literature and Its Professors, Atlantic,* August 1867, 252–55; Howells to Annie Howells, February 8, 1873 (Harvard).

Nation, October 29, 1868, 355, and February 3, 1870, 77.

"The Next President," *Atlantic,* May 1868, 628–32. On *Atlantic* and politics see Austin, 32–33, 149; Louis Budd, "Howells, the *Atlantic Monthly* and Republicanism," *American Literature,* May 1950, 139–56.

There are numerous letters to and from Howells and contributors or prospective contributors to the *Atlantic.* The bulk of the replies are, of course, among the Howells papers at Harvard. *Atlantic* letters he wrote can be found in almost any research library one cares to investigate. See *Letters, passim;* Jewett Papers (Harvard), Taylor Papers (Cornell), Stedman Papers (Columbia), etc., etc. See Austin, 146–50; and on relations with Fields, "Real Conversations . . . ," 8; "Recollections . . . ," 594; Fields's vacation: *Letters,* I, August 24, 1869; Austin, 39, 156–60. *Guardian Angel: Literary Friends,* 153; Eleanor M. Tilton, *Amiable Autocrat,* 1947, 283–91; Austin, 75–78; *Nation,* May 30, 1867, 432. Mrs. Stowe: *Literary Friends,* 138–40; *Letters,* I, 146–50; Holmes to Stowe, September 25, 1869, Morse, editor, *Life and Letters of O. W. Holmes,* 1897, II, 228–30; Forrest Wilson, *Crusader in Crinoline,* 1941, 535, 551; Mott, 505; *The Atlantic Monthly and Its Makers,* 49–50; Austin, 266–99; G. W. Curtis to Howells, September 3, 1869 (Harvard); Lowell to Edmund Quincey, September 15, 1859 (perhaps the most acute contemporary analysis of the episode), Howe, editor, *New Letters of James Russell Lowell,* 1932, 146–47.

III

Howells to W. C. Howells, October 21, 1868 (Harvard).

Letters, I, 132–33; 141–42; *Literary Friends,* 195; H. H. Boyesen, "Mr. Howells at Close Range," 1; "Real Conversations . . . ," 9–10.

Mary Howells' death: W. C. Howells to W. H. Smith, October 12, 1868; Annie Howells to Mrs. Smith, January 4, 1869 (Comly Papers, Ohio); *Letters,* I, 136–37; II, 140; Howells to Mrs. Upton, March 9, 1910 (Western Reserve Hist.).

Squire Mead: *Letters,* I, 138, 141–43, 149.
"Forget death": *A Hazard of New Fortunes,* 68.

IV

Norton, "Reminiscences of Old Cambridge," *Pub. Cambridge Hist. Soc.,* I (1905), 11–23; Lowell, *Fireside Trends,* 1864, 81, also 70, 78, 87; Higginson, *Old Cambridge,* 1900, 49, also 14, 29, 32, 36; *Letters,* II, 221; John Holmes to C. E. Ware, August 16, 1871, W. R. Thayer, editor, *Letters of John Holmes to James Russell Lowell and Others,* 1917, 81–82; on Cambridge social life as contrasted with Boston see Lathrop, 397; Howells was lyrical about it throughout *Literary Friends* (especially 179–81, 194, 232, 251, 286); cp. *Letters,* II, 178; *Atlantic* editors, Higginson, 69.

Dante Club: Samuel Longfellow, *Life of Henry Wadsworth Longfellow,* 1886, III, 62–64, *et passim; Literary Friends,* 182–94. For Longfellow's liking of Howells see *Literary Friends,* 195; J. J. Piatt, "An Acquaintance with Longfellow," *Hesperian Tree,* 1903, 136; Samuel Longfellow, III, 71, 382; *Letters,* I, 176. Howells' recollection of the doorbell rule was not entirely consistent: cp. H. E. Monroe, "Statesman and Novelist," *Lippincott's,* January 1887, 130, and *Literary Friends,* 188. Cp. Greenslet, *Under the Bridge,* 76–77.

Venetian Life: see Woodress; Norton's review was September 6, 1866; Lowell and Curtis in October issues; see Howells to J. S. Hart, July 10, 1871 (Cornell); Howells to Comly, November 19, 1866 (Ohio); *Letters,* I, 112–15; *Contemporary Review,* August 1866, 594–95; H. James, "William Dean Howells," *Harper's Weekly,* June 19, 1886, 394.

Lowell: the friendship is writ large in *Literary Friends,* in *Letters,* in Norton, editor, *Letters of James Russell Lowell,* 1894, and Howe, editor, *New Letters of James Russell Lowell,* 1932. Cp. Woodress, "The Lowell-Howells Friendship: Some Unpublished Letters," *New England Quarterly,* December 1953, 523–28; "Real Conversations, I . . . ," 8; "Commemoration of the Centenary of the Birth of James Russell Lowell," *Proc. Am. Academy of Arts and Letters,* 1919, 33; Clark and Foerster, *Lowell,* xlv–lxxxiv, *passim.* Justin McCarthy, *Reminiscences,* I, 194.

M.A.: the quotation is Lowell to Leland, July 8, 1867, E. R. Penrell, editor, *Charles Godfrey Leland,* 1906, I, 295–96. Leland was voted his M.A. at the same time as Howells: Child to Lowell,

June 23, 1867, Howe and Cottrell, editors, *The Scholar Friends . . .* , 1952, 18.

Academic offers: *Letters*, I, 138, 139, 155, 330–31, 333–35, 384–86; II, 136; Morison, *The Development of Harvard University*, 1930, 453; Woodress, 160–62; Howells to Mira Dock, December 17, 1911 (N.Y. Public).

V

See Philip Wiener, *Evolution and the Founders of Pragmatism*, 1949, vii. Ralph Barton Perry, *The Thought and Character of William James*, 1936, I, 110–11, 273; *The Letters of William James*, I, 253; II, 10, *et passim;* Virginia Harlow, *Thomas Sergeant Perry*, 1950, 46; *Yankee from Olympus*, 210–11, 223; *Letters*, I, 426; Matthiessen, *The James Family*, 1948, goes with Perry to make the Jameses America's most effectively documented family. John S. Clark, *Life and Letters of John Fiske*, 1917, 209, 378, 405–06, 515; Ethel Fisk, editor, *Letters of John Fiske*, 165 *et passim*.

On Darwinism: see Wiener, and Perry; H. W. Schneider, *A History of American Philosophy*, 1946, 319–437; R. H. Gabriel, *The Course of American Democratic Thought*, 1940, 143–289; R. Hofstadter, *Social Darwinism in American Thought, 1860–1915;* H. H. Clark, "The Role of Science in the Thought of W. D. Howells," *Transactions Wisconsin Academy of Science, Arts, and Letters*, 1953, 263–303; A. E. Jones, Jr., "Darwinism and Its Relationship to Realism and Naturalism in American Fiction, 1860 to 1900," *Drew University Bulletin*, December 1950, 3–21; Robert Frost, "New Hampshire," *Collected Poems*, 1930, 208.

Pragmatism: Wiener, 5, 97, 106, 145, 190–91, 199–200.

For Howells reviews in the *Atlantic* see Gibson and Arms. As early as October 1866, the *Atlantic* printed Charles B. Sprague's careful but unsparing argument for "The Darwinian Theory"; cp. Hofstadter, 1–17.

Cambridge skepticism: Perry, I, 464–66; Wiener, 47, 78, 100–01.

Henry James, Sr., and religion: J. H. Young, *The Philosophy of Henry James, Sr.*, 1951; Norton, *Letters,* II, 379; *Letters*, I, 134–35; Perry, I, 133, 153; cf. Matthiessen, 3–66, 136–205; Howells to Comly, October 29, 1868 (Ohio); Howells to W. C. Howells, October 31, 1868 (Harvard); *Letters*, I, 165–67.

Agnosticism: *Literary Friends*, 149, 202–03, 229; Howells to Comly, December 13, 1869 (Ohio); Thomas Huxley, "Agnosticism,"

Nineteenth Century, February 1889, 169–94; "A Counsel of Consolation," *In After Days,* 1910, 5; *Literary Passions,* 202; cp. Theodore Dreiser, "The Real Howells," *Ainslee's,* March 1900, 277.

VI

W. James to H. James, April 13, 1868, in Perry, I, 271; cp. Harte to Howells, August 5, 1869 (Harvard).

Henry James: *Letters,* II, 394–99, and see *Letters* of both men *passim;* James, *Notes of a Son and Brother,* 1914, 437; *The Middle Years,* 1917, 35; "A Letter to Mr. Howells," *North American Review,* April 1912, 558–59; "Mr. and Mrs. James T. Fields," *Atlantic,* July 1905, 26–27; Howells quoted by A. H. Quinn, "The Art of William Dean Howells," *Century,* September 1920, 676; McCabe, "Literary and Social Recollections," *loc. cit.,* 551. Cp. Leon Edel, *Henry James, The Untried Years,* 1953, 268–78; and "Real Conversations . . . ," 10.

Kilmer, *op. cit.,* 293; James, "William Dean Howells," *Harper's Weekly,* June 19, 1886, 394; Howells to C. Johnson, *Outlook,* March 31, 1894, 581; Austin, 31.

Suburban Sketches and experimentalism: 1869 Journal (Harvard); W. James to Henry, Perry, I, 204, 316; *Book Buyer,* July 1897, 559; *North American Review,* January 1871, 236–37; H. James, "William Dean Howells," *op. cit.,* 394. There is an excellent account of *Suburban Sketches* and its milieu in F. C. Marston, Jr., *The Early Life of William Dean Howells, a Chronicle, 1837–71,* unpublished dissertation, Brown, 1944. *Atlantic* essays, e.g., James, "The Novels of George Eliot," October 1866; T. W. Higginson, "Literature as an Art," December 1867; Curtis, see *Trumps,* 1861, 499; and *Harper's,* June 1859, 124–25; Taylor, see prefaces to *John Godfrey's Fortunes,* 1869, and *The Story of Kennett,* 1866; Howells to Taylor, April 11, 1866 (Cornell); Taylor to Stedman, April 15, 1866, *Life and Letters of Bayard Taylor,* 1884, II, 456–57; Howells review of *Story of Kennett, Atlantic,* June 1866; De Forest, see Howells review of *Miss Ravenal's Conversion, Atlantic,* July 1867; *Atlantic* reviews: see Carl Van Doren, *The American Novel,* 1921, 134–35; Howells review of Charles Reade, *Griffith Gaunt,* December 1866; H. W. Beecher, *Norwood,* June 1868; Björnson, *Arne; The Happy Boy; The Fisher-Maiden,* April 1870; cp. George Arms, "The Literary Background of Howells' Socialism," *American Literature,* November 1942, 271–74; and *Letters,* II, 251–52. See Everett

Carter, *Howells and the Age of Realism,* 1954, 43–111; Floyd Stovall, "The Decline of Romantic Idealism, 1855–1871," and Robert Falk, "The Rise of Realism, 1871–1881," in H. H. Clark, editor, *Transitions in American Literary History,* 1953, for various points of view toward the development of realism and Howells' relation to it.

Chapter Eight

Harte: *Letters,* I, 158–61, *et passim;* Fisk, 209; Geoffrey Bret Harte, *Letters of Bret Harte,* 1926; George Stewart, *Bret Harte: Argonaut and Exile,* 1931; *Literary Friends,* 114–15, 191; Howells to Higginson, March 1, 1871, Hellman, 29; Howe, *Atlantic . . . Makers,* 68; Bernard De Voto, editor, *Mark Twain in Eruption,* 1940, 275.

Letters, I, 162.

Their Wedding Journey: Letters, I, 162–63; Howells to Taylor, September 1, 1870 (Cornell); Howells to Comly, August 5, September 5, 1869, October 23, 1871 (Ohio); Howells to Annie Howells, April 26, 1872 (Harvard); *Book Buyer,* July 1897, 550; Howells to Keeler, September 23, 1871 (UCLA); Henry Adams, *North American Review,* April 1872, 444; *Letters and Journals of T. W. Higginson,* 262; Jewett to Howells, October 17, 1871 (Harvard); *Life of John Hay,* 1, 357. Cf. William N. Gibson, "Materials and Form in Howells's First Novels," *American Literature,* May 1947, 158–66.

I

Godkin to Norton, May 6, 1871, *Godkin Letters.*

Fiske to his mother, April 30, 1877, Fisk, 363–64. Cp. Mildred Howells, introduction to *Mrs. Farrell,* 1921, v–vi.

Mark Twain: see *Letters, passim; My Mark Twain,* perhaps the greatest short American literary biography; A. B. Paine, editor, *Mark Twain's Letters,* 1917, I, 389–90, 422 *et passim;* Paine, *Mark Twain, a Biography,* 1912, *passim;* O. W. Firkins, *William Dean Howells, A Study,* 1924, 224; De Lancey Ferguson, *Mark Twain: Man and Legend,* 1943, 77–78; K. R. Andrews, *Nook Farm, Mark Twain's Hartford Circle,* 1950, *passim; Mark Twain in Eruption,* 300; Ferris Greenslet, *Life of Thomas Bailey Aldrich,* 1908, 94, 113–14, 143, 145; *Crowding Memories,* 146; Greenslet, *Under the Bridge,* 89–90; Mary Lawton, editor, *A Lifetime with Mark Twain,*

1925, 39, 92, 317; Twain to Howells (series) (Harvard); Booth
Tarkington, *Pen Portraits*, 23; W. H. Rideing, *Many Celebrities*,
1914, 154; E. Earnest, *S. Weir Mitchell*, 1950, 241; Gamaliel Brad-
ford, *As God Made Them*, 1929, 186. M. A. D. Howe, *John Jay
Chapman and His Letters*, 1937, 254.

Howells' effect: cf. *Twain Letters, passim,* especially I, 223, 229 ff.,
263, 273, 327; *Letters, passim;* Perry, *And Gladly Teach*, 1935,
140–41; Bernard De Voto, *Mark Twain at Work*, 1942, *passim;*
Harlow, *Perry*, 209; Andrews, 158, 191–92; John B. Hober, "Mark
Twain's *A Connecticut Yankee:* A Genetic Study," *American Liter-
ature,* November 1946, 213; *North American Review,* April 1912,
557; *Mark Twain in Eruption*, 302; Twain, *What Is Man? and
Other Essays*, 1917, 228, 235, 239; Twain on *Foregone Conclusion,
Twain Letters,* I, 222; on *Lady of the Aroostook*, I, 346; on *A
Modern Instance,* I, 421–22. Cp. Ferguson, 180–81; Paul J. Carter,
"The Influence of William Dean Howells Upon Mark Twain's Social
Satire," *University of Colorado Studies,* July 1953, 93–100;
Wagenknecht, *Mark Twain: the Man and His Work*, 1935; Rosa-
mund Gilder, editor, *Letters of Richard Watson Gilder*, 1916,
398–99.

II

See "Recollections of an *Atlantic* Editorship," *Atlantic,* November 1907, 594–606; Mott, 505–06; Howe, *Atlantic . . . Makers,* 50–
51; *Josiah Gilbert Holland*, 185–86; for Osgood see *Literary Friends*,
121–22; Aldrich to Howells, October 25, 1895, in Greenslet, 191–92;
for Boston Fire see Henry M. Rogers, *Memories of 90 Years*, and
Howells, "Among the Ruins," *Atlantic,* January 1873.

Boyesen, "Howells at Close Range," 8; Fiske, in Fisk, editor,
Letters, 205, 210; cp. Aldrich to Stedman, February 20, 1881, in
Greenslet, 141; Stedman to Howells, October 1871, in *Stedman Life*,
I, 455; Howells to Comly, December 12, 1823 (Ohio).

Atlantic . . . Makers, 70, 76; on Contributor's Club see *Letters*,
I, 228, 230; Howells to Stoddard, December 9, 1826 (Anthony
Papers, N.Y. Public); Howells to W. H. Bishop, December 18,
1876 (Yale); "Recollections . . . ," 597; Harlow, *Perry*, 52; *Atlantic Supplement,* February 1880. I think it significant that, apart
from the letters and memories of Twain and Howells, it is not easy
to find references to show that guests at the dinner or members of
the public were much impressed by the fiasco at the Whittier

Dinner over which one school of Twain interpreters has made so much.

Howells and contributors: *Literary Friends,* 136; *Atlantic,* November 1907, 603–04, 720, 595–96; cp. Greenslet, *Aldrich,* 161; Jewett to Howells, September 18, 1877 (Harvard); cp. Matthiessen, *Sarah Orne Jewett, passim;* Addison, *Lucy Larcom,* 189; Howells to Taylor, December 28, 1873 (Cornell); Stedman, *Letters,* I, 536–37, 464; Bellamy to Howells, August 21, 1881 (Harvard); J. D. Ferguson, "New Letters of Paul Hamilton Hayne," *American Literature,* January 1934, 368–70, cp. Hubbell, editor, *Last Years of Timrod,* 109; A. H. Starke, "William Dean Howells and Sidney Lanier," *American Literature,* March 1831, 79–82, cp. Howells to Taylor (on "Corn"), March 27, 1877 (Cornell); George Cary Eggleston, *Recollections,* 148–49; Paul Buck, *Road to Reunion,* 225; James, *Atlantic,* December 1915, 26.

Atlantic and the West: *Atlantic,* November 1907, 600–02; Mott, 495, 504, 506, 508; Austin, 27, 43–44; *Literary Friends,* 114–15; Perry, *And Gladly Teach,* 174. Cp. B. T. Spencer, "The New Realism and a National Literature," *PMLA,* December 1941, 1116–32.

Atlantic and Europe: Howells to Higginson, October 18, 1873, Hellman, 32–33; *North American Review,* April 1912, 554–55; *Atlantic,* November 1902, 596–97; *Letters,* I, 170, 172. See Virginia Harlow's excellent biography of *Thomas Sergeant Perry, passim.* Cp. Helen McMahon, *Criticism of Fiction, A Study of Trends in the Atlantic Monthly, 1857–98,* 1953.

III

The standard indictment of the Gilded Age, full of Populist indignation and rhetoric, is Parrington's, which has needed the ample correction it has had from Gabriel, *The Course of American Democratic Thought,* 1940, 1956; Merle Curti, *The Growth of American Thought,* 1943; Walter Fuller Taylor, *The Economic Novel in America,* 1942; Richard Hofstadter, *The Age of Reform,* 1955, among others.

There is an excellent summary of Howells' political experience of this period in Louis J. Budd, "Howells, the *Atlantic Monthly,* and Republicanism," *American Literature,* May 1952, 139–56. The full Howells-Hayes correspondence, including letters from Mrs. Howells, is neatly available in the Rutherford B. Hayes Library, Fremont, Ohio. See also Williams, *Hayes,* and Williams, editor,

Diary and Letters of Hayes; Howells to Comly, July 28, 1826 (Ohio) ; Howells to Hon. Poley W. Chandler, June 4, 1928 (Library of Congress). The Garfield Papers at the Library of Congress contain interesting communications between Garfield and Howells as well as W. C. Howells. See also Hinsdale, editor, *The Garfield-Hinsdale Letters,* 103, 123; and Mason Wade, editor, *Journals of Francis Parkinson,* 1947, II, 558 (and cp. Howells to Garfield, December 31, 1872, Library of Congress).

Atlantic and socio-economic problems: see Budd, "Republicanism," and Arms, "Literary Background . . ."; Follett and Follett, *Some Modern Novelists,* 100–02. *Wedding Journey,* 219; Caro Lloyd, *Henry Demarest Lloyd,* 1912, I, 59–61, 62–64, 72, 281; Allan Nevins, *A Study in Power,* II, 140–41, 331. C. F. Adams to Howells, December 5, 1880 (Harvard); *Literary Friends,* 219–20; "Carlo Goldoni," *Atlantic,* November 1877, 604.

IV

A Chance Acquaintance: Harlow, *Perry,* 51; *New York Sun,* February 25, 1917; Howells to Comly, October 22, 1871, and December 12, 1873 (Ohio); H. James review *Foregone Conclusion, North American Review,* January 1875; Boyesen, "Howells at Close Range," 7; *Letters,* I, 180; E. Purcell, *Academy,* 1879, 364–65; *Letters,* I, 174–75; *Literary Friends,* 149; *Nation,* June 1890, 454; Orcutt, *Celebrities Off Parade,* 127; A. L. Dawes, "The Moral Purpose in Howells's Novels," *Andover Review,* January 1889, 27; "The Earlier and Later Work of Mr. Howells," *Lippincott's,* December 1882, 607; A. S. Van Westrum, "Mr. Howells and American Aristocracies," *Bookman,* March 1907, 68; M. A. D. Howe, editor, *Later Years of the Saturday Club,* xvi–xvii, 67–76; Morse, editor, *Holmes,* II, 44; F. J. Stimson, *My United States,* 1931, 79; *A Chance Acquaintance,* 1874, 21, 260, *et passim;* Higginson, *Short Studies of American Authors,* 1879, 36; cp. T. S. Perry, "William Dean Howells," *Century,* March 1882, 683; Orr, "International Novelists and Mr. Howells," *Contemporary Review,* May 1880, 746. See also, "The Gentleman as Socialist: William Dean Howells," in Cady, *The Gentleman in America,* 1949, 184–205.

Lady of the Aroostook: Higginson, *Short Studies,* 36, *New York Times,* February 25, 1921, and *Letters,* I, 265–66.

V

E. M. McGill, editor, Clara Reeve, *The Progress of Romance*, 1930, III, 6–7, 13, 67; Scott, "Essay on Romance," *Misc. Prose Works*, VI, 129–30, and *Journal*, I, 118; cp. G. E. Smock, *Scott's Theory of the Novel*, unpublished dissertation, Cornell, 1934; Hawthorne, *The House of the Seven Gables*, 1890, 13; Howells review of Dickens' *Our Mutual Friend*, *Round Table*, December 2, 1865, 200; review of H. James, *Hawthorne*, *Atlantic*, February 1880, 282; *Literature and Life*, 1902, 29–30. An excellent account of the topic may be found in Louis Budd, "William Dean Howells' Defence of the Romance," *PMLA*, March 1952, 32–42. W. C. Brownell, "The Novels of Mr. Howells," *Nation*, July 15, 1880, 51; James Hart, *The Popular Book*, 104; *Criticism and Fiction*, 1891, 124; Hellman, 38.

A Foregone Conclusion: *Book Buyer*, July 1897, 559; Journal begun in 1869 (Harvard); H. James, *North American Review*, January 1875, 207–14; *Nation*, January 7, 1875, 12–13; George Saintsbury, "New Novels," *The Academy*, March 13, 1875, 264; cp. Stedman, *Letters*, I, 526; Woodress, 208, and "Howells' Venetian Priest," *Mod. Lang. Notes*, April 1951, 266–67.

Private Theatricals, see *Letters*, I, 189, 190, 205, 209–10. Austin 161-62, errs in identifying the Fields-Howells exchange over a new story in November 1875 as over *Foregone Conclusion* (which had gone into book form on December 3, 1874, and been widely reviewed). Cf. "Ricus," "A Suppressed Novel of Mr. Howells," *Bookman*, October 1910, 201–03.

VI

Scudder, "New York in Recent Fiction," *Atlantic*, April 1890, 563; S. Kirk, "America, Altruria, and The Coast of Bohemia," *Atlantic*, November 1894, 701; H. James, review *Italian Journeys*, *N. Am. Rev.*, January 1868, 336; review Howells' *Poems*, *Independent*, January 8, 1874, 9; *Letters of Celia Thaxter*, 72; Whipple, "The First Century of the Republic in Literature," *Harper's*, March 1876, 527; *The Correspondence of Bayard Taylor and Paul Hamilton Hayne*, 1945, 59–60, cp. 63–64, *et passim;* Stedman, *Letters*, II, 338; E. Purcell, *Academy*, 1879, 365; W. C. Brownell, "The Novels of Mr. Howells," *Nation*, July 15, 1880, 50.

On Howells and debts for realism, see Kilmer, 291–92; Quinn,

258; Cooke, 61; Howells and Björnson, *Critic*, July 16, 1887; Arms, "Literary Sources . . . ," 150 ff.; on Taine, see Carter, 96 ff., but cp. H. James's review of Taine, *Atlantic*, April 1872. On Turgenev, see Royal A. Gettman, *Turgenev in England and America*, 1941; 53 ff.; Harlow, *Perry*, 78 ff., 254; *Letters*, I, 232, 282, 379; *Literary Passions*, 169–72, H. James, Sr., to Turgenev, July 19, 1879, in Perry, I, 138–39.

Turgenev on Howells: Hay to Hayes, December 22, 1879 (Hayes Memorial) and Hayes to Howells, same day, *Letters*, xx, I, 280; Howells to Hayes, December 26, 1879, and Hayes to Howells, January 20, 1880 (Hayes Memorial); Marrion Wilcox, "The Works of William Dean Howells," *Harper's Weekly*, July 4, 1896, 655; H. James, *Letters*, I, 49.

The Undiscovered Country, 1880: for Hawthorne see 109–10; *Book Buyer*, 559. Arthur Barker, "New Novels," *Academy*, September 18, 1880, 200; W. H. Bishop to Howells, May 5, 1880 (Harvard); Spencer, *Regionalism in America*, 233–35; *Literary Friends*, 229; *Lippincott's*, December 1882, 607; *Life and Letters of John Fiske*, 209; Higginson, *Scribner's*, Sept. 1880, cp. Hellman, 42; Brooks Adams, *International Review*, August 1880, 149–54; Appleton to Howells, February 28, 1880 (Harvard); Brownell, 49, 50.

Chapter Nine

Belmont; see *Letters*, I, 244–45, 250, 270–71, 278, 283–84, 311; Lathrop, "Literary . . . Boston," 390–91; *Authors at Home*, 205; *Critic*, November 27, 1886, 260; *Letters of John Fiske*, 372, 468; Clara Clemens, *Mark Twain, the Letter Writer*, 47; "Real Conversations," 10–11; Howells to Hayes, May 17, 1880 (Hayes Memorial).

Atlantic Breakup and Osgood: *Letters*, I, 293–94; Howells to Comly, May 16 and 27, 1881 (Ohio); on salary see Rood, 42; Boyesen, "Howells at Close Range," 7. *Critic*, June 20, 1884, estimated that Howells, James, and Cable were making about $8,000 per book on sales of 20,000 copies plus serial rights. Cp. J. W. Harper, Jr. to Chas. Fairchild, May 13, and Fairchild to Harper, May 14, 1885 (Harvard); also Howells to Conway, April 22, 1881 (Columbia).

I

Professional Writer: Howells to W. C. Howells, March 4, 1888 (Harvard); "Howells at Home," *Current Literature,* 1898, 402; Boyesen, "Howells at Close Range," 8; *Literary Digest,* June 12, 1920, 54, 56; H. E. Monroe, "Statesmen and Novelists," 128; Mrs. Daniel Chute French, *Memories of a Sculptor's Wife,* 158; "Howells at Home," *N. Y. Tribune,* January 25, 1880; Howells to Higginson, August 31, 1886, Hellman, 45; "Mr. Howells' Work," *Literary News,* May 1886, 155.

Fiction and Method: Brooks, "Howells at Work," 284, 286; "Howells at Home," *Current Literature,* 1898, 402–03; Howells to Matthews, May 27, 1914 (Columbia); R. Grant, *Later Years of the Saturday Club,* 1927, 71; *Literary Digest,* June 12, 1920, 54; Howells to children of Jefferson, O., Schools, March 18, 1881, unidentified newspaper clipping; Monroe, 730; Rood, *Ladies' Home Journal,* 157; Arms, "A Novel and Two Letters," *Journal Rutgers Library,* December 1944, 9–13; *Letters,* I, 355–56.

II

See Kirk and Kirk, cii–cvi; *Letters,* I, 299–300.

Modern Instance: W. de Wagstaffe, "The Personality of Mr. Howells," *Book News Monthly,* June 1908; cp. *Letters,* I, 227; Howells to Gilder, September 4, 1881 (Harvard); "Howells at Home," *Current Lit.,* 402; "Howells at Close Range," 7.

Letters, I, 303–311. *Literary Friends,* 209; Howells to Higginson, April 8, 1882. Hellman, 43.

H. E. Scudder, "A Modern Instance," *Atlantic,* November 1882, 712; cp. *Letters,* I, 332–33; on titles: Howells to Higginson, April 8, 1882, Hellman, 42–43; Howells to Harvey, July 28, 1903, Johnson, *George Harvey,* 86–87; Gilder to Howells, September 4, and October 8, 1881 (Harvard); *N. Y. Times,* February 25, 1912. "Earlier and Late Work . . . ," *Lippincott's,* 607; C. P. Woolley, "Mr. Howells Again," *New England Magazine,* December 1893, 409–10; Cable to Howells, March 3, 1882, January 27, 1883; W. H. Bishop to Howells, January, 1883 (Harvard).

See Howells to ?, March 24, 1882, in Gibson and Arms, 29–30; Trilling, "Book Reviews," *New Yorker,* September 24, 1949, 89.

III

Gilder to Howells, March 27, 1882 (Harvard); Howells to Osgood, March 13, 1883 (Columbia); cp. *Autobiography of William
Allen White,* 1946, 106.

Winifred: Mary Mapes Dodge to Howells, March 13, 1877 (Harvard). *Letters,* I, 271, 283, 289, 301, 311; Howells to Hayes,
December 1 (Hayes Memorial); Howells to Mrs. Fields, January
23, and July 10, 1881 (Huntington); Howells to W. C. Howells,
August 21, 1881 (Harvard).

London: *Letters,* I, 315–21; *Letters of Bret Harte,* 212; Gosse,
"The Passing of William Dean Howells," *Living Age,* July 10, 1920,
98–99; Howells to Gosse, September 9, 1882 (British Museum).
"To W. D. Howells," *From Shakespeare to Pope,* N.Y., 1885,
iii; to Howells, December 10, 1882, L. Charteris, editor, *Life
and Letters of Sir Edmund Gosse,* 1931, 154–55, *et passim;* cp.
Howells to Gosse, August 1, 2, 8, 26, 1882 (Gosse Papers, British
Museum); *Oscar Wilde Discovers America,* 205, 355, *et passim;
Life of Herbert Spencer,* 504; *Hay,* I, 409; *Letters,* I, 341–42;
"Mr. Howells in England," *Literary Digest,* June 19, 1920, 37.
Cp. recurrent reviews in *Academy* and elsewhere, and Clarence
Gohdes, *American Literature in Nineteenth Century England,* 1944,
46 *et passim;* David Douglas to Howells, November 22, 1884
(Harvard).

James article: Gilder to Howells, September 21, 1881 (Harvard);
Howells to Gosse, November 16, 1882 (British Museum); *Letters,*
I, 329, 336–37, 338. Archer, "The Novelist as Critic," *Illustrated
London News,* August 8, 1891, 175; *Atheneum,* November 25,
1882; *Blackwood's Magazine,* January 1883, 136–61—cp. T. M.
Coan, *Studies in Literature,* 1883, 1–61; "American Novels," *Quar-
terly Review,* January 1883, 201–29; *Yankee from Olympus,* 301;
Howells to Brander Matthews, September 10, 1899 (Columbia);
James to Howells, February 21, 1884, *James Letters,* I, 103–05.
"Editor's Easy Chair," *Harper's,* April 1884; James, "Daudet,"
Century, August 1883; Gilder to Howells, December 16, 1882 (Har-
vard); Howells to B. Taylor, November 24, 1868 (Cornell); "Howells'
Novels" *Westminster Review,* October 1884, 347–75. Cp. A. Orr,
"International Novelists and Mr. Howells," *Contemporary Review,*
May 1880, 741–65; F. Wedmore, "To Millicent, from America,"
Temple Bar, June 1886, 241.

Joseph Pennell, *Adventures of An Illustrator*, 1925, 110 *et passim; James Letters*, I, 30–31, 71–74; cf. W. James to H. James, January 23, 1883, Perry, 389; *North American Review*, April 1912, 560–61; Howells to Gosse, June 15, 1883 (Brotherton College, Leeds).

IV

Robert Grant, *The Late Years of the Saturday Club*, 70; cf. Garland, *A Son of the Middle Border*, 324; *Barrett Wendell and His Letters*, 323–24; Justin McCarthy, *Reminiscences*, I, 208–09; Ticknor, *Glimpses of Authors*, 179–90; Howells, *Impressions and Experiences*, 99–100; Howells to Gosse, December 9, 1883 (British Museum); Wedmore, 241; Lodge, *Early Memories*, 344; *Letters*, I, 362.

Howells to Gosse, October 26, 1885 (British Museum), cp. Garland, "A Great American," *N. Y. Evening Post*, March 5, 1921; *Letters*, I, 363; W. H. Bishop, "Mr. Howells in Beacon Street, Boston," *Critic*, November 27, 1886, 259–60 (also *Authors at Home*, 1888); *Letters of John Fiske*, 514–15; Howells to Higginson, January 28, 1895, Hellman, 44; *Literary Friends*, 163.

Date of *Indian Summer:* Howells to Gosse, April 3, December 9, 1883 (British Museum); Alden to Howells, March 17, 1884 (Harvard). *Lapham:* Howells to Gosse, December 24, 1884 and January 25, 1885 (Leeds), March 9 (announcing completion), 1885 (British Museum); in the notebook which Howells kept in his pocket for recording creative ideas as they germinated while he was meditating his novels, all the *Indian Summer* entries precede all those for *Lapham* (Harvard). *Indian Summer:* see introduction by W. M. Gibson, *Indian Summer*, 1951, vii–xxii; Howells to Lounsbury, November 22, 1885 (Yale); Howells to Gosse, December 9, 1883 (British Museum); Alden to Howells, March 17, 1884 (Harvard); "A Dream," *Knickerbocker*, August 1861, 146–150; *Indian Summer*, 1886, 179; *Letters of William James*, I, 253.

V

Howells to W. C. Howells, November 5, 1882 (Harvard); W. B. Trites, "William Dean Howells," *Forum*, February 1913, 217; Garland, "Meetings with Howells," *Bookman*, March 1917, 1–2; Tarkington, introduction to *Lapham*, 1937; xxi; cf. *Barrett Wendell . . . Letters*, 60; S. Baxter, "Howells' Boston," *New England Magazine*,

October 1893, 136; Clarence Buel to Howells, May 9, 1885 (Harvard); F. J. McConnell, *By the Way*, 88; *Letters of William James*, I, 307–08; S. Weir Mitchell to Howells, June 4, 1888 (Penn.).

Women and self-sacrifice: G. H. Badger, "Howells as an Interpreter of American Life," *International Review*, May 1883, 384; *Twain Letters*, I, 286; Garland, "William Dean Howells," *Art World*, March 1917, 411; "Sanity in Fiction," *North American Review,* March 1903, 345; Smith, "An Hour with Howells," *Frank Leslie's Magazine*, March 17, 1892, 118; H. C. Vedder, *American Writers of Today*, 1894, 56; De Forest to Howells, December 6, 1886 (Harvard); cf. Johnson, *George Harvey*, 86; and Hart, *The Popular Book*, 57, 91–93, 98; Gohdes, 143; James review of *Foregone Conclusion*, *Nation*, January 1873, 12; Johnson, "Sense and Sentiment," *Outlook*, 1895, 304; "Politics, But a Good Thing," *N. Y. Times*, October 13, 1894, 9; Dawes, "Moral Purpose in Howells' Novels," 34; Howells' introduction to *Their Husbands' Wives*, ii; F. J. Mather, Jr., review *The Kentons*, *Forum*, October 1902, 221. *The Rise of Silas Lapham*, 338–39. Taine quoted by John Durand to Howells, April 10, 1888 (Harvard).

VI

Julian Hawthorne, "Novels and Agnosticism," *Confessions and Criticism*, 1887; "Novel Writing as a Science," *Catholic World*, November 1885; Mabie, "A Typical Novel," *Andover Review*, November 1885; Marrion Wilcox, "The Works of William Dean Howells," *Harper's Weekly*, July 4, 1896, 655–56; *Life and Letters of Gosse*, 178–180; Gosse, "The Passing of William Dean Howells," *Living Age*, July 10, 1920, 99; *Letters*, I, 361, 364; see September 9, 1883, entries in "Venice" notebook (Harvard). Wister, 712. *Impressions and Experiences*, 45; *Through the Eye of the Needle*, 168; *My Mark Twain*, chapter 16. Cp. Arthur Mann, *Yankee Reformers in the Urban Age*, 1954, 1–23. W. James, *Varieties of Religious Experience*, 163.

INDEX

BELMONT, MASSACHUSETTS HOUSE

WILLIAM DEAN HOWELLS

CAMBRIDGE

HARVARD UNIVERSITY

WASHINGTON

CAMBRIDGE

BROADWAY

HARVARD ST

BRATTLE ST EAST

COLLEGE WHARF

BRIGHTON

CHARLES

OLD FORT 1775

VENICE

"That Venice from which I shall never be exiled"